PENGUIN ⊗ CLASSICS

# THE AGE OF BEDE

ADVISORY EDITOR: BETTY RADICE

ST BRENDAN was born in Kerry *c.* A.D. 486 and died at Annadown *c.* 575. He became a monk and a priest; he founded several monasteries of which Clonfert in Galway was the most famous. The story of his voyage was very widely read in Latin and in several vernacular languages.

BEDE was born in 673. He himself tells us that he became a monk at an early age and lived most of his life at Jarrow. Scholar, teacher and writer, he wrote biblical and other works. He has been described as the 'Father of English History'. His historical works include *Life of Cuthbert* and *Lives of the Abbots of Wearmouth and Jarrow*, both in *The Age of Bede* (a Penguin Classic). Bede died in 735.

Little is known of the priest EDDIUS STEPHANUS except that he wrote his *Life of Wilfrid* between 710 and 720 A.D. He knew Wilfrid well and accompanied him on one of his journeys to Rome.

J. F. WEBB is a priest of the RC diocese of Wrexham, N. Wales.

D. H. Farmer (B.Litt. Oxon) was Reader in History at Reading University until 1988. He is author and editor of several books on ecclesiastical and monastic history such as *Benedict's Disciples* (2nd edition, 1999), *The Age of Bede* (a Penguin Classic, 1983), *St Hugh of Lincoln* (3rd edition, 2000) and *The Oxford Dictionary of Saints* (1978; 4th edition, 1997). This has been translated into Italian, Slovakian and Roumanian. A work on Anglo-Saxon missionaries in Europe is in preparation. He has also been principal consultant for the new twelve-volume edition of *Butler's Lives of the Saints* (1995–9).

# The Age of Bede

*Bede: Life of Cuthbert*
*Eddius Stephanus: Life of Wilfrid*
*Bede: Lives of the Abbots of Wearmouth and Jarrow*
*The Anonymous History of Abbot Ceolfrith*
with *The Voyage of St Brendan*

*Translated by* J. F. WEBB
*Edited with an introduction by* D. H. FARMER

Lives of the Abbots of Wearmouth and Jarrow
*and* The Anonymous History of Abbot Ceolfrith
*translated by* D. H. FARMER

PENGUIN BOOKS

PENGUIN BOOKS

Published by the Penguin Group
Penguin Books Ltd, 80 Strand, London WC2R ORL, England
Penguin Group (USA), Inc., 375 Hudson Street, New York, New York 10014, USA
Penguin Books Australia Ltd, 250 Camberwell Road, Camberwell, Victoria 3124, Australia
Penguin Books Canada Ltd, 10 Alcorn Avenue, Toronto, Ontario, Canada M4V 3B2
Penguin Books India (P) Ltd, 11 Community Centre, Panchsheel Park, New Delhi – 110 017, India
Penguin Books (NZ) Ltd, Cnr Rosedale and Airborne Roads, Albany, Auckland, New Zealand
Penguin Books (South Africa) (Pty) Ltd, 24 Sturdee Avenue, Rosebank 2196, South Africa

Penguin Books Ltd, Registered Offices: 80 Strand, London WC2R ORL, England

www.penguin.com

First published 1965
Reprinted with revisions and new introduction 1983
Reprinted with revisions 1988, 1998
Reprinted 2004

016

Translation copyright © J. F. Webb, 1965
Introduction and Notes copyright © D. H. Farmer, 1983, 1988
Translation of Lives of the Abbots of Wearmouth and Jarrow
and of The Anonymous History of Abbot Ceolfrith
copyright © D. H. Farmer, 1983, 1998

Printed in England by Clays Ltd, St Ives plc

ISBN-13: 978-0-14-044727-9

www.greenpenguin.co.uk

# Contents

# Introduction

*by D. H. Farmer*

THE five texts presented in this volume are important sources for the early history of the Christian Church in England and Ireland. The saints described in them lived in the sixth and seventh centuries. Each was an attractive pioneer both of monasticism and of the primacy of the spiritual. In an age and environment in which the heroic was deeply appreciated, each of them embodied a heroism comparable to, yet different from, that of mythical gods and warriors. They fought spiritual battles against invisible diabolical enemies with the weapons of prayer, fasting and solitude; yet each also contributed powerfully to building Christian cities, communities of monks. Each obtained posthumous and permanent, as well as transient, glory.

These men came from different backgrounds and had contrasting temperaments. Brendan was the earliest, an Irish monk, abbot and founder. But his *Navigatio* is the latest of the five documents and arguably the least rich in authentic personal detail. It is, however, both an attractive and a rewarding document, part fact and part fiction, which represents a long Irish monastic tradition of which the historical Brendan (d. 575) is one famous example. Better known personalities in the same tradition are Columbanus (d. 615), whose writings, missionary activity and monasteries (especially Bobbio and Saint-Gall) made him the most famous Irish apostle in Western Europe, and Columba of Iona (d. 597), especially important in south-west Scotland and through his disciples in Northumbria also.

Cuthbert was a Northumbrian, born in 634. He was trained as a young man by Irish monks at Melrose. After a few years as guestmaster in the abortive foundation at Ripon, followed by the famous Synod of Whitby (663/4), he became prior of Lindisfarne. He was attracted, however, to a more complete solitude, realized

9

first on St Cuthbert's Isle close by and later on the island of the Inner Farne, where he lived as a hermit until 685 when he was called to be a bishop. Lindisfarne was his see, but he lived as bishop for only two years. He died in 687 at the age of fifty-three.

Wilfrid was a Northumbrian also. Like Cuthbert, he became both monk and bishop, being trained first by Irish monks at Lindisfarne and later at Rome, the centre of Christendom. He went to Rome for the first time as a young man, staying for a while at Lyons on his way. Here he experienced the ideals and lifestyle of the Merovingian bishops. After his return to England he became the spokesman for the 'Roman' side at the Synod of Whitby and, soon afterwards, bishop of Northumbria. He experienced extremes of favour and disgrace, was expelled from his see and appealed to Rome for reinstatement. After a second expulsion he again appealed to Rome, not against the division of the Northumbrian diocese but against his virtual deposition and loss of monasteries he had founded in Northumbria, Mercia and even Sussex, whose apostle he had become in exile. Eventually he was reinstated as bishop of Hexham, where he died in 709. Important as a church builder, as the propagator of the Rule of St Benedict and as a pioneer missionary in Frisia as well as Sussex, he was also a controversial figure in life and after death. His *Life* by Eddius Stephanus, now often called simply Stephen, a fervent partisan, was written in about 720. Whatever its faults, it has the merit of being the first historical biography to be written by an Anglo-Saxon.

Bede's *Lives of the Abbots* is a document rather different from the others. First, it concerns several abbots, not just one. Secondly it is a work of local history as well as biography. Thirdly it was written by England's pioneer historian within the monastery ruled by the abbots it describes, probably within ten years of the death of one of its principal characters, Ceolfrith. Of the five works included in this volume it is the shortest, but also the richest in authentic detail. It provides attractive character sketches, vivid details about the daily life, the endowments and the art treasures of England's largest monastery of the seventh century. It is now completed by the contemporary anonymous Life of Ceolfrith.

The *Voyage of St Brendan* was immensely popular in the Middle Ages. This is shown by the unusually large number – 116 – of surviving Latin manuscripts, and by the existence of vernacular translations in Middle English, French, German, Flemish, Italian, Provençal and Old Norse. It is still immensely readable today. Recently the journeys of Dr Timothy Severin in his ship *Brendan* have proved the possibility of the Hebrides, the Faeroes, Iceland and Newfoundland being reached by a craft built on traditional early medieval principles. His book *The Brendan Voyage* is a fascinating record of his journey.

Nevertheless, great caution is necessary in claiming that the *Navigatio* is an authentic biography. For one thing the work appears *c.* 200 years after the death of the historical Brendan (*c.* 486–575). He was a monk and abbot whose main area of activity was western Ireland: Mount Brandon in the Dingle peninsula is named after him. His most important monasteries were Clonfert, Annadown, Inishadroum and Ardfert. He is said to have visited Columba at Hinba (Argyll), to have founded a monastery at Llancarvan (Wales) and journeyed in Brittany with St Malo. These stories reveal a tradition that, like some other Irish abbots of his time, he was a great traveller. His cult can be traced back to the ninth century, but could well be older. However, both his *Life* and the *Navigatio* were most probably written in the eighth century.

The earliest surviving manuscript of the *Navigatio* dates from the ninth century. It is an abridged copy, so it is witness to at least one earlier manuscript, of uncertain date. It is written in a Carolingian minuscule hand: it belonged to, and was quite likely written at, the monastery of St Maximin at Trier. It is now in the British Library (Add. MS 36,736). It is clearly the product of an environment very different from that of Brendan himself: its handwriting contrasts sharply with the Irish or Northumbrian scripts of the Cathach of Columba, the Lindisfarne Gospels or the Book of Kells.

The *Navigatio* is usually, and probably correctly, described as the work of an expatriate Irish monk of the late eighth century. His name is unknown. He was familiar with Irish hagiography, geography and folklore: he wrote good Latin but with some insular characteristics. The six earliest surviving manuscripts all come from the Rhineland or the Low Countries. Monks of Irish origin had settled in this area, either through voluntary exile for Christ or because they had taken refuge there from Viking harassment. Their monasteries were built at such places as Metz, Trier, Liège, Cologne and Utrecht. There presumably they would have followed the Rules of Columbanus or another Irish abbot before the Rule of St Benedict replaced them.

The author of the *Navigatio* knew the *Life* of Brendan and wrote his attractive story to harmonize with it. As it stands, his work is a fascinating mixture of fact, fantasy and literary borrowing. Its basic theme, the quest for a paradise on earth, can be traced back through early Christian writings to Greek, Roman and Egyptian literature. Parallels can be drawn with the Book of Enoch or the Shepherd of Hermas. But the closest resemblances are to the literature of Visions, some of which originated in Ireland and probably made use of pre-Christian Irish elements. The story of an adventurous sea-voyage is common in early Irish literature.

The appearance of Judas Iscariot in the story as an example of the damned and of a Hibernicized Paul the First Hermit as an example of the saved show, with other passages, that this is no historical biography. The use of numbers seems to be symbolical, not historical. His companions number thirty-three, he goes round an island for three days, forty days are spent in preparatory fasting, supplies are also for forty days, for forty years the hermit Paul was brought up in 'Patrick's monastery', and the island was so wide that forty days' wandering did not bring the travellers to the further shore.

The general influence of Scripture and the monastic rule are clear in these and other passages. Wherever the monks go they sing the psalms: so also do the birds. The journeys are marvellously timed to coincide with the Christian festivals. But this dream world has some genuine details. Travelling monks may well have encountered whales, icebergs and volcanoes; Irish settlement in some northern islands has been confirmed by archaeologists, while Viking sagas of Iceland tell of the displacement of Irish monks who had settled there before them. Given the long time-gap between Brendan's death and the appearance of the *Navigatio*, there is little chance of its recording accurately the speech and the journeys of the historical Brendan and his community, whose comradeship in prosperity and adversity is such an attractive feature of the story. Brendan and his followers are written about as representatives of the Irish monastic system who embarked with faith into the unknown. Whatever may be thought of identifying striking details of the story, there can be no doubt of the imaginative charm of this fairy-like tale or of the skilful ingenuity of its author.

Irish monasticism, glimpsed in the *Navigatio*, was a movement of great interest and significance. Its dependence on Eastern regimes as well as the unusual circumstances of Irish society combined to give it a character of its own. This was in many ways unlike that of most Benedictine monasteries in the West.

The principal apostle of Ireland, St Patrick, a Briton who set up his episcopal see at Armagh, was not a monk himself, but his writings show that he encouraged monasticism for men and women. But within a century of his death in *c.* 461 the monasteries emerged as the most important element in the life of the Christian Church in Ireland. Lack of evidence prevents our knowing exactly how this happened. There were no towns in Ireland, nor had it ever been part of the Roman Empire. This meant that the structure of civil government in dioceses, into which the organization of the Christian Church fitted so admirably elsewhere, was lacking. Owing to the absence of towns an Irish urban episcopate could not flourish. Irish society was tribal in structure: the extended family was the significant unit. When the family became Christian, it was natural for it to remain together as a group. From this developed the early Irish monasteries.

Monasteries were numerous and often large numbers of inmates were claimed for them. Within them several different forms of life were represented. Often there were a few hermits, esteemed and influential. There were also cenobites, or community monks, who lived under the verbal rule of the local abbot or one of the written rules such as that of Columbanus. But, it would seem, there were also even larger numbers of married layfolk attached to the monastery, still part of the family unit, who pursued normal lay occupations such as agriculture and cattle-rearing. Such people were, however, called 'monks'. Presumably this section of the monastery was the one which became involved in cattle-rustling and even in 'wars' mentioned in Irish chronicles. Their existence makes less incredible the claim that Irish monasteries sometimes numbered some thousands of inmates. The head of the whole establishment was the abbot; he was of the same family as the founder and even sometimes a layman. Monasteries would often remain in the hands of the same family from one generation to another.

The importance of the abbot in Ireland led in practice to the diminution of the power of the bishop. The bishop remained superior to the abbot in his Orders, which he could receive only from another bishop. But sometimes he seems to have been sub-ordinate to, and dependent on, the abbot. Bede, who heard of this system at Iona, rightly regarded it as novel and unheard of. It was certainly quite different from the tradition, doctrine and practice of the rest of the Christian Church, both in East and West. Long before this time the Christian Church had been organ-ized in territorial sees, situated in towns, whose dioceses were often coterminous with the units of civil administration. From these urban centres Christianity eventually spread into the countryside: it is often forgotten that the word *pagani* (pagans) originally meant country-dwellers.

The mission of Augustine to England in 597 (the very year of Columba's death on Iona) brought Christianity to the Anglo-Saxons who had settled extensively in the south and east of Britain. By the conversion of Ethelbert, king of Kent, then the most important of the Anglo-Saxon kings, and the establishment of dioceses at Canterbury, Rochester and later London, a small but firm bridgehead was built. In spite of reverses after Augustine's early death in 604, Christianity spread throughout the whole country through the labours of Irish and Frankish as well as Italian missionaries. Within less than a century a fully articulated, normal diocesan system under one metropolitan (later two) was set up over the whole of Anglo-Saxon England. In this ultimate fulfilment of the grand strategy, if not of all the details of Gregory the Great (the pope who had sent Augustine), Theodore of Tarsus was the most important single influence. This Greek monk, unexpectedly promoted to the see of Canterbury by the Pope after a plague had wiped out most of the English episcopate, ruled from 665 until his death in 690 at the age of nearly ninety.

The contact between 'Irish' and 'Roman' Christianity in England, sometimes in conflict but eventually in fusion, is illustrated in the other Lives printed in this volume. The dramatic confrontation at the Synod of Whitby, with Wilfrid as the principal spokesman for the Roman side and Colman for the 'Irish', soon led to the consolidation of local centres of diverse origin into a united, organized, nationwide church under territorial bishops. These were more numerous than before, and were in closer contact with each other and with the papacy, whose influence was considerable in England in the seventh century. English monastic missionaries such as Willibrord and particularly Boniface would be its principal supporters in Western Europe in the eighth century. This creative synthesis, of cultural as well as religious importance, was achieved in England partly through the achievements of Wilfrid, Cuthbert and the abbots of Wearmouth and Jarrow.

Although Cuthbert was educated in an Irish monastery, he should be regarded as a transitional, moderate figure rather than a reactionary. After the Synod of Whitby, at which he took no known part, he became prior of Lindisfarne in his early thirties. Here, according to Bede (ch. 16), some of the brethren preferred their old way of life to that of his rule, but he won them over by patient persistence.

It was not surprising that there was trouble at Lindisfarne. Founded by Aidan, the deeply respected apostle of Northumbria who had come from Iona at the invitation of King Oswald in 633, it became the most important Christian centre in Northumbria (and arguably in England) during the next thirty years. But after Whitby its bishop, Colman, left England in 664 for Iona and eventually Inisboffin in western Ireland with thirty of his monks, rather than accept the 'Roman' Easter calculation. The Iona reckoning had been abandoned some years before by southern Ireland: only the north and Iona stood out. At the Synod of Whitby Northumbria opted for universalism, Europeanism and the papacy against insularity and parochialism. This did not mean that all Irish influence ceased forthwith, nor that men like Cuthbert rejected at a stroke all their previous sympathies. Much was admirable about the Irish tradition: austerity, learning, calligraphy, pioneer missionary endeavour. But on the crucial issues of the date of Easter and the place of the bishop in the Church the future lay with Wilfrid and Theodore.

Bede's *Life of Cuthbert* was written by a devoted adherent of the Roman outlook and a scholarly partisan of the Roman Easter, but Bede was also a sympathetic admirer of Irish saints like Aidan. Cuthbert exemplified both elements in Bede's outlook. His Irish training did not prevent his accepting the decision of Whitby, which he implemented at Lindisfarne: at the end of his life he warned his disciples against the danger of schism, telling them to have 'no dealings with those who had wandered from the unity of the Church either through not celebrating Easter at the usual time or through evil living' (ch. 39). This was in 687, more than twenty years after Whitby: the reference to Irish diehards is clear.

The earliest *Life of Cuthbert* had been written by an anonymous monk of Lindisfarne about 700, or soon after the discovery of Cuthbert's body being incorrupt had given fresh impetus to an existing cult. Using this source, Bede wrote a verse *Life of Cuthbert* in 716. About 721 he wrote the *Prose Life*, translated below. He also wrote of Cuthbert in his *History of the English Church and People* (iv, 27-32).

The *Prose Life* is really a rewriting of the earlier *Anonymous Life*, but with ten chapters of new material (3, 6, 8-9, 19, 23, 31, 35, 43 and 46) which add considerably to our knowledge of the saint. Those derived from Herefrith, written in a style different from Bede's, are specially authentic and important. Throughout the work Bede developed certain elements, interpreted events, sometimes giving a different emphasis: he also provided sources and made comparisons. Above all he improved the style. Detailed comparisons have been made more than once between the two *Lives* and some recent writers prefer the simplicity of the earlier anonymous work. But medieval preference for Bede is clearly reflected in the number of surviving manuscripts of each: seven of the anonymous *Life* and thirty-eight of Bede's. Moreover Bede's text was chosen for the two outstanding illustrated manuscript *Lives* of Cuthbert produced at Durham in the twelfth century. These are now Oxford, University College MS 165 and British Library, Yates Thompson MS 26.

In the opinion of this writer, the medieval preference for Bede was justified. If the anonymous *Life* had been fully adequate, there would have been no need for the Lindisfarne monks to commission Bede to write another. This invitation revealed not only their confidence in his ability and skill, but also a real need for some additional account of Cuthbert for posterity. Fifty years and more after the Synod of Whitby, Lindisfarne, the ancient core of Irish influence, and Wearmouth–Jarrow, the newer centre of Roman influence, were on very friendly terms. The affectionate tone of Bede's preface entirely confirms this impression. So does his request to be inscribed on the Lindisfarne list of monks and benefactors so that he could share in the spiritual benefits of their Masses and prayers.

Bede's admiration for Cuthbert was evident, unsurprising and shared with the monks of Lindisfarne. Bede and Cuthbert were both monks; both knew and valued the Rule of St Benedict; both were men of unity and regretted Colman's departure. Even though Bede found fulfilment in his community and his studies while Cuthbert (like Francis later) found it in solitude and the world of nature, the agreements between them were far more significant than the differences. Both were thoroughly orthodox Christians and disciples of the great monastic tradition of which St Benedict was an important, but by no means the earliest figure. Their two communities shared interest in the texts of the Bible which both assiduously copied. The Lindisfarne Gospels (written before 698 'In honour of St Cuthbert') owed its text and several other features to Bede's monastery of Wearmouth–Jarrow.

Bede's *Life of Cuthbert*, being an example of hagiography, exemplifies the nature and purpose of this particular literary form. This was to stress that the saint was a man of God and shared in divine qualities and even in the power of miracles. For Bede, as for Gregory the Great before him, these were to be expected in the early days of Christianity in England just as they had been prominent in the early Church, as testified in the *Acts of the Apostles*. In his commentary on Mark, Bede stressed that the Church 'was nourished with miracles in order that she might grow firm in the faith. When we plant bushes, we water them until they stand firm, but once they have taken root, the watering ceases' (Lib. IV cap. xvi; P.L. 92, 299–300).

Several of the miracle-stories he relates are modelled at least in their literary expression on scriptural examples; others on incidents in Gregory's *Dialogues* and other similar works. It is often difficult or impossible to determine the original event behind particular miracle stories. But frequently they yield an unexpected harvest of historical detail which is otherwise unknown. Thus (ch. 3) a story of how the wind changed direction at Cuthbert's prayer and so prevented some monks at Tynemouth from being carried out to sea in rafts also reveals that the peasants jeered at the monks for abolishing the pagan ways of worship. Such evidence is very seldom recorded. Again, a prophecy by Boisil about Cuthbert (ch. 6) tells us that he owned both a horse and a spear when he entered the monastery: this reveals his comparatively high social status. These are examples of interesting details which can be gleaned from these miracle-stories.

But Bede's contemporaries expected some elements which modern readers do not. People of an unscientific age, sometimes uncertain about secondary causality, would have been most surprised if religion did *not* offer marvellous events of one kind or another as confirmation of divine power. Such was expected by the sophisticated as well as by the ignorant in the late Roman Empire and the age of the barbarian invasions. If Christianity were to prove superior to paganism, its power in such matters, as well as its teaching, would have to surpass those of the pagan gods. Bede's *History of the English Church and People* contains many marvellous events of this kind; so did the anonymous *Life of Cuthbert* which was the principal source for his own *Life* and which contributes considerably to its slightly unreal atmosphere.

The *Life* is specially valuable for the light it throws on Cuthbert's monasteries: Melrose, Ripon, Lindisfarne and the Inner Farne. As a young monk at Melrose, he 'watched, prayed, worked and studied harder than anyone else ... being robust and strong, he was fit for whatever work he cared to undertake' (ch. 6). This energetic zeal, a lifelong characteristic, was complemented by pleasant affability. The latter found full expression when Cuthbert was appointed guestmaster in his twenties at Ripon, a short-lived foundation of Melrose (ch. 7). A special interest of his, as of his master Boisil, was the Gospel of John. This they studied intensively during Boisil's last week on earth. They were able to complete it rapidly because they concentrated on the 'simple things of faith which works by love' rather than on the deepest questions of theological dispute (ch. 8). Nor was Cuthbert's contribution to the apostolate of Northumbria negligible. While he was prior of Melrose, he not only counselled monks about the religious life but also preached in villages and remote hill farmsteads, for a week, a fortnight or a month at a time. These journeys, often the occasion for unusual or miraculous events, were specially necessary in times of plague, which could be the occasion for apostasy or the revival of magic.

When he was prior of Lindisfarne, he still showed the same qualities (ch. 16). The departure of Colman and thirty monks with the consequent absence of a bishop must have caused some crisis. Bede hints at unspecified irregularities: 'Some of the brethren preferred their old way of life to that of the rule' as propounded by the teaching and example of Cuthbert, who ruled in the absence of Eata, abbot of Lindisfarne from 664 and later bishop, first at Hexham, then at Lindisfarne and lastly again at Hexham (d. 686). Until 678 there was no bishop at Lindisfarne: York, under Chad and Wilfrid, had again become the principal ecclesiastical centre of Northumbria. This reflected a return to the example of Paulinus rather than that of Aidan. Yet another change of direction was marked by the division of the Northumbrian see in 678, with sees at Hexham and Lindisfarne as well as York. But this is to anticipate.

After many years in the monastery (as Benedict allowed) Cuthbert became a hermit with the approval of the abbot and monks of Lindisfarne. This was in 676. Bede, like most monastic writers of antiquity but unlike many Christians of today, regarded such a change as a promotion, from 'a long and spotless active life ... to the stillness of divine contemplation' (ch. 17). In the same place Bede recorded precious details about the primitive buildings on the Inner Farne, where Cuthbert lived and prayed.

His solitude, however, was not to be permanent. In 685 he

visited Aelfflaed, King Egfrith's sister, abbess of Coquet Island, to whom he hinted that he might become a bishop. Soon after, Egfrith with Trumwine, bishop of Abercorn (near Edinburgh), came to the Inner Farne to persuade him to accept a bishopric for which he had been chosen at a recent synod. He agreed on a change of sees with his old master Eata, by which Cuthbert became bishop of Lindisfarne instead of Hexham. These appointments were part of the further division of Wilfrid's vast see of Northumbria, arranged by Theodore, archbishop of Canterbury, and King Egfrith. The latter was killed in battle the following year (ch. 27).

As bishop, Cuthbert retained his austere monastic regime (ch. 26). He was also conspicuous for feeding the hungry, caring for the poor and consoling the afflicted. He resumed the preaching journeys which he had initiated at Melrose (chs 9, 28, 30). Doubtless on these expeditions he used both the portable altar of wood and the fine jewelled pectoral cross which survive to this day at Durham cathedral with his wooden coffin and other treasures associated with him.

His episcopate lasted barely two years. Early in 687 he retired once more to his hermitage on the Inner Farne. Herefrith, monk and priest of Lindisfarne, was Bede's principal source for the account of Cuthbert's death (chs 37–40). Cuthbert knew he was going to die, gave details concerning his burial and exhorted the Lindisfarne community to persevere in unity and charity, to shun schism at all costs and to carry out his monastic teaching and that of the Fathers.

From his hermitage the monks, who were with him at the end, signified the news of his death by lighting torches. These were seen by the monk keeping watch in the tower at Lindisfarne. Cuthbert was only fifty-three years old when he died. A man of prayer and peace who lived close to nature and had the reputation of being a miracle worker, he had been monk and hermit for most of his life. Yet he became, and still is, northern England's most popular saint.

The first step in this somewhat surprising development took place eleven years after his death. His reputation for sanctity in life, confirmed by miracles after death, was such that Edbert, bishop of Lindisfarne, decided with his community on the 'elevation' of Cuthbert's body. This was the ancient equivalent of canonization: only those honoured by a burial above ground in the church were considered worthy of liturgical cult. Bede recounts the details (ch. 42). When they opened the coffin, they found to their surprise that Cuthbert's body was intact and incorrupt, with the joints still flexible. It had the appearance of a man asleep rather than dead. The bishop, then living in solitude in an island off Lindisfarne, rejoiced in wonder and compared this happening in lyrical terms with some of the biblical miracles.

Edbert died soon afterwards and was succeeded by Edfrith, now identified as the scribe of the Lindisfarne Gospels. This masterpiece of insular script and illumination, written 'in honour of St Cuthbert', was an integral element of the cult and was for centuries kept with Cuthbert's shrine. It is now in the British Library.

The cult of Cuthbert, while grounded on the impact of his holiness in life, grew through extrinsic causes also. One of these was the incorruption of his body; the other the extraordinary story of his relics. Until 875, the year of the second Viking raid on Lindisfarne, the coffin had remained there in the church. But then it was taken to a place of refuge elsewhere in Northumbria. This proved difficult to find, so the shrine, accompanied by clerics from Lindisfarne and containing other treasures as well as Cuthbert's body, rested in turn at Norham, Ripon, Chester-le-Street and other places until it found its permanent home at Durham in 995. The relics were enshrined in a church there in 999.

Later still, after the Norman Conquest and the establishment of Durham as a permanent see with a monastic chapter, the relics were translated into the present cathedral in 1104. There they still rest; Cuthbert's bones under the floor of the chancel where his shrine stood in the Middle Ages; the secondary relics, of unique archaeological interest, are in a secure museum within the cathedral precinct. Durham became the most important pilgrimage centre of the North, while Cuthbert's cult and influence remained strong there and elsewhere until the Reformation. His memory is far from dead today.

In temperament, in the external circumstances of his life and in his historical reputation, Wilfrid contrasts sharply with Cuthbert. Both were Northumbrian monks of noble birth: their differing ideals and practice were complementary rather than contradictory; both were necessary to the Church of the seventh century.

Wilfrid was born within a year or two of Cuthbert but lived nearly a quarter of a century longer. His first education was at Lindisfarne, where he must have met Aidan. But he tired of its insularity and desired to see the Christian Church in other countries. Enfleda, queen of Northumbria, encouraged him and enabled him to travel to Canterbury and Rome, where he studied Scripture and Canon Law. On his way back he stayed for three years at the important political and commercial centre of Lyons, where he experienced the patronage and lifestyle of the bishop, an aristocrat who mixed with dukes and counts as their social equals, inheriting the traditions of public service and patronage from the late Roman Empire. Sometimes such men combined public munificence with private austerity. Wilfrid also saw at close quarters, as a guest of the bishop, the day-to-day working of the local Church.

It is not known where or when he became a monk, but it was probably during this period of his life. On his return to England, he obtained patronage from Alcfrith, sub-king of Deira (roughly the equivalent of Yorkshire), who gave him the abbey of Ripon, from which a community from Melrose had withdrawn rather than accept the Roman Easter. At Ripon Wilfrid introduced the Rule of St Benedict, a momentous move with important consequences.

Soon afterwards, at the important Synod of Whitby, Wilfrid was chosen as principal spokesman for the 'Roman' side, his learning and eloquence in the vernacular outweighing his comparative inexperience. This was his big chance and he took it eagerly. Bede's famous account in his *History* (iii, 25) is fuller than that of Eddius (ch. 10). The conflict had arisen in Northumbria because churches of Roman and Irish origin followed divergent customs in the same area. This diversity was manifest in the court: King Oswiu had learnt his Christianity from the monks of Iona while his queen had been brought up in Kent with its strongly Roman tradition. Disagreement centred on the rival calculations for the date of Easter. This often differed by a week or more. It is not sufficiently appreciated moreover that different dates for Easter led inevitably to different dates for Lent, Ascension Day and Pentecost, because Easter is the pivot of the liturgical year.

By now southern Ireland had conformed and some of the most intransigent Romanists, such as Ronan, were of the Irish race. Thirty years earlier the Irish abbot Cummian had complained that Iona seemed to think that Rome was wrong, Alexandria was wrong, Gaul was wrong and only Iona and a tip of Ireland were right. Wilfrid likewise stood for universalism against insularity: 'Do you think,' he said, 'that a handful of people in one corner of the remotest of islands is to be preferred to the universal Church of Christ which is spread throughout the world?'

King Oswiu, who had summoned the council, having heard both sides, opted firmly and unexpectedly for the Roman side 'with a smile'. Their calculation was believed by some to be the practice of St Peter and was certainly that of many of his successors in the Roman see, of the council of Nicaea and of nearly all the churches in Europe. The argument in favour of conforming with the rest of the Christian Church (including most of Ireland) was overwhelming. But it was a bitter blow to the diehard bishop of Lindisfarne, Colman, who retired to Ireland rather than accept this decision. Wilfrid's reputation, on the other hand, stood high. Not surprisingly, helped again by his patron Alcfrith, he was chosen to be Bishop of York (chs 11–12).

While Wilfrid was being consecrated in Gaul, Oswiu had appointed the Irish-trained Chad as bishop of Northumbria. The existence of two rival candidates presumably reflects a political struggle between King Oswiu and his son Alcfrith. When Wilfrid returned, he found Chad established at York; with his patron dead or in exile, he could only retire to his monastery at Ripon. But the new archbishop of Canterbury, Theodore, on visitation in the north, put an end to this irregular situation. Chad's consecration was uncanonical because it was performed by schismatical British bishops. Theodore had him reconsecrated and transferred to Lichfield, the new Mercian see, while Wilfrid was enthroned as bishop of York, with the charge of all Northumbria. It is agreeable to note that everyone, including Eddius, spoke well of Chad (chs 14–15).

Wilfrid now began the most prosperous period of his life. The new king Egfrith and his queen Etheldreda, from East Anglia, considerably older than himself, both favoured Wilfrid and made him extensive grants of land. His diocese was coterminous with the kingdom and so extended at its maximum to most of the land between the Forth and the Wash. Wilfrid restored the ruined church of York, started by Paulinus, its first bishop, and built afresh fine churches at Ripon and Hexham. These significant buildings were suitably and lavishly adorned (chs 16, 17, 22): they were also endowed equally generously. Lands were given which had been left by Britons when they fled westwards, while Hexham was provided with extensive properties close at hand through the queen, and the king gave more distant properties in the Pennines. Some abbots and abbesses, rightly anxious about the permanence of their monasteries, made over their estates to Wilfrid in return for his protection (ch. 21). Now and later Wilfrid held extensive lands which were comparable with those held by Merovingian bishops; but in Anglo-Saxon Northumbria no previous bishop had been so powerful, and his considerable wealth was one factor in his fall from royal favour.

The immediate causes of his fall were manifold. Already in 673 at the important council of Hertford, Theodore had embarked on the policy of dividing dioceses within the existing kingdoms. Now in 678 he turned his attention to Northumbria. This area was obviously far too large for one bishop to care for it adequately as a pastor. It was unfortunate that Theodore used Wilfrid's difficulties to divide his diocese over his head. Wilfrid's lifestyle, extensive wealth and numerous retainers were criticized and envied. Moreover Etheldreda's marital problems had been a contributory factor. Here, unexpectedly, Bede is more revealing than Eddius. Twice married, but retaining her virginity, Etheldreda refused to consummate her marriage with Egfrith, who was far younger than herself. With Wilfrid's help and advice, pursuing her desire or her vow to become a nun, she had left Egfrith and joined the monastery of Coldingham before founding her own nunnery at Ely. Egfrith had married again: the new queen, Ermenburga, was bitterly hostile to Wilfrid. Egfrith wished to be rid of Wilfrid and Theodore wished to divide his diocese, with or without Wilfrid's consent. Wilfrid, having lost the king's favour, appealed to the Pope against his virtual deposition without any canonical cause. In so doing, Wilfrid made history, for it was the first time that such an appeal had been made from England. He set out for Rome to plead his case in person.

Adversity in Wilfrid's life was usually the occasion for fresh achievements. On his way to Rome, he took the first step towards the conversion of the Frisians, a work accomplished later by his disciple Willibrord and by Boniface (ch. 26). The element of high adventure too was continued: Aldgisl, king of the Frisians, refused to surrender Wilfrid to his enemies. Shortly afterwards Dagobert II offered him the see of Strasbourg in recognition of Wilfrid's earlier help when he was in exile. Wilfrid had sent him some fighting men to help him regain his kingdom. Chapters 26–28 enable us to glimpse the violent world of seventh-century politics: exile or assassination was the common fate of claimants to the thrones of Frankish or Anglo-Saxon kingdoms.

Eddius's account of Wilfrid's appeal to Rome (chs 29–33) with its lengthy citation of documents (surprisingly not used by Bede) is among the most valuable elements of his work. The papal decision was in Wilfrid's favour. It upheld him in his appeal against virtual deposition and restored him to his see. But at the same time the principle of dividing the diocese was recognized. Wilfrid was enjoined to choose new coadjutors and expel the intruded bishops. Rome's decision was based on limited knowledge and legal precedent in similar cases; it lacked any procedures which could enforce its acceptance. This depended ultimately on the recognition of its jurisdiction and moral authority.

First this was refused in Northumbria, but eventually after Wilfrid's second appeal it was accepted. The consequences of Egfrith's refusal to restore Wilfrid were vital for him, as it led to his becoming the apostle of Sussex, the last pagan stronghold of Anglo-Saxon England; he reached Sussex after being rejected in both Mercia and Wessex, through the machinations (if we are to believe Eddius) of their queens, who were related to the

Northumbrian royal family. His Sussex apostolate lasted from 681 to 686 and appears to have been very successful. Bede's account in his *History* (iv, 13) should be read to complement Eddius.

Meanwhile Theodore wished for a reconciliation and used his good offices with the new king of Northumbria, Aldfrith, to achieve Wilfrid's restoration. This took place in 687 and involved the 'new' reduced see of York with the monasteries of Ripon and Hexham. All these were returned to Wilfrid, but peace lasted for only five years (chs 43–5). Ripon, it seems, was the principal bone of contention, for the king had sequestered some of its lands and given Wilfrid's monastery there to Aethelwine, the bishop of Lindsey who had returned to Northumbria when Mercia reconquered his see in 692. This, at least, seems the most likely explanation of a somewhat obscure incident. Whatever the reason, Wilfrid again went into exile, this time to Mercia, where he acted as bishop, at Leicester rather than at Lichfield. Not much is known of him in these ten years (692–702), but it is likely that he then founded six monasteries which probably comprised Peterborough, Oundle, Brixworth and possibly Evesham, Wing and Withington.

In 703 a council was held at Austerfield, near Bawtry, at which Bertwald, archbishop of Canterbury and most of the English bishops were present (ch. 46). Bede omits all mention of this important gathering and it is not known what other decisions were made. Once again some of the council attempted to remove Wilfrid by interning him in his monastery at Ripon, obtaining his resignation from the episcopate and removing from his ownership and control all his other monasteries. They tried to obtain his consent by urging him in advance to agree to whatever the council decided. This ruthless plan, prepared by king and archbishop, was rejected by some: its proposal was the occasion for Wilfrid's vindication of his life-work. He recalled with passion all he had done for Northumbria: he had brought them to the observance of the 'true Easter', he had introduced the Rule of St Benedict, the Petrine tonsure and the Roman system of singing. What his enemies proposed involved the rejection of papal privileges for his monasteries, so to Rome once again he appealed.

Now seventy years old, he set out once more to put his case

to the Holy See (chs 50–54). Eddius gives the text of his petition, which requested papal directives to the kings of Northumbria and Mercia with the renewal of the papal privileges to his monasteries. Wilfrid was acquitted of all charges against him, while the privileges given by previous popes in his favour were confirmed. Furthermore, a papal letter was written to the kings of Northumbria and Mercia which resumed the case up to now and enjoined Archbishop Bertwald to hold a synod with Wilfrid, Bosa and John and there finally settle the matter. If no agreement were reached, then the parties would have recourse again to the Holy See. In fact Bertwald and the king of Mercia accepted the papal decision, but Aldfrith, king of Northumbria, unwilling to upset the established order in his kingdom, refused. Eventually he changed his mind (chs 58–9).

The final settlement was reached at the synod of the River Nidd in 705. This compromise was worked out with the help of Abbess Aelffled; Osred, the new boy-king of Northumbria, and his counsellors made a peace pact with Wilfrid, which they kept until the end of his life. Wilfrid was restored to the exercise of full episcopal functions in Northumbria, but the extent of his jurisdiction was limited to the diocese of Hexham. This monastery and Ripon were fully restored to him with all their revenues (chs 60–61). For Wilfrid it was peace at last, vindication of all he had stood for, but only partial restoration to the area of his earlier jurisdiction. The other Northumbrian bishops were left undisturbed, or, in the case of John of Beverley, promoted. The final solution was an honourable compromise all round.

Just before his death in 709 Wilfrid provided for the future of his monasteries and distributed his worldly goods. Acca succeeded him at Hexham, Tatbert at Ripon, and the Mercian monasteries would be ruled by his nominees, declared as such by these and a few close followers. Wilfrid also divided his treasure into four: one part for the churches of Rome, one part for the poor, one for his followers who had shared his exile and one for the abbots of Hexham and Ripon, 'so that they may be able to purchase the friendship of kings and bishops'. These divisions fittingly represented four of the main interests of his life. The last of them has been most frequently commented upon: its purpose was to safeguard the permanence of monastic life in his foundations and to deliver them from the current risks of lay control and lay ownership.

Bede's *Lives of the Abbots* is a unique and important document. It gives basic biographical information about Benedict Biscop, founder of Wearmouth and Jarrow, and the equally important Ceolfrith, his successor, who shared his ideals and his policies. It also contains short but unforgettable sketches of Eosterwine and Sigfrid, who both became abbots and both died young. Precious details about the monks' daily occupations, about their numbers and about their land are also provided. Nor are their buildings, libraries and works of art neglected. All in all, such a full and articulate, if summary account, does not occur again in England for several centuries: this work, in fact, became the source and model for monastic chroniclers who accomplished a similar task for monasteries in their own times.

When the greatest historian of the early Middle Ages tells the story of his own monastic home from his own experience, the authority of such a document is very high; so also is its interest. This is both factual and human, reflecting the author's accuracy and his articulate perceptiveness. Its date is not known for certain, but it could not have been written before 716, when Ceolfrith died. It seems likely that it was written before the anonymous *Life of Ceolfrith*. This latter work was written by a monk of Wearmouth or Jarrow. While most of the information given in it is entirely in accordance with Bede's *Lives of the Abbots*, it is centred on Ceolfrith, about whom it tells us more concerning his family, his early life, and the first stages of his cult after death. It is difficult to see why Bede should have omitted this last element if he had been writing after this anonymous *Life*, especially as he mentions the cults of both Eosterwine and Sigfrith.

Bede's account is more complete and balanced. His aim was not primarily to narrate the life of his own dearly loved father abbot, whose unexpected departure caused Bede to interrupt his Commentary on Mark for several months, and whose influence on him from childhood had been deep and lasting. It was to narrate in a balanced way the origins and development of

England's largest and most notable monastery of the late seventh century in a succinct and accurate way. As such it is of permanent historical importance.

The founder of Wearmouth and Jarrow, Benedict Biscop, deserves to be better known than he is. This Northumbrian nobleman (Baducing was his family name) was not only a monastic founder but also an important pioneer in the history of art and education. Vital to all three achievements was his conviction, shared with his contemporary and friend Wilfrid, that it was desirable for England to be enriched, ecclesiastically and culturally, by western Europe and especially Rome.

Biscop was born in 628 and served Oswiu, king of Northumbria, until 653. His career included military service, for which the traditional and expected reward was the granting of land. In 653 he renounced both his career and the prospect of acquiring land in this way, in order to become a monk. First he went to Rome with Wilfrid to visit the tombs of the apostles. Having returned to Northumbria, he went back to Rome (664–5), this time in the company of Oswiu's son Alcfrith, who later became Wilfrid's patron. From Rome he went in 665 to Saint-Honorat, Lérins, a small island off the south coast of France, where he became a monk and took the name of Benedict. This change of name was highly significant as an early indication of his interest in the great monastic patriarch, many of the enactments of whose Rule were to be followed later in Biscop's monasteries.

Biscop spent two years at Lérins, but we next hear of him again, in Rome, in 667. This visit coincided with that of an important group from England. This included the archbishop-elect of Canterbury, Wighard, sent to Rome for consecration after being chosen by Oswiu, king of Northumbria and overlord of other Anglo-Saxon kings, and Egbert, king of Kent. They had agreed on this candidate, himself a member of the household of the archbishop of Canterbury, after the Synod of Whitby. The future archbishop would have the task of unifying the Church after this crisis, as well as that of consecrating new bishops for a hierarchy decimated by plague (ch. 3, *History* iii, 19). Unfortunately, Wighard died in Rome before consecration.

Biscop returned to England in the company of Theodore, the

newly appointed Greek archbishop of Canterbury, in 669: he became abbot of the monastery of SS Peter and Paul, at Canterbury, founded by St Augustine. After only two years' rule he looked round for an opportunity to found his own abbey. He was replaced as abbot of Canterbury by Hadrian, Theodore's African adviser, who had been the Pope's first choice as archbishop. Biscop planned to found a monastery in Wessex, but his patron Cenwalh, its king, died early (ch. 4). He returned instead to his native Northumbria whose new king Egfrith gave him seventy hides of land for his foundation of Wearmouth. Progress there was rapid. With the help of Frankish stonemasons and glaziers whom he imported, the principal buildings were completed in less than two years (ch. 5). The exact size of his community at this time is not known, but his rule was based on the Rule of St Benedict and the customs of other monasteries he had visited. Books also were provided by him from the start.

Once all was in order he visited Rome, yet again, in 679. He returned with diverse treasures, which Bede enumerates in one of the most interesting passages of this work (ch. 6). The books, the pictures (painted on panels), the relics, calendars were all primarily for the monastery, as were the important privileges which attached it closely to the Holy See. Eventually the influence of all these radiated beyond Wearmouth; of more immediate importance for the Anglo-Saxon church as a whole was the presence of Abbot John, the arch-cantor of St Peter's, Rome, who accompanied Biscop on his return. The purpose of his visit was both to assure the doctrinal orthodoxy of the Anglo-Saxons and to teach them the liturgy and the chants as practised at Rome. Not surprisingly, Bede thought this so important that he devoted a chapter in his *History* to it (iv, 16). The religious, artistic and cultural consequences of his presence were incalculable: isolation and insularity were reduced, contacts with the religious and cultural centre of Western Europe increased. And for Wearmouth itself it very probably resulted in the organization of the scriptorium in such a way that books could be produced in uncial script, which was written only in centres where Roman influence was strong.

In 682 Jarrow was founded. King Egfrith again provided land, this time an estate of forty hides (enough for forty families, say 160 persons). This estate was far smaller than that of Wearmouth and the founding community consisted of twenty-two monks, including boys, one of which was most probably Bede himself. The anonymous biographer of Ceolfrith relates the famous story of how, in a time of plague, only the abbot Ceolfrith and a small boy, probably Bede himself, knew the chant well enough to sing it 'with antiphons'. After a few days of monotone recitation, the abbot could no longer endure it, so he and the boy alone sang the antiphons as before. This story illustrates how the foundation of Jarrow met with severe setbacks in early days. In spite of these, however, it prospered and increased in numbers.

This was in large part due to the personal qualities and firm but kindly rule of Ceolfrith himself. Like Biscop, he was of noble Northumbrian birth. He had become a monk at Gilling, but soon moved to Ripon, founded by Wilfrid, where he was ordained priest at the early age of twenty-seven. Visits to Canterbury and to Icanho (probably Iken, Suffolk) under its founder Botulf had increased his monastic experience and his learning, but he also excelled in practical matters, which explains his appointment as baker (or caterer?) on his return to Ripon. Biscop invited Ceolfrith to join him at Wearmouth, where in 676 he acted as prior during Biscop's absence in Rome. He met with opposition from certain monks of noble birth at Wearmouth, who caused his temporary return to Ripon. But Biscop persuaded him to come back to Wearmouth and in 682 appointed him abbot of Jarrow.

Bede tells us that it was always Biscop's intention that these two communities should remain as one. Biscop was still abbot-founder of both houses, but appointed Eosterwine as abbot of Wearmouth (ch. 7). It seems likely that his position, and that of Ceolfrith at Jarrow while Biscop was alive, resembled that of more recent coadjutor-abbots, appointed to help the abbot founder, who was aged or ill or frequently absent, to sustain the burden. It was also doubtless connected with the presumption of Germanic law that monasteries belonged to their founders. Both Wilfrid and Biscop developed monastic life within this particular legal framework, but Biscop soon modified it in one very important respect.

This modification, as we shall see later, took place on his deathbed.

Meanwhile the young abbot Eosterwine assumed effective control of Wearmouth. Bede's portrait of him (ch. 8) is exceptionally attractive. A cousin of Benedict Biscop, Eosterwine used neither his birth nor his office to place him at any distance from the brethren. On the contrary, he identified so completely with them that he shared in their ordinary work of milking, winnowing and threshing, ploughing, gardening, baking, cooking and metalwork. He followed the common regime in everything, eating and sleeping and working with the other monks. Strong but gentle, of distinguished appearance, conspicuous for his cheerful generosity, he won the hearts of his subjects. Unfortunately he died at the early age of thirty-six, after only four years in office.

He had died during the absence of Benedict Biscop, who was on his fifth journey to Rome. As usual, Biscop returned with many treasures, including some panel paintings of Christ, Mary and typological scenes from the Old and New Testament. He also brought two silk cloaks, later exchanged for three hides of land near Wearmouth (ch. 9). The community had elected Sigfrith, a deacon, as abbot; the equal of Eosterwine his predecessor, he too was destined to die young, from a disease of the lungs, presumably tuberculosis (ch. 10).

The subsequent chapters (11–14) which describe the deaths of both Benedict and Sigfrith in 689, are full of interest in several ways. The personal details such as the paralysis of Benedict, the bringing of Sigfrith, equally ill, to his bedside and other elements must surely be due to an eyewitness, possibly Bede himself, then at the impressionable age of sixteen. Even more important are Biscop's deathbed recommendations to his community. He exhorted them to observe the rule and customs which he had carefully arranged from the seventeen monasteries he had visited, to keep his library intact, and to choose his successor according to the Rule of St Benedict. The last of these enactments was the most important, especially as it was accompanied by a strongly expressed warning to his community on no account to choose Biscop's own brother. 'I would far rather have the monastery revert for ever to a wilderness,' he said, 'than have my brother, who has not entered on the way of truth, succeed me as abbot.'

Against the contemporary assumption of family ownership of monasteries (even more explicitly denounced by Bede at the end of his life in his *Letter to Egbert*) Benedict's action has been seen as virtually disinheriting his brother. It is noteworthy that the presuppositions and procedures of the Rule of St Benedict were in this instance preferred to those of Anglo-Saxon law. This is an example of his preference of spiritual fatherhood and monastic inheritance to their natural and earthly equivalents.

Another point also needs to be made. The power and influence of the abbot in St Benedict's Rule was so strong and fundamental that the whole tone and scale of values set in the monastery depended on the character of the abbot more than almost any other factor. In insisting on election of a new abbot who possessed the qualities recommended by St Benedict, Biscop was simultaneously providing in the best possible way for the future quality of his monasteries. He was also arranging for them to be governed according to the Rule of St Benedict.

The precise influence of this in the early years of Wearmouth and Jarrow is not easy to determine. Certainly there is no incompatibility with Benedict's Rule. Some elements such as the singing of the office 'with antiphons' are best understood in the framework of the Rule. Moreover Bede cites the Rule several times and significantly compares Biscop's early life to that of St Benedict described by Gregory. The connection of both Biscop and Ceolfrith with Wilfrid makes Benedictine influence likely. At the present time some scholars (and the Bede museum at Jarrow) emphasize the influence of Benedict's Rule there. But some mixture of other customs was certainly present. This was so in virtually all monasteries of the time. Perhaps Biscop's customs emanating from seventeen monasteries should be compared to some of those from Cluny, Canterbury and elsewhere, which in later ages safeguarded the Rule by legislating for details not explicitly mentioned in it.

Another important influence at Wearmouth and Jarrow, not mentioned here by Bede, is that of Cassiodorus. This influence is certain: Bede himself read and handled the great *Codex Grandior* which came from Cassiodorus's monastery at Vivarium. Cassiodorus was a retired civil servant who founded two monasteries in Italy during the sixth century. They had as part of their explicit aim the preservation of the learning of the past, the detailed study of the text of the Bible and the production of manuscripts. It is likely that other books of his found their way to Wearmouth and Jarrow among the acquisitions of Biscop and Ceolfrith.

Wearmouth and Jarrow were centres, but not the only ones in Europe, where the influences of Benedict and Cassiodorus met. One result of this fruitful fertilization was the emergence of the Benedictine scholar, of whom Bede is an early and notable example. But his knowledge of secular literature was comparatively slight: he was primarily a monastic, scriptural scholar. His development in this direction must surely be ascribed to Ceolfrith more than to anyone else. Since Bede's childhood Ceolfrith had been like a father to him and this relationship continued and deepened after Biscop's death when, both by Biscop's choice and that of the community, Ceolfrith succeeded him in the powers of founding abbot of both Wearmouth and Jarrow. This charge of both monasteries lasted for twenty-eight years, until 716 (ch. 15).

His policy was to complete the work of Biscop. This included building chapels, furnishing them with plate and vestments, doubling the number of books in the library and exchanging lands. The ownership of these lands was guaranteed by a papal indult, and confirmed by the king and the bishops: it needed to be clearly recognized against the possible claims of Biscop's relatives and any would-be intruders. In character Ceolfrith was diligent, zealous, mortified and tactful (ch. 16).

One of the finest achievements of his abbacy was the production of three large complete Bibles, written in uncial hand, of which one (the *Codex Amiatinus*) survives virtually intact at Florence, while there remain a few leaves from another one in the British Library.

The *Codex Amiatinus* (so called because it later belonged to the monastery of Monte Amiato in the Central Apennines) is an enormous volume: the size and weight of it are such that two men carry it in when the student requests to see it. It consists of 1,030 folios (2,060 pages): each double page or opening, measures twenty-seven and a half by twenty and a half inches. It weighs more than seventy-five pounds. It has been credibly estimated that about 1,550 calves were needed to provide the parchment, but recent research suggests that it came from Italy. In either case, only a large and wealthy monastery could have commissioned a volume of this size. Yet Ceolfrith commissioned three.

The *Amiatinus* is the oldest surviving complete Latin Bible in one volume from anywhere in the world. It was more usual in antiquity for the Bible to be bound up in nine volumes or more, as is exemplified in the painting of Ezra in the *Amiatinus* itself. The influence of Cassiodorus is manifest in the planning and execution of this great project. Its text is that of Jerome's Vulgate.

It is probable that it was written in nine sections by seven different scribes. 'Every page,' wrote E. A. Lowe in *English Uncial*, 'was executed by English scribes and painters. The diagrams use rustic capitals, capitulary uncials, and a curious sloping uncial script.' There are also in various places, examples of insular spelling and of insular minuscule script. These, with the dedicatory verses described below, clearly prove its English origin.

The anonymous biographer of Ceolfrith described the enterprise as follows:

The collection of books which he himself or Benedict had brought from Rome he splendidly enlarged: among other things he caused three pandects to be transcribed, two of which he placed in his two monasteries in their churches, so that whoever wished to read a chapter of either the Old or the New Testament, could easily find what he was looking for. As for the third, when he was to leave for Rome, he decided to offer it as a gift to Saint Peter, prince of the Apostles (ch. 20).

It is thus neither affirmed nor denied that the original purpose of the book was to be a present for the Pope: it is not impossible that it was originally destined to be Ceolfrith's own copy, or one to be available for reference or as a model for others. But whatever the original purpose was, it must have been of great importance to justify the enormous expenditure involved both in materials and in deployment of precious skilled labour of the scribes. One of these could have been Bede himself. The exact date of its production is unknown: it could have been as early as the Lindisfarne Gospels (late 690s) or as late as the last few years of Ceolfrith's rule. He resigned his charge in 716 at the age of seventy-four. It was then that he took the precious volume as a gift for the Pope, as, like several other Anglo-Saxon kings and bishops, he wished to end his days at Rome. It is the most impressive artefact to survive from his reign.

The chapters in Bede's work which describe his resignation and departure are very moving (16–18). Diligent and zealous, austere and tactful, he combined in a remarkable degree the qualities of St Benedict's abbot. Conscious that his advancing years made him unable to maintain the standards which he considered proper, he decided to give up his charge and thus enable a younger man to lead his community to a more perfect observance of their rule. When he left, Wearmouth and Jarrow numbered about six hundred monks; their land amounted to 150 hides. The affectionate farewell of abbot and community described by Bede is one of the most moving scenes of monastic literature from the early Middle Ages.

The deep regard the community held for Ceolfrith is also revealed in the letter to Pope Gregory II written by Hwaetberht, his successor, who outlived Bede himself (ch. 19). One of the first actions of his rule had been to obtain the elevation of the bones of Eosterwine and Sigfrith (ch. 20). Bishop Acca of Hexham, disciple and successor of Wilfrid, authorized this, thereby approving the cult of these two as saints. Benedict Biscop was venerated already and Ceolfrith soon would be. Meanwhile he had fallen ill at Langres on his way to Rome, presumably in a large company for security. Faithful to his chosen vocation right up to the end of his life, he recited the psalter twice a day and offered Mass even in extreme weakness (ch. 22). He died on 25 September 716 (ch. 23).

While Bede's account of the abbots of his monastery can be considered a chronicle of local history, the Life of Ceolfrith, below, pp. 213–29, is more of a biography of the most important of Biscop's successors. It survives in only two manuscripts (one of the tenth, the other of the twelfth century), while Bede's work is contained not only in these same two manuscripts but also in another six. Inevitably there is much common ground between the two works, but sufficient differences to make it worth while printing them both in English in the same volume.

The anonymous author seems to have been a monk of Wearmouth rather than Jarrow and one of the monks who accompanied Ceolfrith on his last journey to Rome, which was terminated by his death at Langres. He also describes events of some importance which are not found in Bede's narrative. One of these is the tedium experienced by Ceolfrith in his early days as prior, caused by discontented noblemen. In spite of this, our author emphasizes more than once Ceolfrith's aristocratic origins and provides a delightful anecdote of Ceolfrith's father and his generosity to the poor. Again, he is fuller about Ceolfrith's last journey and he transcribed (though Bede did not) the letter of Pope Gregory to Abbot Hwaetberht in response to his covering letter of recommendation of Abbot Ceolfrith. Each writer recorded elements which the other did not; perhaps the most memorable of the anonymous writer's anecdotes is the famous one of how Ceolfrith and one of the monastery's boys together performed the Divine Office with antiphons after the plague had removed many of the others. This boy is generally thought to have been Bede himself. And if anyone suspects that the scale of the disaster has been exaggerated, it is well to remember that the personnel of the monastery of St Albans was literally reduced to half by the Black Death between Palm Sunday and Easter Sunday in 1348.

The anonymous writer inspires confidence in his accuracy because of his simple, matter-of-fact narrative. If his sentences are sometimes too long and his style too verbose, by these very qualities he provides comparison with Bede, a master of Latin style in every way. The anonymous biographer, like the monk Cuthbert who wrote the moving account of Bede's death, reminds us of the achievements of other monks from Bede's monastery who, like him, laboured hard to achieve a very creditable Latin culture near the ends of the civilized world.

One of the fruits of this culture was the splendid Pandect, later called the *Codex Amiatinus*, appropriately offered to the Bishop of Rome by Ceolfrith and actually presented to him by Ceolfrith's monks. This huge volume is one of the treasures of the Laurentian Library at Florence. Written throughout in uncial characters (seemingly regardless of the considerable cost), it provides one of the best texts of the Vulgate Latin Bible in existence. The dedicatory verses, recorded by our author alone in chapter 37, were subsequently altered when the then pope presented this same

volume to the monastery of Monte Amiato (near Florence) during
the twelfth century. This alteration could easily have resulted in
the Jarrow provenance of this volume not being recorded for
posterity, but the nineteenth-century scholars G. B. de Rossi and
F. J. A. Hort suggested further investigation. The use of ultra-
violet photography restored the original text of the dedication
and showed it to be identical with the text in the anonymous Life
of Ceolfrith. This important discovery effectively confirmed not
only the English origin of this book, but also its identification
with the volume taken by Ceolfrith on his last journey to Rome.

The cult of Ceolfrith as a saint began (as usual) around his tomb.
Reports were made of wonderful and unusual light around it.
Pilgrims came, the monks visited the shrine regularly; other signs
and cures believed to be miraculous soon followed. At an unknown
date his body was brought back to Wearmouth and enshrined.
There it was visited and venerated until the Viking invasions. In
the tenth century, with the revival of monastic life in England
under St Dunstan, some of his monks from Glastonbury claimed
to have translated these relics again, this time to their own
monastery. There he was venerated on his traditional death-day,
25 September.

Of the five texts translated in this book the *Voyage of Brendan*
has immense interest as an imaginative reconstruction of a way
of life attributed to the historical Brendan, of whose life it gives
us little historical detail. Eddius's *Life of Wilfrid* however aims at
being a commemorative biography of a great man, about whom
Bede also wrote with fluency but also a certain reserve. In spite
of its partisan quality and its several inaccuracies, it is largely con-
vincing, although allowances have to be made for it being an
'official' biography. Bede's *Life of Cuthbert* to a considerable extent
depended on the earlier biographer's work, but altered its emphasis; while it tells us much of Cuthbert as a man of prayer and
of miracles, it does not give us even in outline a clear impression
of his historical importance. In his *Lives of the Abbots*, however,
Bede writes as a historian of his own house, describing in detail
what he had seen himself or learnt from other eyewitnesses in
his community. Certainly, an experienced reader of Bede will
detect here and there the way he uses the characteristics of the

heroes of the past to remind his contemporaries of their decline from real or supposed higher standards; but of the five works this is surely the one with the greatest claim to historical accuracy. It is usefully completed by the anonymous *Life of Ceolfrith*.

The characters described in these works were all great men, with considerable appeal to generations other than their own. Brendan and Cuthbert are primarily of insular importance, whereas Wilfrid, Benedict Biscop and Ceolfrith were all Europeans as well as Englishmen, whose achievements in the fields of religion and culture was far greater than that of most of their contemporaries. The rich and contrasting age in which they lived, brought to life for us by the writings of Bede more than any other author, is being rediscovered at the present time by an increasing number of students. The ideals and the scale of values of its great men still appeal across the centuries.

# Bede: Life of Cuthbert

To my holy and most blessed lord and father, Bishop Eadfrid, and to the whole congregation of monks serving God at Lindisfarne, Bede, your faithful servant, sends greeting. It is on your orders that I am writing this customary preface – to let the reader know that the task of writing the book itself was undertaken in brotherly compliance with your wishes. I should also like to inform him, at this point, about what he might otherwise remain ignorant of, and to remind yourselves that I have written nothing about the saint without first subjecting the facts to the most thorough scrutiny and have passed on nothing to be transcribed for general reading that has not been obtained by rigorous examination of trustworthy witnesses. Indeed, before ever beginning to write, I carried out a thorough investigation of the whole of the saint's glorious life, with the help of those who had actually known him. I occasionally mention some of their names in the body of the book so that you can see for yourselves exactly what the sources are.

While the book was still in note form, it was often looked over and revised by our very reverend brother, the priest Herefrith, whenever he came here, and by others who had lived a long time with the man of God, and who were, therefore, more conversant with the details of his life. On their advice I made several amendments. I have tried to avoid all ambiguity or hair-splitting and to write a clear investigation of the truth in simple terms. I have already taken care to let you yourselves examine what I have written, so that what was false could be amended, what was true, confirmed.

When, with the help of the Lord, the book was finished, and had been read for two days before the elders and teachers of your community, and its every detail had been considered, they then

approved all I had written, declaring it fit to be read and transcribed by all whose holy zeal moved them to do so. The dis-
cussions you held among yourselves have brought to light many
other facts, just as important as those I record here and well worth
writing down, except that it hardly seems right to make insertions
and add to a carefully planned and completed work. Furthermore,
since I have been quick to carry out the task you thought fit to
impose on me, may I suggest you crown your kindness by not
being slow to reward me by your prayers. When, in reading my
book, your hearts are raised to a more burning desire for the
Kingdom of Heaven, by the memory of our holy father, do not
forget to intercede with the divine mercy on behalf of one so small,
so that I may be found worthy on earth to long for and hereafter
in perfect bliss to see 'the goodness of the Lord in the land of the
living'. And, when I am dead, pray for my soul and say mass for
me as though I were one of your own household, and be so good
as to inscribe my name on the roll with your own.

You, my lord bishop, will recall having already promised me
this; in witness whereof you ordered our holy brother, Godfrith,
the sacristan, to put my name in the register of your congregation
even now. You may be aware, holy father, that I have already
produced, at the request of some of the brothers here, a life of
this same father of ours, in heroic verse, somewhat shorter than
this prose life but following the same pattern. You may, if you
wish, have a copy. In the preface to the verse life I promised that
I would later write a fuller account of the life and miracles, a
promise which, as far as God permits, I am now striving to fulfil.
On behalf of our congregation, beloved brethren and masters, I
pray that the Almighty Lord may keep you secure in bliss.

Amen

## CHAPTER I

*How the holy child Cuthbert was warned by an infant
and told that he would be a bishop*

THE beginning of our account of the life and miracles of the blessed
Cuthbert is consecrated by the words which the prophet Jeremiah
uses of the state of perfection of the hermit: 'It is good for a man
to have borne the yoke in his youth; he shall sit in solitude and
be silent, because he will raise himself above himself'[1]; for it was
the sweetness of this way of life which led Cuthbert, in his earliest
youth, to put his neck to the yoke of monastic discipline. Later,
when the opportunity arose, he embraced the hermit's life and
lived a long while in silence, pleased to forgo the speech of men
for the delights of divine contemplation. To fit him for these tasks
the grace of God urged him on, little by little, in the way of truth
from his earliest years. Up to his eighth year, the end of infancy
and the threshold of boyhood, he had no mind for anything but
games and carefree play, so that what was said of Samuel might
well be said of him: 'He did not yet know the Lord, neither was
the word of the Lord revealed unto him.'[2] This is as a prelude
to my praise of his boyhood. Later he came to know the Lord
perfectly and opened the ear of his heart to receive His word.

He loved games and pranks, and as was natural at his age, loved
to play with other children. He was naturally agile and quick-
witted and usually won the game. He would often be still fresh
when the rest were tired and would look round in triumph, as
though the game were in his hands, and ask who was willing
to continue. He used to boast that he had beaten all those of his
own age and many who were older at wrestling, jumping, running, and every other exercise. For 'when he was a child, he
understood as a child', but when a man, 'he put away childish

---

1. *Lam.* iii, 27–8.
2. I *Sam.* iii, 7.

things'. And Providence chose a very suitable way of checking his childish ardour. Bishop Trumwine of happy memory tells the story as he had it from Cuthbert himself:

One day a great crowd of lads were at their usual games in a field, Cuthbert among them, twisting themselves about in all kinds of contortions in the excitement of the game. Suddenly a child no more than three years old ran up to him and began to upbraid him, with all the solemnity of an old man, for his idleness and indulgence in games, saying he would do better to exercise a steady control over mind and body. When Cuthbert ridiculed the idea, the child threw himself wailing to the ground, the tears pouring down his cheeks. The others rushed to comfort him, asking why he had suddenly burst into tears, but to no avail. When Cuthbert himself tried to cheer him up, he cried out: 'Why, most holy priest and bishop Cuthbert, do you persist in doing what is so contrary both to your nature and your rank? How ill it befits you to play with children, you whom the Lord has marked out to instil virtue into your elders!'

Cuthbert took this good-naturedly, listened indeed with rapt attention, and soothed the child's feelings with a friendly show of affection. He forsook his foolish games at once and went home. From then on he showed himself more mature and earnest, as the Spirit, who had spoken to him through the mouth of an infant, spoke to him now in the recesses of his heart.

Let it not cause astonishment that God should check the folly of a child by a child. Did He not, when He thought fit, restrain the foolishness of a prophet by putting human words into the mouth of an ass? One can truly say in His praise, 'Out of the mouths of babes and sucklings Thou hast perfected praise.'

## CHAPTER 2

*How he was lamed by a disease of the knee and
immediately cured by an angel*

It is a true saying that 'unto everyone that hath shall be given,
and he shall have abundance' – that is, whoever has his mind
set on virtue shall be greatly endowed with virtues from above.
The child Cuthbert, as a reward for carefully storing up in his
heart the advice given him by human means, was privileged to
see and talk with an angel. His knee suddenly began to hurt and
a great tumour swelled up, causing the muscles of the knee-cap
to contract. At first he could manage to hop with his foot off the
ground, but the swelling got so much worse that he could hardly
walk at all. One day the servants carried him outside to lie in the
fresh air. Looking up he caught sight of a horseman approaching
from afar, dressed in white, with noble looks, on a steed of un-
paralleled beauty. He rode up, saluted him courteously, and asked,
almost jokingly, if he would mind ministering to a guest such as
him. Cuthbert replied: 'I am only too ready to devote myself to
showing you hospitality, but I am pinned down, for my sins, by
this weakness of the leg. I have been troubled with it for a long
time now and there is no doctor anywhere with skill enough to
cure it.'

The horseman alighted, looked hard at the knee, and said: 'Boil
some wheaten flour in milk and bathe the tumour with it hot,
and you will be healed.'

He mounted and rode off. Cuthbert did as he was bidden and
within a few days was well again. Then he knew that it was an
angel that had given him the remedy, sent by the same power
who had deigned to send the Archangel Raphael to cure Tobias's
eyes. If anyone thinks it strange for an angel to appear on horseback, let him read the history of the Maccabees, where angels on
horseback come to defend both Judas Maccabeus and the Temple
itself.

## CHAPTER 3

*How the winds changed at his prayer and the rafts, which*
*had been carried away, were brought back safe to land*

HENCEFORTH the boy devoted himself to God, and, as he would
later recount to his friends, when he prayed for help against
frequent and pressing difficulties, he often had angels sent to
defend him. He was heard by Him who is wont to listen to the
cry of the poor and deliver them from all their tribulations, because he in turn was kind enough to pray for others in similar
dangers.

There is a monastery near the mouth of the Tyne, on the south
bank, once full of monks, but changed, like everything else, by
the course of time, and now housing a noble company of women.
These monks used to bring the wood they needed for the house
by raft, from a good distance away along the current of the river.
One day they had reached the point opposite the monastery and
were bringing the rafts in when a sudden gale rose out of the
west, scattered the rafts, and dragged them down towards the
mouth of the river. The monks inside the monastery saw what
had happened and launched out to help their brethren labouring
on the rafts; but the fury of the wind got the better of them and
they could do nothing. Giving up hope of human aid they fled
to the divine – while the rafts were floating out to sea, they came
out of the monastery, gathered round the nearest rock and prayed
fervently to the Lord for their brethren who were on the point
of perishing before their very eyes. The answer to their prayers
was long delayed, but when it did come it was clearly the work
of God's providence, manifesting the power of Cuthbert's prayers.
He himself was standing on the opposite bank of the river among
a great crowd of peasants. The rafts floating out to sea looked
like five birds bobbing up and down on the waves. While the
monks opposite were watching in sorrow, the peasants began to
jeer at their way of life, as though they deserved such misfortune

for spurning the life of the ordinary man and introducing new, unheard-of rules of conduct. Cuthbert stopped their insults.

'Do you realize what you are doing? Would it not be more human of you to pray for their safety rather than to gloat over their misfortune?'

But they, boors both in thought and speech, fulminated against him.

'Nobody is going to pray for them. Let not God raise a finger to help them! They have done away with all the old ways of worship[1] and now nobody knows what to do.'

The saint listened to them and then knelt down and prayed, bending low to the ground. At once the wind changed right about and bore them safe and sound to land at a very convenient spot beside the monastery. Seeing this, the country people burnt inwardly with shame at their impiety. They gave due credit to Cuthbert's faith, and from then on never ceased to praise him. The man who told me the story, a worthy brother of this monastery, said he had often heard one of that very group, a simple peasant, incapable of lying, tell the tale before a large audience.


## CHAPTER 4

*How, when he was with some shepherds, he saw the soul of*
*St Aidan borne heavenward by angels*


WHEN Christ, by whose grace the lives of the faithful are directed and guided, decided to call his servant to a higher and harder way of life, to earn a greater and more glorious reward, Cuthbert, at the time, happened to be looking after a flock of sheep committed to his charge, away up in the hills. One night when his companions had gone to sleep and he was keeping watch and praying as usual, he suddenly saw light streaming from the skies, breaking the long night's darkness, and the choirs of the heavenly

1. i.e. pagan worship.

host coming down to earth. They quickly took into their ranks a human soul, marvellously bright, and returned to their home above. The youth was moved by this vision to give himself to spiritual discipline in order to gain eternal happiness with the mighty men of God. There and then he set about thanking God and exhorting his companions in a brotherly way to praise Him.

'What wretches we are, given up to sleep and sloth so that we never see the glory of those who watch with Christ unceasingly! After so short a vigil what marvels have I seen! The gate of Heaven opened and a band of angels led in the spirit of some holy man. While we are still in the deepest darkness, he has the happiness of looking forever on the halls of heaven and their King. I think he must have been some holy bishop or layman of great distinction since he was led in with such splendour and light by retinues of angels.'

In this way Cuthbert fired the hearts of the shepherds with the love and honour of God. Next day he was told that Aidan, Bishop of Lindisfarne, a man of outstanding holiness, had passed into the Kingdom of Heaven at the time of his vision. He delivered the sheep back to their owners and decided to enter a monastery.

## CHAPTER 5

*How God provided food for him on a journey*

WHILE he was seriously contemplating entering on a higher course of life, he received a great grace to strengthen his resolve, and, incidentally, to show quite clearly that those who seek the Kingdom of Heaven and its justice will, by the mercy of providence, not lack bodily sustenance. He was travelling alone one day and, about the third hour, chanced to turn into a distant village. He went to the home of a devout married woman, wishing to rest a while; he was more worried about food for his horse than for himself, for winter was just beginning. The woman made him welcome and pressed him to let her prepare him a meal. But the saint would not permit it; he could not eat as it was a Friday, a day on which many of the faithful, in honour of the Death of our Lord, are wont to prolong their fast till the ninth hour. The woman, being hospitality's own self, insisted.

'You will not find another village on your way, nor even a house; and it will take you till sunset to reach your destination. At least take something with you, otherwise you will be fasting the whole day, perhaps even till tomorrow.' But his zeal for religion got the better of her insistence and he set out still fasting and remained in that state till vespers. When it came to vesper time he saw that he would not be able to finish the journey that day; he saw too that there was no human dwelling within reach. He suddenly noticed some shepherds' huts, very makeshift constructions, built for the summer, and deserted. He went in, meaning to stay the night, tied the horse to the wall, and gave it a bunch of straw he had gathered from bits blown out of the roof. He passed the time in prayer. Looking up from his psalms he saw the horse lift its head up and start to pull straw out of the roof. Suddenly a bundle wrapped in a linen cloth fell down with the straw. When his prayers were over he got up to find out what it was and discovered half a loaf still warm and some meat wrapped in the cloth, enough for one meal.

'O God,' he said, 'I was fasting for the love of Thee and in return Thou hast fed both me and my animal, blessed be Thy Name.'

He broke the bread and gave half to the horse. From that day on he was much more ready to fast, now that he knew he had been fed in his solitude by Him who, when there was no one else to provide, had sent the very birds, day after day, with food for Elijah in the wilderness. His eyes are ever on them that fear Him and hope in His mercy, so that He may, in the words of the Psalmist, 'snatch their souls from death and feed them in time of famine.'[1] The holy priest Ingwald from our monastery at Monkwearmouth heard this from Cuthbert when the latter was a bishop. Ingwald, thanks to his ripe old age, has ceased to gaze on earthly things with the eyes of the flesh; his heart is completely taken up with the things of Heaven.

---

1. *Psalm* xxxii, 18–19 (A.V. xxxiii, 18–19).

## CHAPTER 6

*Boisil's prophecy. Cuthbert arrives at Melrose,*
*is welcomed and remains there*

OUR venerable servant of God, meanwhile, was hastening to leave the world and take upon himself monastic discipline. Spurred on by his heavenly vision of the joys of eternal bliss, he was ready to suffer hunger and thirst in this life in order to enjoy the banquets of the next. The community of Lindisfarne, he knew, was well adorned with holy monks, under whose example and teaching he might make good progress, but the reputation for sublime virtue enjoyed by Boisil, priest of Melrose, led him to enter there. By chance Boisil was standing at the monastery gates when he arrived and thus saw him first. Cuthbert dismounted, gave his horse and spear to a servant (he had not yet put off secular dress), and went into the church to pray. Boisil had an intuition of the high degree of holiness to which the boy he had just been looking at would rise, and said just this single phrase to the monks with whom he was standing: 'Behold the servant of the Lord,' imitating Him who, at the approach of Nathaniel, exclaimed: 'Behold an Israelite indeed, one in whom there is no guile'. An old veteran, Sigfrith, priest of Jarrow monastery, told me the tale; he was there with Boisil at the time, a mere youth in the first steps of the monastic life. Now he is living the life of perfection. He has only a few feeble breaths left in him and is thirsting for the joys of the future life.

Boisil said no more. He welcomed Cuthbert and when he explained the purpose of his visit, namely to leave the world behind him, Boisil received him with great kindness into the community. Boisil himself was prior. A few days later the priest Eata arrived, then Abbot of Melrose and later Abbot and Bishop of Lindisfarne. Boisil told him about Cuthbert, explained how well disposed he was, and gained permission for him to receive the tonsure and become one of the community. Once admitted, Cuthbert was careful to keep up with the rest in observing the rule. He excelled them in zeal for strict discipline. He watched, prayed, worked, and read harder than anyone else. Like Samson the Nazarite he carefully abstained from all alcoholic drink, but he was not so severe with himself as regards food lest his work should suffer. He was robust and strong, fit enough to carry out everything he chose to put his hand to.

## CHAPTER 7

*How he entertained an angel and, in seeking to give him earthly food, was rewarded in turn with bread from heaven*

A FEW years later when King Alhfrith, for the salvation of his soul, gave Abbot Eata ground at Ripon[1] to build a monastery, the abbot transferred some of the monks to live there, under the same rule as they had at Melrose. Cuthbert was one of them. He was appointed guestmaster and is said to have had an angel sent to him as a guest to test his devotion.

One morning he left the inner monastery buildings to go to the guest chamber and found a youth sitting inside. He gave him the usual sort of kindly welcome, thinking, naturally, that he was a man. He got him water to wash his hands, washed his feet himself, dried them, put them in his bosom, and humbly chafed them with his hands. The youth was asked to wait till after terce, when a meal would be ready; otherwise if he left at once he would faint with hunger in the winter cold. He thought the lad had travelled all night through the wind and snow and had put in at the monastery at dawn to rest. But the youth said he must leave immediately and hurry to a far distant place. Cuthbert asked question after question and finally adjured him in God's Name to stay. As soon as terce was over it was dinner time, and a table was set and food brought.

1. When Eata showed himself unwilling to accept Roman practices, Alhfrith drove him and his Celtic monks away from Ripon, and gave the land and monastery to Wilfrid (*Cuthbert*, ch. 8; and *Wilfrid*, ch. 8).

'Now eat and get your strength back,' Cuthbert urged him, 'while I go and get you some warm bread. I hope it will be ready.'

When he came back the youth had vanished. The ground was covered with fresh snow but there were no footsteps to be seen. The man of God was amazed. He puzzled over what had happened and then went to put the table back in the storehouse. At the door there was a wonderfully fragrant odour. He looked about to see where it was coming from and there beside him were three loaves, unusually white and fine. Trembling he said to himself: 'Now I know that it was an angel, come not to be fed but to feed. He has brought bread such as cannot be produced on earth, whiter than the lily, sweeter than roses, more delicious than honey. Such food, it is obvious, comes not from this world of ours but from the paradise of joy. No wonder he refused human food when he can enjoy in Heaven the bread of eternal life.' The manifest virtue of this miracle moved the saint to even greater zeal for good works, and as his virtues increased, so did the grace that was given him. Angels would often appear and talk with him and when he was hungry he would be refreshed with food by the special gift of God. Cuthbert was a very pleasant, affable man; he generally restricted himself to citing the lives of the fathers when he wanted to find models of godly living for his brethren, yet sometimes, in all humility, he would mention his own spiritual graces. Sometimes he did this openly, sometimes he talked in the third person as though it were someone else. His audience always knew that he was speaking like St Paul, who at times would recount his virtues openly, at times as though speaking of another – when, for example, he says: 'I knew a man in Christ, above fourteen years ago, such an one caught up even to the seventh heaven,' and so on.[1]

1. 2 *Cor.* xii, 2.

## CHAPTER 8

*How Cuthbert was cured of a disease, and how the dying
Boisil prophesied what was in store for him*

ALL the ways of this world are as fickle and unstable as a sudden
storm at sea. Eata and Cuthbert and all the rest were thrown out
of Ripon and the monastery they had built was given over to other
monks. This change of place did not weaken our athlete of Christ
in his determination once taken to do battle for Heaven. He
followed the words and actions of Boisil with undiminished
fervour, but he was struck down about this time by a plague which
was ravaging the length and breadth of the country. (My source
for this is Herefrith, a priest of the saint's own community and
later Bishop of Lindisfarne, who had the story from Cuthbert
himself.) The monks spent the whole night in prayer, for they felt
they could not do without him on account of his holiness. His
reply next morning when one of the monks mentioned the
vigil – for they had kept it quiet from him – was: 'Then what am
I lying here for? God will certainly have heard the prayers of so
many good men. Fetch me my shoes and stick.' He got up there
and then and tried to walk with the stick. Day by day his strength
came back until he was quite recovered; only the swelling on the
thigh seemed to move inwards, and for almost the whole of his
life he was troubled with some internal pain, so that, to quote
the apostle, 'strength was made perfect in weakness'.

Boisil saw that he was better and prophesied that he would
never again be stricken by the same malady. 'At the same time,'
said Boisil, 'I warn you not to lose the chance of learning from
me, for death is upon me. By next week my body and voice shall
have lost their strength.'

Cuthbert knew that he was telling the truth.

'Then tell me what is the best book to study, one that can be
got through in a week.'

'St John the Evangelist,' Boisil answered. 'I have a commentary in seven parts. With the help of God we can read one a day and perhaps discuss it if we want.'

It was done as he said. They were able to finish quickly because they dealt not with the profound arguments but with the simple things of 'the faith which worketh by love'. On the seventh day, when the reading was finished, illness overtook Boisil, and – this I recount with gladness – he entered into the joy of eternal bliss. He is believed to have unfolded all Cuthbert's future during that week. He was a prophet and a very holy man. Three years before the epidemic came he foretold it to Abbot Eata and did not conceal the fact that he would perish. Eata, he said, would not be carried off but would die of what the doctors called dysentery. His prophecy turned out right. He hinted to Cuthbert that he would be a bishop. Afterwards, when he was living a hermit's life, Cuthbert would not mention the predicted honour, except occasionally to his brethren.

'If,' he would lament, 'I could live in a tiny dwelling on a rock in the ocean, surrounded by the swelling waves, cut off from the knowledge and the sight of all, I would still not be free from the cares of this fleeting world nor from the fear that somehow the love of money might snatch me away.'

## CHAPTER 9

*How Cuthbert was most assiduous in preaching the word*

On Boisil's death Cuthbert became prior, an office which he carried out for many years with holy zeal. Inside the monastery he counselled the monks on the religious life and set a high example of it himself, and outside, in the world, he strove to convert people for miles around from their foolish ways to a delight in the promised joys of Heaven. Many who had the faith had profaned it by their works. Even while the plague was raging some had forgotten the mystery conferred on them in baptism and had fled to idols, as though incantations or amulets or any other diabolical rubbish could possibly avail against a punishment sent by God the Creator. To bring back both kinds of sinners he often did the rounds of the villages, sometimes on horseback, more often on foot, preaching the way of truth to those who had gone astray. Boisil did the same in his time. It was the custom at that time among the English people that if a priest or cleric came to a village everyone would obey his call and gather round to hear him preach. They would willingly listen and even more gladly put his words into practice as far as they had understood them. Such was his skill in teaching, such his power of driving his lessons home, and so gloriously did his angelic countenance shine forth, that none dared keep back from him even the closest secrets of their heart. They confessed every sin openly – indeed they thought he would know if they held anything back – and made amends by 'fruits worthy of repentance', as he commanded. He made a point of searching out those steep rugged places in the hills which other preachers dreaded to visit because of their poverty and squalor. This, to him, was a labour of love. He was so keen to preach that sometimes he would be away for a whole week or a fortnight, or even a month, living with the rough hill folk, preaching and calling them heavenwards by his example.

## CHAPTER 10

*How after he had spent the whole night praying in the sea, animals ministered unto him as he came out of the water, and how one of the monks, ill with fear at the sight, was restored by his prayers*

INSIDE the monastery the man of God performed more and more signs and wonders, and his reputation kept pace. There was a nun called Aebbe, a real mother to the Lord's handmaids, in charge of the convent of Coldingham, honoured for piety and nobility alike, for she was King Oswiu's sister. She sent to Cuthbert to ask if he would come and exhort the community. So kind a request could not be refused. He came and stayed a few days, showing them the way of righteousness in deed as well as word. He was in the habit of rising at the dead of night, while everyone else was sleeping, to go out and pray, returning just in time for morning prayers. One night one of the monks watched him creep out, then followed him stealthily to see where he was going and what he was about. Down he went towards the beach beneath the monastery and out into the sea until he was up to his arms and neck in deep water. The splash of the waves accompanied his vigil throughout the dark hours of the night. At daybreak he came out, knelt down on the sand, and prayed. Then two otters bounded out of the water, stretched themselves out before him, warmed his feet with their breath, and tried to dry him on their fur. They finished, received his blessing, and slipped back to their watery home. He was soon home and was in choir at the proper time with the rest of the monks. But the brother who had spied on him from the cliffs returned with faltering steps, fear-stricken and distressed. He prostrated himself before Cuthbert and, in tears, craved pardon for his stupidity and presumption, quite sure that Cuthbert knew the cause of his discomfort.

'Why, what is wrong, what have you done?' asked the saint. 'Have you been spying on my night's work? I will forgive you, but only if you promise not to tell anyone while I am still alive.'

In this he followed his Master, who, when He had revealed the glory of His Majesty on the mount, warned the disciples, saying: 'Tell no man until the Son of Man be risen again from the dead.'[1] The brother promised, received a blessing, and was freed from the guilt and embarrassment he had so rashly incurred; but the silence he preserved while Cuthbert was living he more than made up for once the saint was dead.

1. *Matt.* xviii, 9.

## CHAPTER 11

*How he promised a calm sea to some sailors cut off by a
storm and how his prayer for food was answered*

MEANWHILE the man of God began to grow strong in prophecy,
foretelling the future and revealing to those near him events that
were happening elsewhere.[1] Once he had to go to the land of the
Niduari, a tribe of Picts, to settle some business or other. Two of
the brethren travelled with him by boat. (One of them, who afterwards became a priest, brought this miracle to general notice.)
They arrived after Christmas, hoping to take advantage of the
calm sea and favourable winds to return soon. For this reason
they did not trouble about provisions, but matters turned out very
differently from what they expected. No sooner had they landed
than a violent storm arose, cutting them off completely, and they
languished for some days, hungry and cold. Cuthbert, however,
did not waste this leisure time in idleness, nor did he merely sleep
through it. Night after night was spent in prayer. The Feast of
Epiphany was approaching, and in his usual blithe and affable
way he tried to raise his companions' spirits:

'Why do we remain listless and unresourceful?' he asked. 'We
ought to be thinking over every possible way of saving ourselves.
The land is bleak with snow, clouds lour in the sky, there is a
gale raging and the sea is a fury of waves, we are dying of hunger
and there is no chance of human aid. Then let us storm Heaven
with prayers, asking that same Lord who parted the Red Sea and
fed His people in the desert to take pity on us in our peril. I believe
that, unless our faith falters, He will not let us go fasting, today
of all days, the day which He has singled out for such wondrous
proofs of His Majesty. Let us move on and look for the banquet
He will surely provide for us to keep His festival with joy.' He led
them to the bank where he usually spent the whole night praying,

1. Gregory, *Dialogues* ii, 11.

and there they found three cuts of dolphin meat, ready to cook, as though prepared by human hand. They went down on their knees and thanked God.

'You see,' said Cuthbert, 'what comes of trusting and hoping in the Lord. He has given his servants food, and in giving them three lots has shown how much longer they are to stay here. Pick up the gifts Christ has sent us. Come, let us eat and refuse to be daunted.'

Three days of fierce storm were followed by a calm sea and a blue sky, and they were wafted home with fair winds following.

### CHAPTER 12

*How on a journey he foretold that provisions would be brought by an eagle*

HE had gone out one day to preach as usual, taking a boy with him for company. Long before reaching their destination they were tired out. Cuthbert said to the boy, to test him: 'Tell me, son, where do you intend to eat today? Will you be able to turn in at friends on the way?'

'I was thinking about that myself,' answered the lad. 'We did not bring anything with us when we set out, and there is no one to ask a meal from. We cannot cover the rest of the journey fasting, without doing ourselves an injury.'

'Learn to have constant faith and hope in the Lord,' answered Cuthbert. 'He who serves God shall never die of hunger.' He looked up and saw an eagle flying high overhead. 'Do you see that eagle up there? God is quite capable of sending us food by it.'

They were making their way along a river, talking about such things, when they suddenly saw the eagle settling down on the bank.

'There,' said the saint, 'is the servant I was telling you about. Run and see what God has sent and bring it back quickly.'

The boy brought back a big fish which the bird had just caught.

'What!' said the saint. 'Did you not give the servant its share? Cut it in two, quickly now, and give half to the bird.'

The boy did as he was told. They put in at the next village and had the rest boiled. They and the family who cooked it for them had a most enjoyable meal. Cuthbert preached to them and praised God for His bounty, for 'blessed is the man whose hope is in the Lord and who has not sought after vanity or idle folly'. Then they resumed their journey to those they had set out to teach.

## CHAPTER 13

*How, while preaching to the people, he foresaw that the devil would send a phantom fire, and how he put it out*

HE suddenly realized, while preaching the words of life to a great crowd in a small village, that the ancient enemy, the devil, was present, come to hinder his work of salvation. He set out at once in his sermon to forestall the plot he knew to be hatching. He suddenly interrupted his discourse with this warning:

'My dear brethren, whenever you hear the mysteries of the Kingdom of Heaven being preached, you must be on your guard to listen with complete attention and not let the devil distract you with foolish worries from hearing what concerns your eternal salvation: for he has a thousand crafty ways of harming you.'

He immediately took up the thread of the sermon. All at once that wicked enemy sent down mock fire on to a nearby house. Sheets of flame, fanned by the wind, seemed to sweep through the whole village, and the noise of their crackling rent the air. Cuthbert managed, with outstretched hands, to restrain a few of the villagers, but the rest, almost the whole crowd, leaped up and vied with each other in throwing water on the flames. But real water has no effect on phantom fire, and the blaze raged on, until through Cuthbert's prayers the father of lies fled, taking his false fire with him, into the empty air. The crowd came to their senses, knelt before Cuthbert and, red in the face with shame, begged pardon for their fickleness, saying that they knew now that the devil did not cease for even an hour in his warfare against man's salvation. Cuthbert strengthened the weak and irresolute and carried on with his exhortations.

## CHAPTER 14

*How Cuthbert checked the flames of a house that was really on fire*

ONE day on his travels – for, like the apostles, he went everywhere preaching the way of salvation – he came to the house of a holy woman who was much given to good works. He often visited her because she was his old nurse, indeed he always called her mother. She lived towards the west of the village. No sooner had he entered the place than a house in the eastern quarter caught fire through carelessness and began to blaze. A wind sprang up from the same direction, tore away wisps of blazing straw from the roof, and scattered them far and wide. As the fire got hotter it kept back the men who were throwing water, finally forcing them to retreat. This holy woman ran back to her home in great consternation to find Cuthbert and implore him to pray; otherwise the whole village would be destroyed, her house with it.

'Do not worry, mother, keep calm. You and yours will be safe, no matter how fierce the flame.'

He went out and lay full length on the ground in front of the door. Before he had finished praying the wind had changed to the west and put the house the man of God had entered completely out of danger. In these two miracles he imitated the wonders of two of the fathers. In foreseeing and getting rid of phantom fire he followed the most holy and reverend father Benedict, who cast out a fire kindled by our ancient foe in the form of a burning kitchen, and in extinguishing and changing the direction of great sheets of flame he is comparable to the venerable Marcellinus, bishop of Ancona. When that city was burning Marcellinus stationed himself in front of the flames and damped them by prayer when the efforts of the whole city had proved useless. No wonder that the tried and faithful servants of God should have power over ordinary fire; hard daily practice has taught them both to subdue the fires of their own flesh and 'to quench all the fiery darts of the wicked one'. The following prophecy fits them aptly: 'When thou walkest through the fire thou shalt not be burned, neither shall the flame kindle upon thee.' Myself and those like me, knowing well our own weakness and helplessness, would not dare take any such measures against fire; we are not even sure of escaping scot-free from the undying fire of future punishment. But the loving kindness of Our Saviour is mighty and abundant. He will give us grace, unworthy though we are, to extinguish the flames of vice in this world, and escape the flames of punishment in the next.

## CHAPTER 15

### *How he exorcized the wife of a sheriff even before he reached her*

FROM having shown what power the venerable Cuthbert had against the deceits and frauds of the devil, we can now go on to reveal his strength in combating the fiend's undisguised fury. There was a sheriff of King Ecgfrith, called Hildmer, a man dedicated to good works along with all his household and therefore specially loved by Cuthbert. He visited Hildmer whenever he happened to be in the neighbourhood. His wife, though zealous in almsgiving and all the other fruits of virtue, was suddenly possessed of a devil. She was so sorely vexed that she would gnash her teeth, let out frightful howls, and fling her arms and legs about. It was terrifying to see or hear her. The convulsions gradually exhausted her, and she was already at death's door, or so it seemed, when her husband galloped off to fetch Cuthbert.

'My wife is ill,' he pleaded. 'She is very near her end. Send a priest before she goes, to give her the Body and Blood of the Lord and to bury her in holy ground.'

He was ashamed to admit that she whom Cuthbert was used

to seeing well was now out of her mind. Cuthbert went off to see whom he could send when it suddenly came to him that she was in the grip of no ordinary illness; she was possessed. He returned.

'I will not send anyone else. I ought to go back with you and see her myself.'

As they were going along the sheriff began to weep. The bitterness of his anguish was apparent from the floods of tears. He was afraid that when Cuthbert found she was mad he might think she had served God up to now only in feigned faith. But the man of God gently soothed his fears.

'Do not weep. Your wife's condition will not astonish me. I know, even though you are ashamed to admit it, that she is afflicted by a demon. I know too that before I arrive the demon will have left her and that she herself will come running out to meet us as sound as ever. She will take the reins, bid us come in quickly, and treat us with all her usual attention. It is not only the wicked who are stricken down in this way. God, in his inscrutable designs, sometimes lets the innocent in this world be blighted by the devil, in mind as well as in body.'

Cuthbert continued to console and instruct his friend in this vein, and as they approached the house the evil spirit, unable to bear the coming of the Holy Spirit with whom Cuthbert was filled, suddenly departed. The woman, loosed from the chains of the devil, jumped up as though woken from a deep sleep, rushed out in gratitude to the saint, and caught hold of his bridle. Her bodily and mental strength soon returned completely. She asked him to dismount and come in to bless the house, and waited on him with her most devoted attention. She admitted quite openly that at the first touch of his bridle all trace of her affliction had vanished.

## CHAPTER 16

*How he lived and taught in the monastery at Lindisfarne*

WHEN the venerable servant of God had passed many years in the monastery at Melrose, where he had distinguished himself by many signs of spiritual power, Abbot Eata transferred him to the monastery at Lindisfarne, to teach the true rule of monastic life in his capacity as prior and to illustrate it by his own perfect example. Eata was Abbot of Lindisfarne too. Let no one be surprised to hear that Lindisfarne, as well as being an episcopal see (a fact which I have already mentioned), is also the home of an abbot and community, for indeed it is. The episcopal residence and the monastery are one and the same, and all the clergy are monks. Aidan, the first bishop, was a monk and he and his followers kept to the monastic life – hence every bishop of Lindisfarne has exercised his office in this way. The abbot, who is elected by the bishop and a council of monks, rules the monastery, while the clergy – priests, deacons, cantors, lectors, and the rest – live the full monastic life together with the bishop. Blessed Pope Gregory showed himself a great devotee of this way of life, as can be seen from the reference he makes in his reply to Augustine. He was the first bishop Gregory sent to the English and had written to ask what sort of life the clergy should lead. I quote from the letter: 'You, brother, have been brought up in the monastic rule. Now that the faith has been brought to the English you must not start living apart from your clergy. Introduce that way of life practised by the fathers of the early church, none of whom claimed as his own anything that he possessed – for everything was held in common.'[1]

So when Cuthbert came to the church and monastery of Lindisfarne he handed on the monastic rule by teaching and example; moreover, he continued his custom of frequent visits to

1. Bede, *History* i, 27.

the common people in the neighbourhood, in order to rouse them up to seek and to merit the rewards of Heaven. He became famous for miracles, for his prayers restored sufferers from all kinds of disease and affliction. He cured some who were vexed by unclean spirits not only by laying on of hands, exhorting, and exorcizing – that is by actual contact – but even from afar, merely by praying or predicting their cure, as in the case of the sheriff's wife.

Some of the monks preferred their old way of life to the rule. He overcame these by patience and forbearance, bringing them round little by little through daily example to a better frame of mind. At chapter meetings he was often worn down by bitter insults, but would put an end to the arguments simply by rising and walking out, calm and unruffled. Next day he would give the same people exactly the same admonitions, as though there had been no unpleasantness the previous day. In this way he gradually won their obedience. He was wonderfully patient and unsurpassed for courage in enduring physical or mental hardship. Though overwhelmed by sorrow at these monks' recalcitrance, he managed to keep a cheerful face. It was clear to everyone that it was the Holy Spirit within giving him strength to smile at attacks from without. Such was his zeal for prayer that sometimes he would keep vigil for three or four nights at a stretch, so they say, without ever sleeping in his bed – and there was nowhere to rest outside the dormitory. Whether he was praying alone in some secret place or saying his psalms, he always did manual work to drive away the heaviness of sleep, or else he would do the rounds of the island, kindly inquiring how everything was getting on, relieving the tedium of his long vigils and psalm-singing by walking about. He would upbraid the monks for their softness in being annoyed if any restless brother should awaken them at the wrong moment.

'Nobody vexes me,' he would say, 'by waking me up. In fact I am pleased, for by driving away my drowsiness he has made me turn my mind to doing something useful.'

So full was he of sorrow for sin, so much aflame with heavenly yearnings, that he could never finish mass without shedding tears. He would imitate, as was only fitting, the rite he was performing, by offering himself up to God with a contrite heart. He urged his people to lift up their hearts and give thanks to the Lord God more by the yearnings of his own heart than by the sound of his voice, more by sighs than by chanting. His thirst for righteousness made him quick to reprove wrong-doers, but his gentleness made him speedy to forgive penitents. Often as they were pouring out their sins he would be the first to burst into tears, tears of sympathy with their weakness, and, though he had no need, would show them how to make up for their sins by doing the penance himself. He wore quite ordinary clothes, neither remarkably neat nor noticeably slovenly. The monastery follows his example to this day. The monks are discouraged from wearing expensively dyed cloth and are expected to be content with natural wool.

By these and other similar spiritual works the venerable prior fired all good men with the desire to emulate him, and recalled the wicked and the rebels against the rule from their obstinacy in error.

## CHAPTER 17

*How he banished demons from the Farne Island and
built himself a dwelling-place there*

AFTER many years in the monastery he finally entered with great joy and with the goodwill of the abbot and monks into the remoter solitude he had so long sought, thirsted after, and prayed for. He was delighted that after a long and spotless active life he should be thought worthy to ascend to the stillness of divine contemplation. He rejoiced to have attained to the condition of those of whom the psalmist proclaims: 'They shall go from strength to strength; the God of gods shall be seen in Sion.'[1] To learn the first steps of the hermit's life he retired to a more secluded place in the outer precincts of the monastery. Not till he had first gained victory over our invisible enemy by solitary prayer and fasting

---

1. *Psalm* lxxxiii, 8 (A.V. lxxxiv, 7).

did he take it on himself to seek out a remote battlefield farther away from his fellow men. The Farne is an island far out to sea, unlike Lindisfarne, which is an island in the strict sense of the word only twice a day, when cut off by the tide. When the tide is out it is joined to the mainland. (The Greeks call this kind of tide *'rheuma'*.) The Farne lies a few miles to the south-east of Lindisfarne, cut off on the landward side by very deep water and facing, on the other side, out towards the limitless ocean. The island was haunted by devils; Cuthbert was the first man brave enough to live there alone. At the entry of our soldier of Christ armed with 'the helmet of salvation, the shield of faith and the sword of the spirit which is the word of God' the devil fled and his host of allies with him. Cuthbert, having routed the enemy, became monarch of the place, in token of which he built a city worthy of his power and put up houses to match. The structure was almost circular in plan, from four to five poles in diameter, and the walls on the outside were higher than a man. Out of piety he made the walls higher inside by cutting away the solid rock at the bottom, so that with only the sky to look at, eyes and thoughts might be kept from wandering and inspired to seek for higher things. This same wall he built not with cut stone or bricks and mortar but with rough stones and peat dug out of the enclosure itself. Some of these stones were so big that four men could hardly lift them, but with the help of angels he managed to fit them into the wall. There were two buildings, an oratory and one for living in. He finished off the walls inside and out by digging away a lot of the soil. The roofs were of rough-hewn timber and straw. Near the landing-place there was a bigger house for the visiting brethren to stay in, with a spring close by.

## CHAPTER 18

*How his prayer brought forth water out of the dry land.*
*His life as a hermit*

THE dwelling-place, built on almost solid rock, had no water supply. So one day he summoned the brethren – for he had not yet cut himself off from his visitors – and said:

'The place I have chosen, as you can see, is without a well. Pray with me, I beseech you, that He who "turns the solid rock into a standing water and the flint into fountains of water" may, "giving glory not unto us but to His Name", open a spring of water for us on this rocky ground. If we dig in the centre of my little enclosure I believe He will "make us drink from the river of His pleasures".'

They dug a pit and found it next morning full of water springing up from beneath. Without a doubt it was the prayers of the saint that had brought forth water from ground of the driest, hardest kind. This water, strangely enough, kept its original level, never spilling over on to the ground nor sinking as it was drawn out. God in his bounty willed that there should never be any less, nor any more, than was needed.

Once the brethren had helped him to build the place, he lived completely alone. At first, if they came over to visit him, he would go out and see to their needs; he would, for instance, wash their feet in warm water. Sometimes they made him take off his shoes and let them return the compliment, for care of his own body was so far from his thoughts that he kept his soft leather boots on his feet for months on end without ever removing them. If he put new boots on at Easter they would not come off till the next Easter and then only for the Washing of the Feet in church on Maundy Thursday. The monks found long thick calluses, where the boots had chafed his shins through all his prayers and genuflexions.

But as time went on his zeal for perfection led him to shut

himself away from sight within the hermitage, rarely talking to visitors even from inside, and if he did so then only through the window. Thus he learned to live a hermit's life of prayer and fasting. He used to keep the window open and enjoy seeing his brethren and being seen by them, but in the end he blocked it up and opened it only to give a blessing or for some definite need.

## CHAPTER 19

*How, at a word, he drove the birds away from the crops*
*he had sown with his own hands*

AT first he took bread from his visitors and water from his own well; then he thought it would be better to follow the example of the fathers and live by his own hands. He asked for implements to work the land with and wheat to sow, but though he planted in spring there was nothing ready by mid-summer.

'It's either the nature of the ground,' he said to the brethren, 'or the will of God, but the wheat certainly is not growing. So bring barley and we shall see whether that will produce anything. If God does not see fit to give increase, then rather than live off others I shall return to the monastery.'

The barley was brought long past the proper time for planting, when there was no hope of it growing, but it soon sprang up and brought forth a very good crop. When it began to ripen the birds came down and set about devouring it. (This tale was told by the pious servant of God himself, for it was his custom, being by nature friendly and cheerful, to strengthen the belief of his colleagues by recounting some of the blessings with which his own faith had been rewarded.)

'Why are you eating crops you yourselves did not grow?' he asked the birds. 'Perhaps you have greater need of them than I. If God has given you permission, then do as He bade you; if not, be off with you, stop damaging other people's property.'

They flew off at his first word and did no further damage. These two miracles of the venerable servant of God are reminiscent of

the doings of two of the fathers. In bringing water out of the rock
he reminds one of a similar miracle performed by St Benedict –
only he brought it forth more abundantly because there were
more people in need – and in driving away the birds he was following the example of St Antony who, by words alone, restrained
wild asses from trampling his little garden.

## CHAPTER 20

*How the ravens said their prayers and brought the man of
God a gift to make up for the harm they had done*

THIS is the place to recount another of the blessed Cuthbert's
miracles similar to one of our father Benedict's, in which human
pride and obstinacy are openly put to shame by the humble
obedience of birds. One day some ravens which had long inhabited
the island were seen tearing the straw from the roof of the visitors'
house and carrying it off to build their nests. The saint reproved
them with a slight gesture of the right hand and told them to
leave the monks' property alone. They merely scorned his command.

'In the Name of Jesus Christ, depart forthwith!' he shouted. 'Do
not dare remain to do more damage.'

They flew off shamefacedly almost before he had finished speaking. Three days later one of a pair of them returned, and finding
Cuthbert digging, stood before him, with feathers outspread and
head bowed low to its feet in sign of grief. Using whatever signs
it could to express contrition it very humbly asked pardon. When
Cuthbert realized what it meant, he gave permission for them all
to return. Back they came with a fitting gift – a lump of pig's lard.
Cuthbert would often show this to his visitors, inviting them to
grease their shoes with it.

'What care should not men take,' he would say, 'to cultivate
obedience and humility when the very birds hasten to wash away
their faults of pride by prayers, tears, and gifts.'

The birds stayed on the island many years to set men a good

example of reform, building their nests but never presuming to do harm to anyone. Let no one think it ridiculous to learn a lesson in virtue from birds. Does not Solomon instruct us: 'Go to the ant thou sluggard, consider her ways and be wise'?[1]

## CHAPTER 21

### How even the sea served him

Not only the inhabitants of air and ocean but the sea itself, following the examples of the air and the fire cited above, showed respect for the venerable old man. No wonder; it is hardly strange that the rest of creation should obey the wishes and commands of a man who has dedicated himself with complete sincerity to the Lord's service. We, on the other hand, often lose that dominion over creation which is ours by right through neglecting to serve its Creator. The very sea, I say, was quick to lend him aid when he needed it.

He set about constructing within the walls of his dwelling a small shed which should be big enough for his day to day requirements. It was to be built towards the sea with the floor over a long deep cleft hollowed out by the constant action of the waves. It was to be twelve foot long, for that was the length of the cleft, so he asked the monks to bring him some planks of that length for floorboards the next time they came. They willingly agreed, received his blessing, went off home and forgot all about it. Back they came on the appointed day but without the wood. He gave them a very warm welcome, commending them to God with the usual prayer, then asked: 'Where is the wood?' Then they remembered. They confessed they had forgotten and asked him to pardon their negligence. The kindly old man soothed their anxiety with a gentle word and bade them stay till next morning: 'For I do not believe God will forget my wish.' They complied with his request. The following morning when they went out there was

1. *Prov.* vi. 6.

a piece of wood of the correct length thrown up by the tide right under the site of the shed. They marvelled at the sanctity of a man whom the very elements obeyed, and blushed with shame at their own slackness in needing to be reminded by inanimate nature what obedience is due to saints.

## CHAPTER 22

*How he exhorted many who came to him to the ways of salvation and pointed out the weaknesses in the snares of our old enemy*

Now Cuthbert had great numbers of people coming to him not just from Lindisfarne but even from the remote parts of Britain, attracted by his reputation for miracles. They confessed their sins, confided in him about their temptations, and laid open to him the common troubles of humanity they were labouring under – all in the hope of gaining consolation from so holy a man. They were not disappointed. No one left unconsoled, no one had to carry back the burdens he came with. Spirits that were chilled with sadness he could warm back to hope again with a pious word. Those beset with worry he brought back to thoughts of the joys of Heaven. He showed them that both good fortune and bad were transitory in this world. To men beset with temptation he would skilfully disclose all the wiles of the devil, explaining that a soul lacking in love for God or man is easily caught in the devil's nets, while one that is strong in the faith can, with God's grace, brush them aside like so many spiders' webs.

'How often have the demons tried to cast me headlong from yonder rock; how often have they hurled stones as if to kill me; with one fantastic temptation after another they have sought to disillusion me into retreating from this battle-field; but they have never yet succeeded in harming either soul or body, nor do they terrify me.'

He very often stressed that the brethren ought not to marvel at his way of life, as though it were especially exalted to prefer to cast aside the cares of the world and live apart.

'It is the monastic life you ought to stand in awe of. In that life everything is subject to the abbot; the times of prayer, fasting, vigils, and work are governed by his will. I have known many abbots who for purity of mind and depth of prophetic power have far surpassed my poor self – Boisil, for example, a man to be named with all honour and veneration. He was old and I but a youth when he brought me up in the monastery at Melrose. While he was instructing me he prophesied my whole future accurately. One of those prophecies has yet to happen; would to God it might not.'

Here he referred to Boisil's prophecy that he would one day be a bishop. His desire for a more secluded life made him tremble at the thought.

## CHAPTER 23

*How Abbess Aelfflaed and one of her nuns were cured by his cincture*

CUTHBERT did not cease to perform miracles of healing even though far removed from mankind. There was a holy handmaid of Christ, Aelfflaed, who, as one of the joys of her virginal state, had charge of a great company of nuns. She looked after them with motherly love, adding to her royal rank the yet more noble adornment of a high degree of holiness. She had a deep affection for Cuthbert. She herself told the following story to that most reverend priest of the Lindisfarne church, Herefrith, who in turn told it to me.

She had been seriously ill for a long time and seemed almost on the point of dying. The doctors could do nothing for her. By God's grace she was suddenly removed from danger of death though not entirely cured; the internal pain went and she regained the use of her limbs but still could not stand upright nor move about except on all fours. She began to fear that the condition might be permanent, since she had long since given up hope of getting any help from doctors. One day oppressed by these sad thoughts her mind wandered to the peaceful life Cuthbert led.

'How I wish I had something belonging to my dear Cuthbert!' she sighed. 'As I trust and believe in God I know for certain that I should be quickly healed.'

Shortly afterwards someone arrived with a linen cincture sent by Cuthbert. She was delighted with the gift and realized that her wishes had been made known to him by heavenly means. She girded herself with it and next morning was able to stand up straight. Two days later she was completely well. A few days after this one of the nuns was seized with excruciating pains in the head. She got daily worse until it seemed unlikely she could last much longer. The venerable abbess paid her a visit, saw how ill she was, and bound up her head with the cincture. The pain left her that very same day and she was cured. She took off the cincture and hid it in her locker. When it was required by the abbess a few days later it was nowhere to be found, neither in the locker nor anywhere else. This was God's doing: by those two miracles of healing he manifested Cuthbert's holiness to the faithful, and then removed the cincture lest it should lead the faithless to doubt such sanctity. Had it been allowed to remain, the sick would have flocked to it and if anyone through lack of merit were left uncured, the fact would be taken not as a proof of that person's unworthiness but as a reason for disparaging the relic. So, as I said, by a merciful dispensation of Divine Providence, first the belief of the faithful was strengthened, and then all danger of disparagement by the envious or unbelieving was removed.

## CHAPTER 24

*What he predicted about King Ecgfrith in answer to
Aelfflaed. He foretells his own consecration*

THAT same holy virgin Aelfflaed, mother of the handmaids of Christ, sent to Cuthbert on another occasion begging him in God's name to come and talk over some important matter. He took a boat and sailed with his brethren to the appointed meeting place,

Coquet Island, so called because it lies opposite the mouth of the Coquet. It was renowned for its monasteries. In the course of conversation, after Cuthbert had answered her queries at length, she suddenly broke off and flung herself before him, adjuring him by the awful name of the King of Heaven and His Angels to tell her how long her brother Ecgfrith would last and who was to rule after him.

'I know you can tell me,' she said, 'if only you will, for the spirit of prophecy is strong in you.'

Her oath frightened him, yet he still shrank from revealing the truth.

'It surprises me,' he answered, 'that a sensible woman, and one so well versed in the scriptures should think of calling human life long. Does not the psalmist declare "our years are reckoned as a spider's web"? Does not Solomon exclaim: "If a man live many years and rejoice in them all, yet let him remember the days of darkness, for they shall be many. When they come the past is reckoned as vanity."?[1] Then how much shorter must a man's life appear when he happens to be in his last year with death at the gates?'

She wept at such dire prophecies, then wiped her face and with true feminine audacity adjured him by the Divine Majesty to say who would be her brother's heir, since he had neither children nor brothers. Cuthbert was silent for a while, then said: 'Do not say there is no heir. One will come whom you will embrace with as much sisterly affection as though he were Ecgfrith's own self.'

'Then tell me where he is!' she cried.

'Look at the sea,' he replied. 'It abounds in islands. God could easily provide a ruler for the English from one of them.'

She realized he was hinting at Aldfrith, the supposed son of Ecgfrith's father, who was away in Ireland being educated. She knew also that Ecgfrith wanted to see Cuthbert a bishop and she wanted to know whether the proposal would be carried out. She began again:

'Oh how divided in aim are the hearts of men! Some enjoy the wealth they have gained, others love riches but never have any

1. *Psalm* lxxxix, 9 (A.V. xc, 9); *Eccl.* xi, 8.

to enjoy. You spurn worldly glory when offered you and reject a bishopric – than which there is nothing higher in the sight of men – in preference to that barren fastness.'

'I know I am not worthy,' he replied, 'but I know too that the decree of the Supreme Ruler cannot be escaped, no matter where one might flee to. If however, I am forced to shoulder a burden, I do not think it will be for long. After two years, perhaps, I shall be allowed to go back to my accustomed solitude and peace. Now I command you in the Name of our Lord and Saviour not to tell anyone what I have said while I am still alive.'

He expounded many other questions for her and gave her necessary advice, then went back to the Farne to cultivate the solitary life.

Shortly afterwards there was a great synod presided over by Archbishop Theodore of happy memory, in the presence of King Ecgfrith, at which Cuthbert, by general consent, was elected Bishop of Lindisfarne. Letters and messengers were sent to him repeatedly, but he refused to move. The King himself and that most holy bishop, Trumwine, with numerous devout and influential personages sailed across, knelt down and adjured him by the Lord, and wept and pleaded with him, until at last he came forth, very tearful, from his beloved hiding-place and was taken to the synod. Very reluctantly he was overcome by their unanimous decision and compelled to submit to the yoke of the episcopacy. The consecration was postponed till the end of winter, which was just then beginning. His prophecy was completely fulfilled; next year Ecgfrith was slain by the Picts and the throne went to his bastard brother Aldfrith recently returned from his studies in Ireland, where he had willingly exiled himself for the love of learning.

## CHAPTER 25

*How as bishop elect he cured the ailing servant of one
of the king's bodyguards with holy water*

AFTER his election the man of God returned to his island and
went on fighting the good fight in secret with unabated zeal. Then
his holy bishop, Eata, called him to Melrose to converse with him.
On the way back one of King Ecgfrith's bodyguards came to meet
him and asked him to turn aside on an urgent matter, namely
to confer a blessing on his house and homestead. Cuthbert arrived
at the house and was most hospitably treated. One of the servants
was ill.

'Thanks be to God, holy father,' said the man, 'for your kindness
in coming to visit us and enter our home. Your coming will, I
feel sure, be a great boon to us. Our servant is tormented with
some foul disease and is in such pain today that he seems more
like a dying than a sick man. His extremities look dead already
and he is only just breathing.'

Cuthbert blessed some water and gave it to Baldhelm, another
servant, ordering him to give it to the sick man to drink. The third
time it was poured down his throat he fell into a deep sleep –
a complete contrast to his previous condition. This happened in
the evening. He passed a quiet night and the following morning
his master found him restored to full health. Baldhelm is still alive
and now a priest of the church at Lindisfarne, an office which
he adorns with every virtue. It is sweeter than honey to him to
recount Cuthbert's miracles to any who care to know them; he
told me this one himself.

## CHAPTER 26

### *His way of life as a bishop*

THIS venerable man of God, Bishop Cuthbert, following the teaching and practice of the apostles, adorned his office with good works. He protected the flock committed to him by constant prayer on their behalf, by wholesome admonition and – which is the real way to teach – by example first and precept later. He delivered 'the poor man from him that was too strong for him, the poor and the needy from him that despoiled them'. He took care to comfort the sad and faint-hearted and to bring back those that delighted in evil to a godly sorrow. He strictly maintained his old frugality and took delight in preserving the rigours of the monastery amidst the pomp of the world. He fed the hungry, clothed the destitute, and had all the other marks of a perfect bishop. These outward signs and wonders in which he excelled give adequate proof of his virtue. It has been my task to give a brief account of some of them.


## CHAPTER 27

### *How he saw in spirit, though absent from the scene, the destruction of King Ecgfrith, as he had predicted*

WHEN King Ecgfrith led his army against the Picts and devastated their lands with brutal and ferocious cruelty – an extremely rash move – then Cuthbert knew that his prophecy to Aelfflaed was nearing fulfilment. He set off therefore to Carlisle, to speak with the queen, who had arranged to stay there in her sister's convent to await the outcome of the war. The day after his arrival the citizens conducted him round the city walls to see a remarkable Roman fountain that was built into them. He was suddenly disturbed in spirit. He leaned heavily on his staff, turned his face dolefully to the wall, then straightening himself and looking up to the sky he sighed deeply and said almost in a whisper: 'Perhaps at this moment the battle is being decided.'

A priest who was standing by realized what he was referring to, and burst out imprudently with: 'How do you know?'

'Do you not see how strangely disturbed the air is? Who can fathom the judgements of God?'

He hurried straight back to the queen and spoke to her in secret. 'Tomorrow being Sunday you cannot travel. Monday morning at daybreak leave in your chariot for the royal city. Enter quickly for perhaps the king has been slain. Tomorrow I have been invited to a neighbouring monastery to dedicate the chapel, but as soon as the dedication is over I shall follow you.'

On the Sunday morning at the end of his sermon, as the congregation were expressing their approval, he took up this prophetic theme again:

'Brethren, I beseech you to watch as the apostle warns you. Stand firm in the faith, play the man, lest sudden temptation find you unprepared. Be mindful rather of the Lord's command: "Watch and pray lest ye enter into temptation." ' (Now there had recently been a devastating pestilence in the area which had carried off numbers of people in a great wave of destruction. They thought he meant the plague would return.) He continued: 'One day, when I was living alone on the Farne Island, some of the monks came over to see me on Christmas Day to persuade me to leave my abode and pass so sacred and so joyful a feast in their company. I gave way to their earnest requests and came out. We sat down outside and banqueted. In the middle of the meal I said to them: "Brethren, I implore you, let us act prudently and be on our guard lest through taking neither care nor heed we be seduced by temptation."

' "For goodness' sake," they replied, "let us enjoy ourselves today – it is Christmas, the birthday of Our Lord Jesus Christ."

' "Very well, let us," I replied. As things went on and we were enjoying our dinner, feeling convivial and telling stories, I broke in again to warn them to be earnest in prayer and vigils and to be ready against all temptation.

' "Well said," they answered. "You give excellent advice but there are plenty of fast days, plenty of time for vigils and prayers. Today we are rejoicing in the Lord. This is the day the angels announced Christ's birth to the shepherds, giving them glad tidings of great joy, a joy to be celebrated by them and all mankind."

'To which I answered: "Very well, let us do so." When however, while we were still feasting and passing the day merrily, I repeated the self-same words of warning a third time, they realized I was not anxious without good reason and they began to be afraid:

' "Let us do as you say. It does indeed behove us to be ever on the watch, our loins ever girt against the snares of the devil and all temptations."

'I must confess I knew as little as they did whether some new temptation would attack us or no, but I felt an instinctive warning that one should be on constant guard against sudden storms of temptation. The following morning they left for Lindisfarne and returned to find one of their brethren dead of the plague. The disease raged for month after month, lasted a whole year and carried off almost that whole renowned company of spiritual fathers and brothers. So now brethren, persevere in prayer so that, should tribulation befall you it will not find you unprepared.'

Because of this story they naturally thought he was warning them against the plague. Next day a fugitive from the battle arrived, whose tale of woe threw light on Cuthbert's dark hints. The same day, nay, the very same hour that Cuthbert received the message as he stood by the fountain, the king and all his bodyguards had been slaughtered by the enemy.

## CHAPTER 28

### *How he predicted his own death to Hereberht the hermit*

SHORTLY afterwards he was invited to Carlisle to ordain some deacons to the priesthood and to give the religious habit with his blessing to the queen. There was a holy priest called Hereberht, long bound to Cuthbert in spiritual friendship, living the hermit's life on an island in that great lake from which the River Derwent flows. He used to come to Cuthbert every year to take counsel about his eternal salvation. Hearing that he was staying at Carlisle, Hereberht came to him, seeking, as usual, to be fired with an ever-increasing love for the things of Heaven. While they were regaling each other with draughts of celestial wisdom Cuthbert said casually: 'Remember, brother Hereberht, to ask me now whatever you need to ask. This is the last time we shall see each other with the eyes of the flesh, for I know the time is at hand when I must lay aside my earthly tabernacle; the time of my departure is nigh.'

Hereberht flung himself at his feet and sobbed.

'In the Lord's name, do not leave me. Think of your friend and ask the Divine Mercy to grant that, as we have served Him together on earth, so we may journey forth together to see His glory in Heaven. You know I have always striven to follow your commands, and whenever ignorance or human frailty has led me astray I have always chastised myself as you judged fit.'

The bishop prayed fervently and was immediately given to know that his prayer was answered.

'Rise up, brother; do not weep. Rejoice and be glad, for the Divine Mercy has granted our prayer.'

This was borne out by the course of events. Hereberht departed, and they saw each other on earth no more, but their souls left their bodies at one and the same moment and were soon carried to the celestial kingdom by an angel host, to be united with each other in the beatific vision. Hereberht's death was preceded by a long racking illness, inflicted perhaps by God in His mercy, to make sure that, if previously he had lagged behind Cuthbert in merit, he might now be made equal to his intercessor through suffering and so deserve to depart this life with him at the same time and be received into the same eternal bliss.

## CHAPTER 29

### *He sends a priest with holy water to the wife of a bodyguard of the king*

ONE day, as he was going round the diocese giving saving counsel in all the houses and hamlets of the countryside, and laying his hand on the newly baptized so that the grace of the Holy Spirit might come down upon them, he came to the house of a member of the royal bodyguard whose wife lay ill and seemed to be dying. The man ran to meet him, knelt down and thanked God that he had come, brought him into the house, and made him most welcome. After the formal hospitality of having his hands and feet washed, the bishop sat down. Then the man told him that his wife was desperately ill and begged him to bless some holy water to sprinkle on her.

'I am sure,' he said, 'God will grant her a speedy recovery, or if she must die, put an end to her long agony and take her without delay.'

Cuthbert had water brought, blessed it, and gave it to a priest to sprinkle over the sick woman. The priest entered her bedroom and found her lying there looking like a corpse. He sprinkled the bed, sprinkled her, opened her mouth, and poured a little of the life-giving draught down her throat. The patient was quite unaware of what was being done, but as soon as the water touched her an astonishing thing happened: she was immediately restored to full health both of body and mind. She came to, blessed and thanked the Lord for deigning to send such guests to cure her, and then, rising from her bed, ministered to those who had ministered to her, the patient tending the physicians. What a pleasant sight to see that of all the members of so noble a household the lady of the house herself was the first to offer a drink to her guest, a guest whose blessing had just then removed the chalice of death from her own lips! She followed the example of

Peter's mother-in-law who, as soon as Christ had cured her of the fever, 'forthwith rose and ministered unto Him and His disciples'.

## CHAPTER 30

*He cures a girl of pains in the head and side by anointing her with oil*

HERE is another miracle similar to the last and testified to by many eyewitnesses, among whom there is the holy priest Aethilwald, one of Cuthbert's retinue at the time and now abbot of Melrose.

Cuthbert was making his usual preaching mission through the villages and had come to one where there were a few nuns. They had fled from their own monastery for fear of the barbarian army shortly before, and had been lodged in the village by Cuthbert. One of them, a relation of Aethilwald, was seriously ill, seized with pains in the head and all down one side, so that the doctors had given her up. Cuthbert's companions pointed this out to him and begged him to heal her. Full of pity for her wretchedness he anointed her with holy oil. She began to improve from that very moment and in a few days completely recovered.

## CHAPTER 31

*How a sick man was healed with bread blessed by Cuthbert*

IT would hardly be right to omit to mention a miracle performed by the power of that same venerable man but without his being actually present. You have already heard of the sheriff Hildmer – it was his wife Cuthbert exorcized. Hildmer himself was later confined to bed with a dangerous illness and grew daily worse till it seemed he could hardly last another minute. His friends had crowded round the bed to console him, when one of them suddenly remembered that he had in his pocket a piece of bread which Cuthbert had shortly beforehand blessed and given him.

'I am sure this will restore him to health,' he said, 'unless our slowness to believe prevents it.'

They were all laymen but very devout, and having discussed the matter each one said he had not the least doubt that Hildmer could be healed by partaking of the bread. They filled a cup with water, dropped a tiny piece of bread in, and gave it him to drink. The moment the water the bread had made holy entered his stomach all internal pain left him and his body ceased to atrophy. Once the pain was gone, health and strength returned, inciting him and all who saw or heard of the unexpected recovery to praise Cuthbert's holiness and marvel at the strength and sincerity of Hildmer's faith.

## CHAPTER 32

*How, on a journey, he restored to life a youth who was brought to him dying*

ONCE when this most holy shepherd of the Lord's flock was doing the round of his sheepfolds, he came into a rough mountain area whither many had gathered from the scattered villages to be confirmed. Now there was no church nor even a place in the mountains fit to receive a bishop and his retinue, so the people put up tents for him while for themselves they made huts of felled branches as best they could. Cuthbert preached twice to the milling crowds and brought down the grace of the Holy Ghost by imposition of hands on those newly regenerated in Christ. In the middle of the ceremonies some women appeared bringing in on a litter a youth all wasted away by a long nagging disease. They laid him down at the edge of the wood and sent to Cuthbert to ask permission to bring him forward for a blessing. When the youth had been brought in Cuthbert saw how gravely ill he was and bade everyone move farther off. He had recourse to his usual armoury, prayer, gave a blessing and drove away the disease for which the doctors, despite their skill in concocting medicines, had

THE AGE OF BEDE

been unable to devise a cure. The youth regained his strength, stood up and gave thanks to God, and went back home with the women who had brought him. And so it came to pass that he who had been carried in prostrate by sorrowing women walked home hale and hearty amid their rejoicings.

## CHAPTER 33

*How, when the plague was on, he restored a dying boy to his mother*

AT this same time the plague broke out and dealt such havoc that of great villages and estates once crowded with inhabitants only a tiny scattered remnant remained, and sometimes not even that. Our most holy father Cuthbert went round the diocese with unflagging zeal, preaching and bringing much-needed consolation to the few people left. In one village he exhorted everyone he found and said to the priest, 'Do you suppose there is anyone else left in the place who needs visiting and speaking to, or can I now move on to the next?'

The priest looked all round and pointed out a woman some distance away, who had just before lost one son and was now holding another, dying, in her arms. Her tear-stained face gave ample proof of both past and present ills. Cuthbert went up to her without delay, blessed the boy, and kissed him.

'Have no fear,' he said to the mother. 'Do not grieve. The child will get better and live, and you will lose no more of your family.'

Mother and child both lived long afterwards, thus proving the prophecy true.

## CHAPTER 34

*How he beheld being carried heavenwards the soul of a man
who had been killed in a fall from a tree*

CUTHBERT knew that he was soon to die and made up his mind
accordingly to lay aside the burden of pastoral office and retire
to a life of solitude. Once free from material worries he might be
able to give himself undividedly to his prayers and psalms, to
prepare himself for death or, rather, eternal life. But he wished
to make a visitation of the diocese first and visit the homes of some
other of the faithful in the neighbourhood to exhort them and
give them the strength they needed. Then he would withdraw
to the joy and refreshment of his longed-for solitude. As he was
going the rounds, that most noble and holy virgin Aelfflaed, of
whom we have spoken above, asked him to come to see her at
one of the estates belonging to her monastery in order to converse
with her and consecrate a church. There were a good number
of people, servants of God, living on this estate. When they had
sat down to dinner, Cuthbert suddenly turned his attention from
the worldly feast to meditate on spiritual things. His limbs went
limp and useless, his face changed colour, his eyes became fixed
in amazement, and the knife fell from his hand to the table. The
priest, his minister, who was standing near, lent over to the abbess
and whispered: 'Ask the bishop what he sees, for his hand did
not tremble and let go the knife without reason. He is having some
kind of vision which is denied us.'

She turned to him at once.

'My lord bishop, I beg you to tell me what you have just seen –
your hand did not slacken and let the knife fall for no reason at
all.'

He tried to conceal the fact that he had seen anything extra-
ordinary by merely laughing it off:

'Well, I cannot eat all day. I must pause sometime.'

But she pestered him into telling.

'I saw,' he admitted, 'the soul of some holy man being borne by the hands of angels into the joy of Heaven.'

'Where did he come from?'

'From your monastery.'

She wanted to know his name.

'You yourself will tell me tomorrow in the middle of mass.'

She sent off at once to the main monastery to see whose soul had been so recently snatched from his body, but the messenger found them all safe and sound and set off back the next morning. On the way he came across a group of men bearing the body of one of their brothers on a cart to burial. He learnt, on asking, that it was one of the shepherds, a good-living man, who had climbed a tree too recklessly and had fallen. His injuries proved mortal and he had passed away at the very time Cuthbert saw him carried heavenwards. On being informed Aelfflaed hastened to the bishop, then in the middle of the dedication ceremonies, and, woman-like, acted as though stupefied, announcing, as if it were fresh news: 'My lord bishop, remember at mass my servant Hadwald who died yesterday of a fall from a tree.'

Then everyone saw, as clear as could be, the extent and scope of Cuthbert's prophetic gifts – not only could he see a soul being carried heavenwards at the very moment of death but also foresee what others would tell him about it later.

CHAPTER 35

*How he gave water the flavour of wine simply by tasting it*

WHEN he had gone through the upper districts of the diocese in order, he came to a convent of virgins close to the mouth of the Tyne, a place we have already mentioned. Abbess Verca, a devout and, in the eyes of the world, a noble woman, gave him a magnificent welcome. When the after-dinner rest was over Cuthbert said he felt thirsty and would like a drink. They asked whether he wanted wine or beer.

'Give me water,' came the reply.

It was drawn from the well and brought. He blessed it, drank a little, and gave it to his priest, who gave it to the man who had brought it, a priest of the monastery. He asked if he might drink from the cup which the bishop had just used.

'Of course. Why not?' Cuthbert answered.

The priest drank, and it seemed to him that the water had taken on the taste of wine. Eager to have witnesses of so great a miracle he handed the cup to a brother standing by. He drank and thought he had wine in his mouth, not water. They gaped at each other in astonishment and afterwards, when they had a chance to talk, confessed that they had never tasted better wine. One of them later came to stay in our monastery at Monkwearmouth, lived with us a long time, and was peacefully buried there. I had the story from him.

## CHAPTER 36

*How certain brethren who had disobeyed him were held
back by a storm at sea*

IN the second year of his episcopate Cuthbert knew that his end was nigh. He laid aside his pastoral duties and went back as soon as possible to his beloved life of solitary conflict, to give the flame of compunction time to burn away the deeply fixed thorns of worldly cares. Nevertheless he would often leave his dwelling to meet and talk to the brethren who came over to visit him.

Perhaps it would not be out of place at this juncture to insert an account of a miracle he worked about this time, to show you quite clearly that saints are to be obeyed in even their most casual commands. Here it is then:

One day some of the monks came over and Cuthbert went out to give them a few words of encouragement. He finished thus: 'Now it is time to go back to my cell. You are ready to go too, but before you set off have something to eat. Take that goose hanging up on the wall, cook it and eat it, and then set sail in the Name of the Lord.'

He blessed them and went in. They ate as he had bidden them, but, since they had plenty of their own food with them, they could not be bothered to prepare the goose. When the meal was over they made to go aboard, but a fierce storm arose making it impossible to row, with the result that they were shut in on the island for a whole week with the seas raging round them, quite unaware of the fault for which they were kept imprisoned. They sought out Cuthbert and anxiously complained about the delay. He merely preached patience, but the seventh day very graciously came out to speak to them, thinking that a word of sympathy might soothe their pain. He entered the visitors' house and, seeing the bird still hanging there uncooked, calmly upbraided them for their disobedience – he was, in fact, rather pleased.

'What! Is that bird still hanging there uncooked? Do you wonder the sea will not let you go? Quickly now, put it in the pot, cook it and eat it, then the sea will calm down and you will be able to leave.'

They obeyed at once and, wondrous to relate, just as the goose began to boil in the pot, the wind died away and the waves lost their fury. They finished eating the goose, saw that the sea was smooth, and set off, arriving home with the wind behind them, overjoyed and not a little ashamed. They blushed at the thought of their disobedience and at their dimwittedness, which despite the chastisements of the Creator had kept them from realizing and correcting their fault. They rejoiced to see that God had such regard for His faithful servant that He would call up the elements to punish those who failed to respect him, and rejoiced also that He cared for them to the extent of performing a miracle to correct their errors.

This story did not come to me from any casual source but from one of that very party, the venerable monk and priest Cynimund. He is still alive and renowned far and wide for his great holiness and great age.

## CHAPTER 37

*The temptations he suffered while ill and the instructions
he gave about his burial just before he died*

As soon as Christmas was over Cuthbert sought out his island
home once more. A crowd of the brethren gathered to see him
off, one of whom, an old monk, strong in the faith though wasted
away through dysentery, said to him, 'Tell us, my lord, when we
may expect to see you again.'

The answer came back as plain as the question (for Cuthbert
knew it was true): 'When you bring back my corpse.'

He was given almost two months to rediscover the delights of
the quiet life and to fit mind and body into the strict discipline of his
old routine; then he was suddenly felled by disease, to be prepared
by the fires of internal pain for the joys of everlasting bliss. Let me
tell you of his death verbatim, just as I had it from Herefrith, a
sincerely devout priest and present abbot of Lindisfarne:

'After being racked by three weeks of continual illness, he met his end
in the following way. He took ill, you know, on a Wednesday, and it was
on a Wednesday too that the disease conquered and he went to his Lord.
I arrived the morning the sickness began – I had already been there three
days previously with the brethren to get his blessing and words of consolation – and now gave the usual signal to let him know I had arrived.
He came to the window, but when I greeted him he could only sigh.

' "What is wrong, my lord? Have you had an attack during the night?"

' "Yes," he said, "it came last night."

'I thought he was referring to his old complaint that used to trouble
him nearly every day, not to anything new. Without further question I
asked for his blessing as it was time to be rowing back.

' "Do as you intend," he said. "Board your vessel and go safely home.
When God takes my soul, bury me here close to the oratory, on the south
side and to the east of that holy cross I myself put up. To the north of
the oratory you will find a stone coffin hidden under the turf, a present
from the holy Abbot Cudda. Put my body in it, wrapped in the cloth you
will find there. Abbess Verca gave it me as a present but I was loath to
wear it. Out of affection for her I carefully put it aside to use as a winding-
sheet."

'Hearing this I exclaimed: "Father, now that you yourself have told me you are dying, I beg you to let some of the brethren stay and look after you."

' "Go now and come back at the proper time."

'I insisted that there should be someone by him but he would not agree. Finally I asked when we were to come back.

' "When God wants. He will show you."

'We carried out his directions. Calling together the brethren in church I ordered constant prayer on his behalf, telling them that I gathered from his words that he would soon be with the Lord. I was anxious to return, but a storm kept us back for five days; events were later to prove that this was the work of Providence. Almighty God, in order that his servant might be purified from every trace of human frailty and to show his adversaries their impotence against his strength of faith, willed him to be cut off from mankind for so long to test him by physical suffering and by exposing him to still fiercer conflict with our ancient enemy. When the storm abated we reached the island to find that he had left his cell and was sitting in the house where we used to lodge. The other monks had to go over to the shore on some necessary errand but I stayed and lost no time in seeing to his needs. One of his feet needed attention; it had been swollen for a long time and had now developed an ulcer and was suppurating. I heated some water and bathed it. I then gave him some warm wine and tried to make him taste it. You could see from his face that what with the illness and lack of food besides his strength was all drained away. When I had finished he sat down quietly on the couch and I sat beside him. He was silent, so I began the conversation.

' "My lord bishop, I can see how much you have suffered since we left you, and I wonder why you would not allow anyone to stay to look after you."

' "It was God's will that I should be left to suffer awhile without help or company. From the time you left the sickness grew steadily worse; and I got up and came out here so that when you did arrive to take care of me, you would be able to find me without having to bother to enter the monastery. From the time I came in here and settled myself down I have not moved a limb but have remained in the same position these five days and nights."

' "But my lord, how can you live like this? Have you gone without food all this time?"

'He turned back the coverlet on which he sat and showed me five onions.

' "This has been my food for the last five days. Whenever my mouth was parched or burned with excessive hunger or thirst I refreshed and cooled myself with these."

'One of the onions was less than half nibbled away. He added: "My assailants have never tempted me so sorely as they have during the past five days."

'I did not dare inquire what kind of temptations they were but contented myself with asking him to let himself be waited upon. He consented and let some of us stay, one of whom was the priest Bede, his personal servant. (It was his position as servant that enabled Bede to know all the presents that Cuthbert had ever received.) Cuthbert wanted him at hand in case he had forgotten to make due return for any of the gifts he had received; if that was so, Bede could remind him and give him time to return the kindness before he died. He especially asked to have another brother by him as a servant. This other monk had suffered for a long time from severe diarrhoea and could not be cured. His piety, prudence, and seriousness marked him out as a worthy witness of the saint's last words and of the way he died. I returned and told the brethren that our venerable father had ordered that he was to be buried on the island.

'"But it seems far more fitting to me," I added, "to ask him to let us bring his body back here to be given a more decent burial with proper honours in the church."

'They agreed and we went to Cuthbert.

'"We do not think lightly of your command, my lord, to be interred here, but it seemed right that we should ask for the honour of bringing your body back to the monastery to remain with us."

'"But it is my desire to rest here where I have fought my fight for the Lord and where I want to finish the course and whence I hope to be raised up by my just judge to receive the crown of righteousness. What is more, it would be less trouble for you if I did stay here, because of the influx of fugitives and every other kind of malefactor which will otherwise result. They will flee for refuge to my body, for, whatever I might be, my fame as a servant of God has been noised abroad. You will be constrained to intercede very often with the powers of this world on behalf of such men. The presence of my remains will prove extremely irksome."

'We pleaded with him a long time, insisting that all this would seem light to us through being a labour of love. At last he gave us this advice.

'"If you feel you must go against my plans and take me back there, I think it would be best to make a tomb in the interior of the basilica – then you will be able to visit it yourselves whenever you wish and also to decide who else from outside may do so."

'We thanked him on bended knee for his permission and advice and went back home. After that we paid him frequent and regular visits.

## CHAPTER 38

*How, though sick himself, he healed his servant of diarrhoea*

'HE grew progressively worse and, realizing that the time of departure was at hand, gave instructions at about the third hour of the day to be carried back to his oratory and little house. We carried him back as he was too weak to walk. When we reached the door we asked him to let one of us go in with him to see to his needs. It was years since anyone but himself had gone beyond that door. He looked around at us all, caught sight of the monk who suffered from diarrhoea – whom I mentioned before – and said: "Let Wahlstod come in with me."

'Wahlstod stayed inside till about the ninth hour, then came out and called me.

' "The bishop commands you to enter. I have some marvellous news for you: from the moment I touched him as I led him into the oratory, I felt my old complaint go. Doubtless this is the action of Heaven's grace, that he who had previously healed so many when strong and well himself should now be able to cure me when he is at death's door. This is a clear sign that bodily weakness is powerless to impair the spiritual force of this holy man."

'This miracle reminds one very forcibly of a cure worked by our venerable and holy father, Bishop Aurelius Augustinus. When he was on his death-bed someone came with a sick man, asking only that the bishop should lay a hand on him and he would be healed. He answered that if he had any such powers he would have first used them on himself. But the man pressed him, saying he had been ordered to come – he had heard in a dream a voice saying: "Go to Bishop Augustinus and he shall cure you with a touch of the hand." At this the bishop placed his hand on the man to bless him and sent him home cured.[1]

---

1. c.f. Possidius, *Life of Augustine*, ch. 29.

## CHAPTER 39

*His last commands to the brethren and how, having received*
*the viaticum, he yielded up his spirit in prayer*

'I WENT in to him,' Herefrith continued, 'about the ninth hour and found him lying in a corner of the oratory opposite the altar. I sat down beside him. He said very little, for the weight of affliction made it hard for him to speak. But when I asked him rather urgently what counsel he was going to leave us as his testament or last farewell, he launched into a brief but significant discourse on peace and humility, and exhorted us to be on our guard against those who, far from delighting in these virtues, actively foster pride and discord:

' "Preserve amongst yourselves unfailing divine charity, and when you have to hold council about your common affairs let your principal aim be to reach a unanimous decision. Live in mutual concord with all other servants of Christ; do not despise those of the household of the faith who come to you seeking hospitality. Receive them, put them up, and set them on their way with kindness, treating them as one of yourselves. Do not think yourselves any better than the rest of your companions who share the same faith and follow the monastic life. With those who have wandered from the unity of the Catholic faith, either through not celebrating Easter at the proper time or through evil living, you are to have no dealings. Never forget that if you should ever be forced to make the choice of two evils I would much rather you left the island, taking my bones with you, than that you should be a party to wickedness on any pretext whatsoever, bending your necks to the yoke of schism. Strive most diligently to learn the catholic statutes of the fathers and put them into practice. Make it your special care to carry out those rules of the monastic life which God in His divine mercy has seen fit to give you through my ministry. I know that, though some might think my life despicable, none the less after my death you will see that my teachings are not to be easily dismissed."

'These and like sayings he uttered at intervals, because the gravity of the disease, as I said before, had weakened his speech. He passed the day quietly till evening, awaiting the joys of the world to come, and went on peacefully with his prayers throughout the night. At the usual time for night prayer I gave him the sacraments that lead to eternal life. Thus fortified with the Lord's Body and Blood in preparation for the death he knew was now at hand, he raised his eyes heavenwards, stretched out his arms aloft, and with his mind rapt in the praise of the Lord sent forth his spirit to the bliss of Paradise.

CHAPTER 40

*How, in accordance with the prophecy contained in the psalm they sang as he died, the monks of Lindisfarne were attacked, but, with the Lord's help, kept safe*

'I WENT out at once and announced his death to the brethren, who were themselves spending the night in prayer and vigil. As chance would have it they had reached Psalm Fifty-nine in lauds, the one beginning: "O God Thou hast cast us off and hast broken us down; Thou hast been angry and hast had compassion on us." One of the monks went without delay and lit two candles and went up, with one in each hand, to a piece of high ground to let the Lindisfarne brethren know that Cuthbert's holy soul had gone to the Lord. They had decided among themselves that this should be the sign of his holy death. The brother in the watch-tower at Lindisfarne, who was sitting up all night awaiting the news, ran quickly to the church where the monks were assembled for the night office, and as he entered they too were singing that same Psalm Fifty-nine. This, as events were to prove, was providential. For after Cuthbert was buried such a storm of trouble broke out that several monks chose to depart rather than bear the brunt of such danger.

'A year later Eadberht succeeded to the bishopric. He was a man of outstanding virtues, completely dedicated to works of charity, and a fine scripture scholar. It was with his accession that the trouble and disturbances were quelled. "The Lord," as the scriptures tell us, "did build up Jerusalem" – that is, the vision of peace – "and gather together the outcast of Israel. He healed the broken-hearted and bound up their wounds." Then the import of the psalm they had been singing when news of Cuthbert's death arrived was made plain – his fellow-citizens of the monastery might be cast down and forced out, but when the blaze of wrath had spent itself they would be brought to life again through the divine mercy. Anyone who glances at the psalm will see that the rest of the verses convey the same meaning.

'We placed the body of our venerable father in the boat and bore it across to Lindisfarne, where it was received by choirs of singers and a great crowd that had turned out to meet it. It was buried in a stone coffin on the right-hand side of the altar in the church of the Blessed Apostle Peter.'

## CHAPTER 41

*How a lotion made from the soil on to which the water used to wash*
*Cuthbert's body had been poured was used to cure a demoniac boy*

CUTHBERT'S miracles of healing did not cease with his death and burial. There was a boy on Lindisfarne possessed by a most brutal spirit. His wits were gone completely, he yelled, howled like a beast, and bit to shreds everything within reach, including his own limbs. A priest whose exorcisms had usually succeeded in putting evil spirits to flight was sent for from the monastery, but he could do nothing with this one. He advised the boy's father to strap him to a cart and bring him to the monastery to be prayed for at the relics of the martyrs. The father did as advised but the martyrs refused to grant the cure – in order to show just how high a place Cuthbert held amongst them. The lunatic boy struck terror into all who saw or heard him by his howls and groans and gnashing of teeth. No one could think of any remedy at all till suddenly one of the priests, instructed in spirit that Cuthbert could restore him to health, went secretly to the place where he knew the water from washing the corpse had been thrown out. He mixed a particle of the earth with water and poured it into the sufferer's mouth. His mouth was gaping wide, a disgusting sight, and he was yelling hideous pitiful cries, but as soon as the water touched him the cries died down, his mouth shut, the glaring bloodshot eyes closed, and his head and whole body sank into repose. He slept well and awoke next morning both from sleep and from madness to realize that he had been freed from the spirit which had beset him through the prayers and merits of Cuthbert.

Everyone was as delighted as they were astonished at the sight of the lad going round the holy places with his father, sound of mind and giving thanks to the saints for their help, while only the day before he had had no idea who or where he was. On his knees before the martyrs' relics, with the whole community standing by and joining their thanks to his, he praised God for releasing him from the scourge of the enemy. He returned home with his faith strengthened. The pit into which the water had been thrown is on view to this day. It is square, with a wooden frame round the sides, and is filled in with stones. It stands near the church where Cuthbert is buried, on the south side. From then on God granted many miracles of healing by means of those same stones and earth.

## CHAPTER 42

*How his body was found incorrupted eleven years later*

THE sublimity of the saint's earthly life was well attested by his numerous miracles. Almighty God in His Providence now chose to give further proof of Cuthbert's glory in Heaven by putting it into the minds of the brethren to dig up his bones. They expected to find the bones quite bare (as is usual with the dead), the rest of the body having dwindled away to dust. They were going to put them in a light casket in some fitting place above ground in order to give them their due veneration. Bishop Eadberht was informed of their decision sometime in mid-Lent and expressed his agreement, ordering them to carry out the ceremony on the 20th of March, the anniversary of the burial. This they did. On opening the coffin they found the body completely intact, looking as though still alive, and the joints of the limbs still flexible. It seemed not dead but sleeping. The vestments, all of them, were not merely unfaded but crisp and fresh like new, and wonderfully bright. The monks were filled with great fear and trembling; they could not speak, did not dare to look at the miracle, and hardly knew where to turn. Taking some of the outer garments with them as a sign of the incorruption – for they were afraid to touch anything that had been next to his skin – they hurried off to the bishop, who was then staying alone in a place some distance from the monastery, a place cut off by the sea at high tide. He used to spend Lent here and the forty days before Christmas in prayer and severe fasting, shedding tears of devotion. It was the place where

Cuthbert had fought his solitary battle for the Lord for a while before going to the Farne. Eadberht received the vestments with joy and gladly listened to the story of the miracle, kissing the clothes with great affection, as though they had been still round the body.

'Put new vestments on the body,' he said, 'in place of those you have removed and replace the corpse in the chest you have made ready for it. For I can assure you that the spot that has been consecrated by so great a proof of heavenly virtue will not be empty for long. And blessed is he indeed to whom the Lord, the fount and author of true happiness, will grant a place of rest therein.'

He expressed his wonder in the following words (which I myself once put into verse):

'What tongue can talk calmly about the gifts of God? What eye has ever seen the joys of Paradise? That will only be possible when we leave behind our earthly bodies and are received into the arc of Heaven by the Lord Himself. See how He now honours the form of an earthly body in token of far greater glories to come! You have caused power to flow from these dear bones of Cuthbert, Lord, filling the Church with the very atmosphere of Paradise. You have bidden decay hold, as you did when you brought forth Jonah into the light of day after three days in the whale's belly. The tribe of Israel, which Pharaoh made to wander forty long years in the desert, you called to be your own people; you preserved Shadrach, Meshach and Abednego in the flames of the fiery furnace and, when earth shall tremble at the last trump, you shall raise us to glory for your Son's sake.'

When the bishop had finished this paean with great emotion and faltering speech, the brethren went off to carry out his orders. The body was wrapped in a new garment, enclosed in a light coffin, and placed on the floor of the sanctuary.

## CHAPTER 43

*Eadberht is buried in Cuthbert's tomb beneath a sarcophagus
containing Cuthbert's remains*

MEANWHILE Eadberht was stricken with a painful disease. It
grew daily more intense and within a short while he died, on the
6th of May to be exact. His wish, to die not suddenly but through
long and wearing illness, had been granted. He was put in
Cuthbert's tomb under the chest containing the incorrupted body.

Even to this day there is no lack of signs and wonders; the very
clothes worn by the saint, both in life and in death, have still the
power to heal.

## CHAPTER 44

*A sick man is cured by praying at the tomb*

ONE of the clergy of the reverend and holy Willibrord, Clement,
bishop of the Frisians, came from abroad and stayed for a few
days as a guest at Lindisfarne. Suddenly he fell gravely ill; his condition gradually worsened and was finally pronounced desperate.
So severe was the pain that life and death seemed equally intolerable. Then he had an inspiration.

'Take me, I beg you,' he said to his servant, one Sunday, 'to
honour Cuthbert's most holy body; for I hope to be delivered from
my agony by his intercession, either by being restored to this
present life or carried off to the life to come.'

The servant obeyed and – no mean task – led him hobbling
along on a stick into the church. Kneeling down at the sepulchre
of our most holy father and God's beloved he bowed his head to
the ground and prayed for recovery. Immediately he felt such

strength flow into him from the saint's incorrupt body that he rose to his feet without the least effort and walked back to his rooms without the aid of servant or staff. A few days later when he was fully himself again he set off on his intended journey.

## CHAPTER 45

### How his shoes healed a paralytic

THERE was a youth in a near-by monastery who had lost the use of all his limbs through that disease which the Greeks call paralysis. His abbot knew that the Lindisfarne monastery housed some extremely skilful physicians, so he sent him there with the request that they should do everything within their power to cure him. In compliance with the abbot's and their own bishop's command they applied every ounce of skill and knowledge they possessed, but all to no effect. The disease advanced from day to day and he became so helpless that in the end he could only open his mouth. His doctors, having so long exerted all their human skill in vain, gave up hope. Lying there despaired of, he had recourse to the Divine Physician, to Him who when sought with sincerity of heart 'pardoneth all our iniquities and healeth all our infirmities'. He asked his servant to bring him a piece of the incorruptible garments from the sacred body, believing that God, by virtue of the relic, would grant the grace of recovery. On the abbot's advice the servant brought the shoes which Cuthbert had worn in the tomb and put them on the lifeless feet of the invalid, for the paralysis had first taken hold in the feet. This was done at sunset when it was time to rest. The invalid immediately fell into a calm sleep. Suddenly, as the hours were drawing on into the silence of the night, first one foot, then the other began to twitch. The servants who were watching over him saw this quite clearly and realized that the power of the saint's relics was at work, travelling upwards through the rest of the body from the soles of the feet. The bell for the night office woke him and he sat up. He knew at once that he was cured – the muscles and all the joints of his limbs felt strong and solid and the pain had gone. He rose and stood all through matins giving thanks to God. In the morning he went to the church, and with the whole community looking on and congratulating him he went round the holy places, praying and offering the sacrifice of praise to his Saviour. There now occurred a most delightful reversal of procedure. He had been carried to Lindisfarne on a cart, completely paralysed; he walked away safe and sound with every member strong and under perfect control.

Let us not forget that this was the work of the unchanging might of God's right hand; His wonders, memorable from of old, cease not to be poured forth in brightness on the world.

## CHAPTER 46

*How Felgild the hermit was cured of a swelling in the face by some of the covering of Cuthbert's cell wall*

ONE ought not to pass over a heavenly miracle granted by the Divine Mercy through part of the fabric of that holy oratory wherein our venerable father did solitary battle for the Lord. He who judges the hearts of men alone knows whether it ought to be ascribed to the merits of Cuthbert himself or to his successor Aethilwald, a man equally devoted to God. There is no reason for not believing that they both had a hand in it, together with the faith of that reverend father, Felgild, through whom and in whom the cure itself was wrought. He was the third heir to Cuthbert's spiritual battleground and is now over seventy, awaiting the end of this life and longing for the life to come. After Cuthbert's death Aethilwald came to the Farne, having been already tested many years in the monastic life until he had reached, step by step, the sublime life of a hermit.

The walls of the oratory were crumbling with age. The planks they were made of had been badly put together and had consequently come apart, leaving the place wide open to the stormy winds. Our venerable Cuthbert, more concerned with the splen-

dours of his heavenly than his earthly abode, had simply stuffed
the cracks with mud or straw or whatever else he could lay hands
on, to avoid having the fervour of his prayer cooled by daily blast
and downpour. When Aethilwald saw the state of the building
he asked the brethren who used to flock to him to bring calf-skin.
This he hoisted up as a shield against the violence of the blasts,
at the corner where he, like Cuthbert before him, had most often
stood or knelt in prayer. There he remained twelve years without
a break until he entered the joys of Paradise. Felgild came next,
and it was then that the right reverend Bishop of Lindisfarne,
Eadfrith, decided to restore the oratory from its foundations up,
since by then it was falling to pieces. When the work was finished
Felgild had many requests from devout people for some small relic
of Cuthbert or Aethilwald. The idea came to him of cutting the
calf-skin into pieces, but he thought he would first try it out on
himself before giving it to anyone else. His face was disfigured
with a red patch and a swelling, the beginnings of which had
been obvious long ago to his colleagues with whom he had lived
the common life. Greater abstinence and comparative neglect of
the body during his life as a hermit, coupled with the fact that
he shut himself up for long periods out of the warmth of the sun
and the fresh air, had made the disfigurement much worse. His
face was now one mass of inflammation. Fearing that the gravity
of his complaint would force him to retire from the solitary life
back to the monastery, he was bold enough to pin his faith on
a cure, hoping that they whose abode he delighted to dwell in
would make him whole again. He put a piece of the leather in
water and bathed his face with it. At once the swelling and foul
scab disappeared.

The first person to tell me this was a good priest of this monastery at Jarrow. He said he saw Felgild's face when swollen and
disfigured and had put his hand through the window to feel it
when it was cleansed. Felgild told the story later himself, saying
that everything had happened just as the priest said, and that,
though he lived in confinement for as many years again, the swelling never returned. Such is the grace of that almighty God whose
property is to cure many even in this world, and to heal all
infirmity of body and mind in the world to come, satisfying our

desires with good things and crowning us forever 'with loving-kindness and tender mercies'.

Here ends the book of the life and miracles
of St Cuthbert, Bishop of Lindisfarne

Eddius Stephanus: Life of Wilfrid

## PREFACE

IN the name of our Lord Jesus Christ. Here begins the humble preface of Stephen the priest to his account of the life of St Wilfrid, a bishop worthy before God. I have no choice but to give way, my honourable masters Bishop Acca and Abbot Tatberht, before the weight of your demands and the will of the whole community – but would that I might be able to accomplish all I should like! The work is difficult, my intelligence and command of rhetoric small; none the less, though the result might come below expectation, the effort will at least pay my debt of obedience. The greatest proof of my respect for you lies in my willingness to satisfy your request even though it demands more than I have to offer. If I produce anything to justify your choice, you must impute it to the grace of God. Relying on the faith and encouragement of you at whose request I begin, I have no doubts about my ultimate success. Everyone realizes that the task you have set me is one you think even myself capable of carrying out. Great profit accrues from the work itself – that of preserving the memory of Bishop Wilfrid, for simply to know what kind of man he was is in itself a sure way to virtue. In short, you can accept everything that popular report claims for him but realize that even then you know only very little about matters of great import, for believe me nobody can possibly have the full story.

I beseech you therefore, readers, credit my report. Take no notice of the thousand envious pricks of our old enemy the devil, but give ear and assent to what I now eloquently put forth. Fortitude always meets with enmity – 'Lightning strikes the peaks first'. Do not imagine I have been so rash and presumptuous as to put down anything which would not be passed as genuine by trustworthy witnesses. I prefer silence to falsehood. Now let us take the journey begun at your request.

# CHAPTER I

## *The birth of Wilfrid and its portent [634]*

I SHALL now embark, with the help of God, on the holy life and merits of blessed Bishop Wilfrid, whom the Lord, in the words of that outstanding teacher St Paul, 'foreknew, predestined, called, justified, and glorified'.[1] A sign from God proved that he was sanctified while still in the womb of his most pious mother, just as clearly as when the voice announced to Jeremiah: 'Before I formed thee in the belly I knew thee: and before thou camest out of the womb I sanctified thee and I ordained thee a prophet unto the nations.'[2] His mother was in confinement, worn out with the pains of labour, her women round her, when a group of men standing outside saw the house suddenly take fire and flames shoot sky high. Everyone started dashing panic-stricken in all directions, trying to douse the flames with water and rescue the inhabitants. But the women of the house came to the door and told them to keep calm: 'Control yourselves; a child has been born into the world.' At first they were amazed; then saw in what had taken place a great work of God, just as when Moses saw the burning bush with the flames crackling yet consuming nothing. Very often, brethren, we hear of the Holy Spirit appearing in the form of fire, for God is a fire consuming sinners and enlightening the righteous.[3] This light God has ordered to be placed on a candle-stick, not hidden under a bushel, and through our holy bishop it has shone openly on almost every church in Britain. This, the meaning of the omen, was entirely borne out by future events.

1. *Rom.* viii. 29–30.
2. *Jer.* i. 5.
3. cf. *Heb.* xii. 29.

108

## CHAPTER 2

## *He chooses God in boyhood [648]*

FROM his boyhood he was obedient to his parents, beloved of all, handsome, well-proportioned, gentle, modest, and controlled, with none of the silly fads common to boys, but, as St James the apostle says, 'swift to hear but slow to speak'.[1] He ministered with humble skill to all his father's visitors, whether the king's companions or their slaves – a fine example of the prophet's dictum 'All shall be taught by the Lord'.[2] When he was fourteen he decided to leave his father's estates to seek the Kingdom of Heaven, for his stepmother was harsh and cruel. His own mother was dead. None the less he managed to clothe, arm, and mount both himself and his servants so that he need not feel ashamed in the royal presence. His father blessed him, as Isaac blessed Jacob and Jacob his own sons, that their seed might multiply a thousand fold, and off he set to Eanfled, King Oswiu's queen, to be presented to her on the recommendation of those noblemen whom he had cared for at his father's house. Thanks be to God, he at once found favour in her sight. He was handsome and very keen-witted, so his request – to be allowed, on the queen's advice and with her protection, to give himself to the service of God – was granted. One of the king's most loving and faithful companions, a nobleman called Cudda, had also resolved, on account of his paralysis, to give up worldly ambition and dedicate himself to monastic life at Lindisfarne. The queen commended the newly arrived Wilfrid to him to join him in the service of God and act as his servant. Wilfrid set about his task with heartfelt zeal. This and the fact that he strove humbly and obediently to carry out the rule with sincere devotion made his master and the older monks love him as a son, and his equals to regard him as a brother. He learnt the whole psalter and several other books by heart. His head was

1. *Jas.* i, 19.
2. *John* vi, 45.

not yet tonsured but he served God in purity and true circumcision of heart, deserving a share in the blessing which Samuel received as Eli's servant.

## CHAPTER 3

### *He longs to visit the threshold of St Peter, Prince of the Apostles*

AFTER a year or two the youthful Wilfrid, prompted by the Holy Ghost, conceived a great desire to visit the See of St Peter, Prince of the Apostles, a road hitherto untravelled by our people, believing that he would wash away every trace of sin thereby and receive a great blessing. He told his master, who in his wisdom realized at once that this longing came from God and gladly agreed that his dear son should set out for the fount of all goodness. On Cudda's advice, Queen Eanfled sent Wilfrid to her cousin Erconberht, king of Kent. She fitted him out handsomely for the journey and sent messages to convey her highest commendations of him to Erconberht. There he was to stay until trustworthy fellow-travellers might be found for him. When the king saw this servant of God occupied, as was his wont, in constant prayer and fasting, vigils and spiritual reading, he began to love him dearly. Wilfrid had previously used St Jerome's version of the psalms; now he learnt by heart the fifth edition, the one in use in Rome. A whole year passed in tedious waiting, till at last, at the queen's prompting, the king found him a guide in Biscop Baducing, a nobleman of outstanding intelligence, who was himself hastening to Rome. Like Jacob he journeyed forth with his parents' blessing, a blessing which was later to stand him in good stead. He was pleasant to all, of keen mind, strong in body, willing to do any good work, with never a sad look to cloud his face. He arrived at Lyons in high spirits and broke the journey there with his companions. Here his austere guide separated from him, just as Barnabas took leave of Paul on account of John whose surname was Mark.

# CHAPTER 4

## *Archbishop Dalfinus makes him most welcome*

BLESSED be God, who protects and defends his servants and sends good men to help them. In this city lived Archbishop Dalfinus [1] of happy memory. As soon as he set eyes on the gentle Wilfrid and saw that his peaceful looks indicated a saintly mind, he took a liking to him, and put up both him and his companions as guests with all hospitality. He treated them as though they were his own, provided them abundantly with all they needed, and expressed the wish to adopt Wilfrid as his own son.

'Stay with me and be trustful,' he said, 'and I shall give you a good part of Gaul to govern in perpetuity and my own niece to be your wife. I shall adopt you as my son and you shall have me for a father and faithful helper in all things.'

The servant of God replied as wisdom had taught him.

'I have made my vows to the Lord and I shall keep them, leaving, like Abraham, my kinsfolk and my father's house to visit the Apostolic See, there to learn the laws of ecclesiastical discipline so that our nation may grow in the service of God. I yearn to receive the reward God promised to those that love Him when He said: "Everyone that hath forsaken father or mother shall receive a hundred fold and shall inherit everlasting life." [2] If with God's help I am still alive, I promise to come back to see you.'

From this and other signs the holy bishop realized that he was a true servant of God and filled with the Holy Spirit. He provided him with his requirements for the journey and sent him off, as he wished, to the Apostolic See with guides and supplies.

1. See page 113, note.
2. *Matt.* xix, 29.

## CHAPTER 5

### How he reaches the See of St Peter in safety

WILFRID and his companions arrived with joy and thanksgiving after a good journey at their long-desired destination – the See of Peter, apostle and Prince of Apostles. Just as that most excellent Doctor of the Gentiles, St Paul, made his way to Jerusalem 'lest by any means I should run or had run in vain', so this most humble light of our race, stirred up by God 'to hear from the ends of the earth the widsom' of this world's rulers, came to Rome.[1] In the oratory dedicated to St Andrew he humbly knelt before the altar over which the four gospels are placed, and adjured the apostle, by the name of the God for whom he had suffered, to obtain for him keenness of mind to learn and teach the nations the message of the Gospel. His prayer was granted, as many will testify. He passed many months in daily visits to the shrines of the saints, at one of which he found a teacher, sent by God and the apostle to be his faithful friend, Boniface the archdeacon, one of the wisest of counsellors. Boniface made him word-perfect in the four gospels, taught him the rule about Easter, of which the British and Irish schismatics were ignorant, and many other rules of Church law, teaching him as diligently as though he were his own son. Later he presented him to the pope, giving a very clear account of the whole purpose of this youthful servant of God's journey. The pope placed his blessed hand on Wilfrid's head, prayed over him, and blessed him. Then he set off in the peace of Christ, armed with the holy relics he had collected in Rome, and so returned safely to his father the Archbishop of Lyons.

1. cf. *Gal.* ii, 1–2; *Matt.* xii, 42.

## CHAPTER 6

*He receives the Roman form of tonsure from Archbishop Dalfinus.
The archbishop's martyrdom [658]*

FINDING Archbishop Dalfinus[1] safe and sound he went in to greet
him like a son, and recounted all the events of the journey, one
after another, to let him see how many blessings he had received.
The bishop thanked the Lord for having watched over him in
his travels and brought him safe home. The boy stayed on for
three years with him, making sound progress under his learned
tutors, and their love for each other steadily grew. Wilfrid had
an ardent desire to receive St Peter's, that is the Roman, form of
tonsure, which goes round the head in the shape of Christ's
own crown of thorns. The archbishop gave it him. As he placed
his hands on Wilfrid's head he intended to make him his heir,
should God will it; but God had it in mind rather to benefit our
own nation.

At that time the wicked Queen Baldhild was persecuting the
Church just like Jezebel who killed the prophets of old. She spared
priests and deacons but had nine bishops put to death, one of
whom was Dalfinus. The dukes, carrying out their evil plan,
ordered him to appear before them. He arrived quite undaunted
at his trial, though he knew full well what was coming. Our
servant of God insisted on accompanying him, despite Dalfinus's
prohibition. With joy he exclaimed: 'What better than that father
and son die at once and go to Christ together!' The holy bishop
received the crown of martyrdom, but the dukes, seeing Wilfrid
stripped and ready to receive his palm of martyrdom, asked who
was the handsome youth preparing himself for death. 'A foreigner
from across the sea, an Englishman,' they were told. 'Then do
not lay hands on him. Spare him,' came their answer. So Wilfrid

---

1. In reality Annemundus was archbishop; his brother Dalfinus was Lyons'
secular ruler. The identity of Baldhild is also doubtful.

in his youth was already worthy to be counted a confessor[1] like St John the Evangelist, who sat unscathed in a cauldron of boiling oil and drank deadly poison without taking hurt. Of him and his brother James the Apostle, Jesus said: 'Can you drink the cup that I am about to drink?'[2]

## CHAPTER 7

### *The welcome he receives from Alhfrith*

ONCE his father Dalfinus had been buried with due honour, Wilfrid set sail with the relics of the saints and with many blessings to protect him. To the delight of the crew, a fair wind sprang up, giving them a pleasant voyage back to the haven of their native land. Alhfrith, who was reigning alongside his father Oswiu, got wind of Wilfrid's arrival, and hearing that he was an adherent of the true Easter rule and an expert in the discipline of the Church of St Peter (to which the king himself was greatly devoted), on the advice of his faithful friend Coenwalh, king of the West Saxons, he ordered him to appear before him. Wilfrid came and greeted him peacefully in the following words: 'Jesus Christ, the Son of God, commanded the disciples and their leader, the apostle Peter, saying: "Into whatsoever house ye enter, first say: Peace be to this house."[3] We must first lay the foundations of this peace within ourselves and establish a harmony between body and soul, in obedience to St Paul's command: "Let the peace of Christ rule in your hearts." Then again Christ orders us to keep peace with our neighbour, saying: "Be wise and keep peace with one another." '[4]

At the end of this address Alhfrith humbly prostrated himself at the feet of God's chosen servant, received his message, and

1. A saint who, though not a martyr, bore witness for Christ by a life of outstanding holiness.
2. *Matt.* xx, 22.
3. *Luke* x, 5.
4. *Col.* iii, 15; *Mark* ix, 50; cf. *Matt.* x, 16.

asked for his blessing. He thought it was an angel of God who spoke. Wilfrid blessed him and they talked together. The wisdom the king showed in his clever questions about details of discipline and government in the Roman Church was balanced every time by the learning and clarity of Wilfrid's answers. The king then begged him by the Lord and by St Peter to remain at court preaching the word of God to himself and the nation, as an organ, so to say, on which the Holy Spirit might play. Wilfrid realized the king's affection for him and agreed to stay. Then their souls intertwined in the most wonderful way, just as we read of David's soul being knit to Jonathan's.

## CHAPTER 8

### *Alhfrith gives him the monastery at Ripon [c. 660]*

THEIR love for each other increased daily. As a proof of this Alhfrith gave the saintly confessor Wilfrid about ten hides[1] of land at Stanforda[2] and then shortly afterwards, for his own soul's good, he gave him the monastery at Ripon and thirty hides of land to go with it. Wilfrid was appointed abbot. This great opportunity for worldly aggrandizement – given by the Lord through the prayers of St Peter – Wilfrid used as a means of almsgiving: widow and orphan, the poor and those beset with any kind of infirmity, all benefited from his charity. You can tell from this that only lack of means had previously restricted his generosity. Behold with awe, my dear brethren, the benefit God bestowed on the king who 'found a goodly pearl and straightway bought it'. And the king was not alone in his love for Abbot Wilfrid; everyone, nobles and commons alike, looked on him as a prophet of God – which indeed he was.

1. A hide was enough land to support one family.
2. This name has been variously identified as Stamford in Lincolnshire, Stamford Bridge near York, or Stainforth (either that near Doncaster or that near Giggleswick).

## CHAPTER 9

### *Bishop Agilberht ordains him priest [c. 663]*

IN those days Agilberht, a bishop of foreign birth, visited Oswiu
and Alhfrith.[1] The latter pointed out Wilfrid to him, as someone
who had come to him from the Apostolic See, and retailed the
good reports he had heard from those who knew him – namely
that he was humble, peaceable, given to prayer and fasting, kind,
temperate. discreet, compassionate, full of the power and grace
of God, modest. prudent, no wine-bibber, pure and open of speech,
willing to learn and a good teacher.

'Therefore I beg you to raise him to the ranks of the priesthood
and he and I shall be inseparable friends.'

To which Agilberht gave this prophetic reply: 'Such a man
ought to be a bishop.'

He complied with the king's request by ordaining Wilfrid a
priest at Ripon. Just as David was chosen by God as a boy, anointed
by Samuel, and after many trials proved worthy to receive the
gift of prophecy, so the holy priest Wilfrid, after many blessings
from the saints of God, received gifts without number from God
Himself, the guardian of his days of poverty.

## CHAPTER 10

### *The conflict between St Wilfrid the priest and*
### *Bishop Colman over the Easter Question [663/4; cf. Bede.*
### *History iii, 25]*

ON a certain occasion while Colman was bishop of York and
metropolitan archbishop,[2] during the reign of Oswiu and Alhfrith,

1. Agilberht, a Frank, had been bishop of Wessex (648–60).

2. Colman was bishop of Lindisfarne, not York: he was never archbishop or
metropolitan.

abbots, priests, and clerics of every rank gathered at Whitby Abbey in the presence of the most holy Abbess Hilda, the two kings and Bishops Colman and Agilberht, to discuss the proper time for celebrating Easter: whether the practice of the British, Scots, and the northern province of keeping it on the Sunday between the fourteenth and twenty-second day of the moon was correct or whether they ought to give way to the Roman plan for fixing it for the Sunday between the fifteenth and twenty-first days of the moon. Bishop Colman, as was proper, was given the first chance to state his case. He spoke with complete confidence, as follows: 'Our fathers and theirs before them, clearly inspired by the Holy Spirit, as was Columba, stipulated that Easter Sunday should be celebrated on the fourteenth day of the moon if that day were a Sunday, following the example of St John the Evangelist "who leaned on the Lord's breast at supper", the disciple whom Jesus loved. He celebrated Easter on the fourteenth day of the moon, as did his disciples, and Polycarp and his disciples, and as we do on their authority. Out of respect to our fathers we dare not change, nor do we have the least desire to do so. I have spoken for our party. Now let us hear your side of the question.'

Agilberht, the foreign prelate, and his priest Agatho bade St Wilfrid, priest and abbot, use his winning eloquence to express in his own words the case of the Roman Church and Apostolic See. His speech was, as usual, humble.

'This question has already been admirably treated by a gathering of our most holy and learned fathers, three hundred and eighteen strong, at Nicaea, a city in Bithynia. Among other things they decided upon a lunar cycle recurring every nineteen years. This cycle gives no room for celebrating Easter on the fourteenth day of the moon. This is the rule followed by the Apostolic See and by nearly the whole world. At the end of the decrees of the fathers of Nicaea come these words: "Let him who condemns any one of these decrees be anathema."'

At the end of Wilfrid's speech Oswiu asked them, with a smile on his face, 'Tell me, which is greater in the Kingdom of Heaven, Columba or the apostle Peter?'

Then the whole synod with one voice and one accord cried: 'The Lord Himself settled this question when He declared: "Thou art Peter and upon this rock I will build my Church and the gates of hell shall not prevail against it. And I will give you the keys of the Kingdom of Heaven; and whatsoever thou shalt bind on earth shall be bound in Heaven and whatsoever thou shalt loose on earth shall be loosed in Heaven.'' '[1]

To this the king added, showing his wisdom: 'He is the keeper of the door and the keys. I will neither enter into strife and controversy with him, nor will I condone any who do. As long as I live I shall abide by his every decision.'

Bishop Colman was told that if, out of respect for his own country's customs, he should reject the Roman tonsure and method of calculating Easter, he was to resign his see in favour of another and better candidate. This he did.

## CHAPTER 11

*Wilfrid is elected to the episcopacy [664]*

THE kings next consulted the councillors of the realm to decide upon whom to elect to the vacant see. The candidate must be of sterling character, acceptable to God and man, and willing both to make the discipline of the Apostolic See his own and to seek to spread it. Their choice was unanimous.

'No better nor worthier man could be found among us than Wilfrid, priest and abbot. He has proved himself wise in all things. We know him to be such as the apostle Paul describes to Titus: "For a bishop must be without crime, as the steward of God: not proud, not subject to anger, not given to wine, no striker, not greedy of filthy lucre; but given to hospitality, gentle, sober, just, holy, continent, embracing that faithful word which is according to doctrine, that he may be able to exhort in sound doctrine and to convince the gainsayers."[2] He has every quality Paul thinks

1. *Matt.* xvi, 18–19.
2. *Titus* i, 7–9.

necessary. We therefore elect him in his prime of manhood to teach the law of God.' Like John the forerunner of the Lord and the prophet Ezekiel, he was chosen at the age of thirty. The election had the backing of the kings and of all the people; St Wilfrid was bidden to accept the rank of bishop in the Lord's name by the whole assembly. First of all he declined, on the grounds that he was not worthy. Later, he thought it better to obey and not try to flee from God's blessing.

We who are still living hold exactly the same opinion about him as was current then.

In speech he was always pure and open, tempering scrupulous regard for truth and solemnity of manner with a persuasive charm. His main topics of conversation were the mysteries of the law, the teachings of the faith, the virtue of continence, and the practice of right living. To everyone he gave varying advice, advice always suitable to the individual character, for he knew, before ever he opened his mouth, exactly what to say and when and how and to whom to say it. He laid special emphasis on prayer, fasting, and vigils, and was forever searching the scriptures and studying the canons of the Church. He had a wonderful memory for texts. In imitation of the saints he spread peace among his brethren. He was full of humility and charity – charity which is worth far more than any other gift, without which every other virtue is vain. He cared for the poor, fed the hungry, clothed the naked, welcomed strangers, brought back captives, and protected the widow and orphan, all so that he might win the reward of eternal life amid the choirs of angels with Jesus Christ our Lord.

## CHAPTER 12

*How he comes to be consecrated in Gaul [664]*

ON his election Wilfrid made the following speech.

'Your royal majesties, it behoves us to take careful thought as to how, with God's help but without criticism from Catholics, we, your candidate, might be raised to the episcopal dignity. Many

English bishops are as much Quartodecimans[1] as the Celts themselves. Of course it is not for me to point the finger at them, but I know I am right. The Holy See does not consider the men they ordain as being in communion with her – any more than she does those who consort with schismatics. In all humility, therefore, let me beg you to send me, under your protection, across the sea to Gaul, where there are many bishops of recognized orthodoxy. There, though unworthy, I can be consecrated without the Holy See raising any objection.'

The kings approved and fitted him out with ship, supplies, and a vast sum of money so that he might reach Gaul in great state. Once he had arrived, a convention was formed of at least twelve Catholic bishops, Agilberht among them. Having received his profession of faith, they consecrated him before all the people with great satisfaction and no less pomp. As their traditions demanded, he was borne into the oratory aloft on a golden throne by the bishops alone, to the accompaniment of songs and canticles from the choir.

Shortly afterwards they sent him to the see of York, commanding him in the Lord's name to keep the faith; just as Paul had commanded his son Timothy to husband well the grace of God which he had received through the laying on of his own hands.

## CHAPTER 13

*The Lord delivers our bishop and his companions from*
*the sea and from the hands of pagans [666; cf. Bede iv, 2]*

ON the crossing back from Gaul, Bishop Wilfrid's party in mid-sea and in the middle of the clerics' songs and psalms of praise, was alarmed by a sudden violent storm and contrary winds, just like the disciples on the Lake of Galilee. The wind howled from the

---

1. Quartodecimans were those who celebrated Easter on the fourteenth day of Nisan, irrespective of whether or not that day was a Sunday. Wilfrid must have realized the injustice of applying the name to the Celtic party; probably Eddius put it into Wilfrid's mouth as a smear.

south-east, and white-crested waves drove them towards the
land of the South Saxons, a region quite unknown to them. Then
the waves left both men and ship high and dry, and drained away
from the land, laying bare the shores, and receded far out to sea.
Forthwith a great horde of pagans approached, intending to seize
the vessel, loot it, carry off captives, and slay without more ado
all who resisted. Our holy bishop, anxious to save his friends' lives,
tried to pacify them with soothing words, and promised a large
sum of money. They were as fierce and stubborn as Pharaoh; they
refused to let God's people free, declaring contemptuously that
everything the sea cast on their shores was theirs. The chief priest
of their idolatry set himself up on a high mound like Balaam and
started to curse God's people, trying to bind their hands by his
magic art. One of the bishop's companions took a stone which
all the people of God had blessed, and hurled it like David from
a sling. It pierced the wizard's forehead through to the brain.
Death took him as it took Goliath, unawares, and he fell back
lifeless on the sand. The pagans then prepared for battle, but they
directed their onslaught against God's people in vain, for God was
on the side of the few. Gideon, at the Lord's command, with three
hundred warriors slew a hundred and twenty thousand of the
Midianites in one attack. Our bishop's companions were small in
number (only one hundred and twenty of them, one for each year
of Moses' life) but, being stout-hearted and well armed, they
formed a pact – that no one should turn his back and flee in battle
but that each should either die with honour or live in triumph.
God can grant either with equal ease. St Wilfrid and his clergy
fell to their knees, raised their hands to heaven, and gained God's
help. For just as Moses, Hur and Aaron lifting up his arms, called
continually to the Lord for help while Joshua, son of Nun, did
battle against Amalek, so did this little band of Christians vanquish
a fierce and untamed pagan host. Thrice they routed them, with
no mean slaughter, losing, strange to say, only five of their own
men all told. Then St Wilfrid prayed again, and God sent back
the tide sooner than usual; so that just as the pagans were
preparing with all their might and main for a fourth battle, and
their king had arrived, the sea flowed in over the whole beach,
and the ship cast off and made for the deep. Thanking God for

the glorious honour He had granted them, they had a fair passage
with the south-west wind behind them and reached harbour at
Sandwich.

## CHAPTER 14

### Chad, meanwhile, is ordained to Wilfrid's see [666]

As time went by without Wilfrid returning, King Oswiu, moved
to envy by our ancient foe, ignorantly let the see be snatched by
a candidate of the Quartodeciman party, a highly irregular procedure and clean contrary to the mind of the Apostolic See. This
Chad, a Celt but a truly devout servant of God and a great teacher,
was ordained in complete defiance of canon law. Wilfrid knew
nothing of the whole affair. When he did return, it was easy to
see who was in the wrong, but Wilfrid withdrew to his old post
as abbot, to a humble life at Ripon for the next few years, remaining there all the time except for the frequent invitations from King
Wulfhere to carry out episcopal duties in Mercia. Wulfhere had
a sincere liking for him. God had raised up for Himself this most
gracious king – amongst whose good works was the gift, for the
good of his soul, of many pieces of land in various places to
our bishop. Wilfrid soon used them to found monasteries. Since
Deusdedit, who followed Archbishop Honorius, had died, the
pious King Egbert of Kent summoned Wilfrid to ordain a good
number of priests and deacons. One of these priests, Putta, later
became a bishop himself.[1]

So Wilfrid carried on honourably, acting as bishop in several
areas and winning universal affection, and then returned to his
own part of the country, bringing with him the singers Aedde [2]
and Aeona and masons and artisans in every kind of trade. He
brought about a great improvement in the church by introducing
the Rule of St Benedict. He was another St Paul, opening in those
parts the great door of the faith.

1. Wulfhere, king of Mercia 659–75; Egbert, king of Kent 664–73; Putta,
bishop of Rochester 669–76.
2. This is probably Eddius himself.

## CHAPTER 15

### *He regains his see [669]*

AFTER three years had gone by, Archbishop Theodore[1] came from Kent to the king of Bernicia and Deira bringing with him from Rome the decrees of the Apostolic See. As soon as he set foot in the kingdom he was told how canon law had been flouted, one bishop, like a thief, grabbing another's diocese. He did not take this lightly. Chad was deposed. Being an extremely meek man and a true servant of God, he realized he had acted wrongly in being consecrated by those Quartodecimans to someone else's see, humbly confessed his fault, accepted the judgement of the bishops, and did penance. It was with Chad's consent then that Theodore installed Wilfrid in York. Our holy bishop returned not wrong for wrong but good for evil, following the Lord's command and David's dealing with Saul where he says: 'I shall not lay my hand upon the Lord's anointed.'[2] His devoted friend Wulfhere had given him Lichfield in Mercia, a place highly suitable for an episcopal see either for himself or anyone he might choose to give it to. So he made overtures of peace to Chad, who was ready to pay the bishops complete obedience. They ordained him through all the ecclesiastical degrees till he was fully consecrated bishop and installed him at Lichfield, where he was given an honourable welcome by the king. He lived a holy life rich in good works and, in due course, went to his fathers, to await the coming of the Lord in that judgement which, for him, ought to be extremely lenient.

1. Theodore (603–90), a Greek monk, was appointed archbishop of Canterbury by the pope in 668.
2. I *Kings* (A.V. I *Samuel*) xxiv, 6–7.

## CHAPTER 16

### The restoration of the church at York [669–71]

WHEN Wilfrid was installed at York during Wulfhere's reign, the stonework of the church which had been first founded and dedicated to God by St Paulinus, in the days of that most Christian king, Edwin, was quite clearly half in ruins. The top of the roof was too old to be serviceable any longer; water streamed through it; the windows had never been glassed in, so birds flew in and out and built their nests inside; the walls were in a disgusting state, decaying and filthy with the mess made by the birds and the rain. Our holy bishop's soul stood still within him, like Daniel's, at the sight of God's house, a house of prayer, looking like a den of thieves. He planned to restore it and make it once more pleasing to God. The decayed ridges of the roof were replaced; the craftsmen made a good job of them, covering them with pure lead. The windows were glazed so that the birds were excluded without shutting out the light too. The walls were washed till they were in the words of the prophet, 'whiter than snow'. The interior of the building was decorated and the altar provided with all kinds of vessels. In addition to all this Wilfrid acquired vast tracts of land for the Church, thus relieving its poverty and enriching it with valuable endowments. What God said about Samuel and all the saints certainly applied to him: 'Whosoever will glorify me, him will I glorify', for he was loved and respected by the whole nation.[1]

---

1. 1 *Kings* (A.V. 1 *Samuel*) ii, 30.

## CHAPTER 17

*The building and dedication of the church at Ripon [671–8]*

IN the midst of all this worldly pomp there grew up in our bishop, by God's grace, an ever-increasing love for that Virgin Bride, the Church, espoused to one husband, the daughter of Charity which is the mother of all goodness. He decked her out with fair rules of discipline, as though with flowers of virtue, making her chaste and modest, continent and temperate and submissive, girt about with garments of every hue. In the words of the prophet, 'All the glory of the king's daughter is within.'[1] Just as Moses, following the pattern God gave him on the mount, built with human hands a tabernacle of various hues to stir up the faith of Israel to the worship of God, so the most blessed Bishop Wilfrid, in the sight of all who believed in their heart and confessed their faith, adorned the bridal-chamber of the true Bridegroom and Bride with gold and silver and every shade of purple: at Ripon he started and completed from foundation to roofbeam a church built of dressed stone, supported with columns and complete with side aisles.

Like Solomon's temple it was consecrated on completion to the Lord. It was dedicated to St Peter, prince of the apostles, to gain the help of his prayers for all who might enter. The altar with its bases was dedicated and vested in purple woven with gold. The people participated in the ceremony and everything was carried out according to the canons. Those most devout and Christian kings, Ecgfrith and Aelwine, the kings beneath them, the abbots and sheriffs, and all kinds of dignitaries besides were present. Wilfrid stood in front of the altar, facing the people, and in the kings' presence read out in a clear voice a list of lands which previous monarchs and now themselves had given him for their souls' salvation with the consent and signature of the bishops and all the ealdormen. He went on to

1. *Psalm* xliv, 14 (A.V. xlv, 13).

enumerate holy places in various parts of the country which the British clergy, fleeing from our own hostile sword, had deserted. God would indeed be pleased with the good kings for the gift of so much land to our bishop. They gave Wilfrid land round Ribble, Yeadon, Dent, and Catlow, and in other places too. When the sermon was over the kings started a feast of three days and nights in which all the people took part, showing kindness to their enemies and treating God's servants with deference. Our holy bishop adorned the house of God even further with a marvel of art hitherto undreamt of: he had had written, for his soul's good, a book of the Gospels, done in letters of purest gold on parchment all empurpled and illuminated, and had ordered jewellers to make a case for them, also of the purest gold and set with precious gems. All these treasures and several more besides are kept in the church to this day as a memorial to him. His remains are here and his name is constantly remembered in the monks' daily prayer.

## CHAPTER 18

### *He restores a child to life*

'GOD is wonderful in his saints,' as the psalmist says; in their works His glory shines. We read in the Old Testament how God's servants did wonders in His name: Elias and Eliseus, for instance, raised the dead to life; and Christ's apostles, following their Master's example, drove out, as He promised they would, every kind of disease in His name. And now, to the glory of God, their successors, of whom our bishop is one, heal the afflicted in exactly the same way. St Wilfrid was out riding one day, going round on his various duties as bishop, baptizing and confirming. Among the people he baptized in the village of On Tiddanufri[1] was a certain woman. Her first-born son had died and she was bitterly distressed, moaning with grief and tired out with the weight of the child – for she had the body with her, wrapped in rags and

---

1. Not identified.

hidden in her bosom. She uncovered its face for the bishop to baptize it with the rest, hoping that it might be brought back to life. Our holy bishop saw that it was dead and stopped, at a loss what to do about it. The woman realized she was found out, fell to the ground, and wept bitterly, boldly adjuring him in the Lord's name to deliver her son from the lion's mouth by bringing him to life again to be baptized. She implored him more and more insistently by all the holiness of the episcopacy, kneeling and clasping his feet, kissing and bedewing them with her tears.

'Most holy lord,' she cried, 'do not dampen the faith of a bereaved woman. Strengthen my belief. Raise him up and baptize him and he shall live for God and for you. By the power of Christ do not delay.'

Then our holy bishop, in no doubt about the power of Christ and seeing in her the faith of the Syro-Phoenician woman, prayed and laid his hand on the corpse. The breath of life returned and the boy breathed again. He handed the child back to his mother, baptized him, and commanded her in God's name to give her son back to him at the age of seven for the service of God. The handsomeness of the boy and her husband's evil advice led the woman to break her promise when the time came. They fled the district. The bishop's reeve, Hocca, searched him out and found him living with a gang of Britons. He removed him by force and brought him to the bishop. The boy lived in the service of God and died in the great plague. How great and wonderful is the mercy of God who, through the power of his servant brought back to life a child dead and unbaptized so that, baptized, he might inherit a life of unending happiness in Heaven.

## CHAPTER 19

*The king's victory over the fierce Picts [671 – 3]*

THE pious King Ecgfrith and Queen Aethilthryth were both obedient to Bishop Wilfrid in everything, and their reign was marked by fruitful years of peace and joy at home and victory over their enemies. Queen Aethilthryth's body did not corrupt in death, an indication that it was unstained in life.[1]

Joas, the youthful king of Judah, during the lifetime of the great high-priest, Joada, pleased God and vanquished his enemies; when the priest died, however, he displeased the Lord and his kingdom diminished. This was the case with Ecgfrith too. While he was on good terms with the bishop, as many will tell you, he enlarged his kingdom by many victories; but when they quarrelled and the queen separated from him to give herself to God, the king's triumphs ceased, and that within his own lifetime. In the early years of his reign while the kingdom was still weak, the vicious tribes of the Picts fiercely resented their being subject to the Saxons; indeed they began to stir up revolt. Swarms of them gathered from every cranny of the north, like ants in summer sweeping up an earthwork to prevent their home from ruin. When the news reached Ecgfrith he quickly mustered a troop of cavalry and putting his trust in God, like Judas Maccabeus, set off with Beornhaeth, his trusty sub-king, and the little band of God's people against a vast army hidden in the hills. Ecgfrith was quite gentle with his people and merciful to his enemies, but quick in battle, impatient of delay. Host upon host of the enemy fell before him. He filled two rivers with the slain and his men crossed dry-shod over the corpses to slay the fugitives. Thus the Picts were reduced to slavery, a condition in which they remained until Ecgfrith himself was slain.

## CHAPTER 20

*Ecgfrith's victory over the king of Mercia [673–5]*

AFTER this Ecgfrith ruled his people with God's bishop in justice and holiness. He was David's equal for quelling his foes and God gave him yet more strength to temper the unruly spirit of the tribes who were rising under their warrior kings. Yet he walked humbly

1. Aethithryth (Etheldreda) *d.* 679 after founding Ely as a double monastery. See Introduction, pp. 24–5. Ecgfrith reigned from 670 to 685.

in the sight of the Lord, rendering Him thanks in all things. King
Wulfhere of Mercia, a man of proud mind and insatiable will,
stirred up all the southern nations against our own, intent not
merely on war but meaning even to enslave us to him as tribu-
taries. His designs were not inspired by God. So Ecgfrith, king of
Bernicia and Deira, a man of unwavering purpose, took the advice
of his counsellors, followed the injunctions of his bishop, put his
trust in God and marched forth against the enemy host, in defence
of Church and fatherland, with as few troops as had Barak and
Deborah. With God's help he laid them low. Countless numbers
were slaughtered, their king routed, and the Kingdom of Mercia
itself put under tribute. Later Wulfhere died (I do not know the
exact cause) and Ecgfrith ruled a wider realm in peace.

## CHAPTER 21

### *Our bishop's virtue*

THESE conquests at one and the same time extended our most
pious King Ecgfrith's territory and enlarged the field of Wilfrid's
ecclesiastical jurisdiction. He was now bishop of the Saxons in
the south and of the British, Scots, and Picts to the north. He was
dearly loved by every race, performed his duties as bishop with
all diligence, ordained priests and deacons to help him in all parts
of the diocese, and steered the barque of the Church on an even
keel through the tossing billows of this world. No wave of con-
viviality swamped him; neither did he let his abstinence cast him
against the rocks of pride. He was habitually temperate at feasts
– and even when alone never drank a full glass, no matter how
small the vessel might be, neither summer nor winter, whether
parched with thirst or faint with cold. There are plenty of witnesses to vouch for this. In praying and keeping vigil, in spiritual
reading and in fasting, where will you find his equal? He himself
testified before the faithful that he had kept his body unspotted
from his mother's womb. Every night, summer and winter, he
washed himself in holy water until Pope John of happy memory
advised him to forgo such rigours on account of his age. Nearly

all the abbots and abbesses made over their possessions to him by vow, either retaining them in his name during their lifetime or naming him heir in their wills. Nobles, men of high position in the world, sent their sons for him to tutor so that they might have the choice either of giving themselves to God or else of returning as grown men with Wilfrid's recommendation to enter the king's service as warriors. These things only served to kindle the flame of envious hate in many hearts, a flame which the devil was quick to fan; but our holy bishop, carrying, in the words of St Paul, armour on the right arm and on the left, bore with equanimity both good fortune and bad. His gifts both to clergy and laity were on such a grand scale that he was second to none in largesse.

## CHAPTER 22

### The building of the house of God at Hexham [672–8]

HE cleaved to God unceasingly, as the psalmist says, placing his hope in the Lord, sweetly rendering his vows to Him to whom he owed everything. At Hexham he built a church to the glory of God and the honour of St Andrew on land given by the saintly Queen Aethilthryth. My poor mind is quite at a loss for words to describe it – the great depth of the foundations, the crypts of beautifully dressed stone, the vast structure supported by columns of various styles and with numerous side-aisles, the walls of remarkable height and length, the many winding passages and spiral staircases leading up and down. Without a doubt it was the Spirit of God who taught our bishop to plan the construction of such a place, for we have never heard of its like this side of the Alps. Bishop Acca, who by God's grace is still with us, decked out this superb edifice with splendid gold and silver ornaments, precious stones and silks and purples for the altars. What description could do justice to the fabric he installed? Let us return to our narrative.

## CHAPTER 23

### *He heals a half-dead boy*

DURING the construction of the highest parts of the walls of the
church, a young man, one of the bishop's masons, lost his footing
on a high pinnacle, fell headlong, and dashed himself on the stone
pavement below. He broke his arms and legs; every joint was put
out. There he lay gasping his last. The masons thought he was
dead and at the bishop's command, took him outside on a bier.
Wilfrid had been praying and weeping but now hastily summoned
all the workmen.

'Let us show how great our faith is by praying together with
one accord that God may send back the soul into this lad's body
and hear our prayers for his life, even as he heard the prayers
of St Paul.'

They knelt down and prayed that he who mocks at every good
thing might have no victory to gloat over in this building. The
bishop prayed after the manner of Elias and Eliseus and gave his
blessing. The breath of life returned to the boy. The doctors bound
up his arms and legs and he improved steadily day by day. He
is still alive to give thanks to God and his name is Bothelm.

## CHAPTER 24

### *How envy is stirred up against our bishop and he is driven from his see [678]*

THE tempter, 'like a roaring lion', to quote St Peter, went prowling
round God's fold looking for an entry, on the watch both night
and day, trying to overcome the strongest soldier first – for, that
done, the rest would easily be conquered. In this skirmish he chose
his usual weapon, one by which he has often spread defilement

throughout the whole world – woman. Iurminburgh, Ecgfrith's queen, greatly envied Bishop Wilfrid. Later, let me tell you, after the king was killed, she changed from a she-wolf into a lamb of God indeed, a perfect abbess and mother of her community. But now she corrupted the king's heart with poisonous tales about Wilfrid, imitating Jezebel in her onslaughts on the prophets and in her persecution of Elias. She used all her eloquence to describe to Ecgfrith all St Wilfrid's temporal glories, listing his possessions, the number of his monasteries, the vastness of the buildings, his countless followers arrayed and armed like a king's retinue. Her darts pierced the king's heart and took effect; from then on the pair of them used their cunning to secure the condemnation of this holy head of the church and to snatch all the gifts left to God by former kings. This certainly showed daring on their part, but in the end their ill-will turned back upon themselves. Balak went against God's will when he summoned Balaam to help him. They did likewise. They secured Archbishop Theodore to further criminal folly, winning him over with bribes, for money will blind even the wisest. Theodore came to them and heard them explain that they intended to humiliate Wilfrid. Without the least excuse he agreed to condemn him although he was completely blameless. While our bishop was absent, Theodore found three men from somewhere or other, not Wilfrid's subjects, and in flagrant contempt of law and precedent proceeded to consecrate them bishops over Wilfrid's own territory. Our holy bishop, when the news reached him, went straight to the king and the archbishop to find out why, when there was no charge against him, his enemies should behave like robbers and defraud him of all the wealth which the kings, for their love of God, had left him. This is the famous public reply he received: 'We do not find you guilty of any crime whatsoever; none the less our decrees against you are to remain unchanged.'

This disgraceful decision by no means satisfied our bishop, and on the advice of his fellow bishops he decided to take the case to the Holy See; just as Paul appealed to Caesar when condemned without reason by the Jews. As he turned away from the royal tribunal, he said to the king's minions who were smirking with delight at his defeat: 'You who are now laughing at my malicious condemnation will be shedding bitter tears a year from today.'

And his prophecy was true. For twelve months later, to the day, the corpse of King Aelfwini[1] was carried into York, at the sight of which the whole population wept and tore their hair for grief and rent their garments.

## CHAPTER 25

### Bishop Winfrid of Lichfield is robbed

WILFRID prepared to set sail with his companions and some of his clergy. The many thousands of monks he was forced to leave behind in the power of the upstart bishops mourned and bewept their fate, imploring God to direct their bishop's journey according to His will. Wilfrid's enemies, finding more scope for their malice in the supposition that he was bound for Etaples and thence by the direct route to Rome, sent envoys off with bribes to Theodoric, king of the Franks, and the wicked Duke Ebroin. They were either to exile him for good or kill his friends and take all his possessions. The Lord freed him from his enemies as though from the hands of Herod himself, for just then Bishop Winfrid, who had been driven out of Lichfield, happened to be on the selfsame route.[2] He fell into their hands and may as well have fallen into the lion's jaws, for they seized him, took all his money, killed many of his friends, and inflicted the extremes of misery on him by leaving him naked. Luckily for our bishop they had mistaken the first syllable of Winfrid's name.

1. Son of King Oswiu, he was born in 661, was sub-king of Deira and died in 679.
2. Winfrid, bishop of Lichfield 672–6.

## CHAPTER 26

### *His journey takes him to Friesland*

FAR from being molested, our holy bishop and his companions were gently wafted on by a westerly breeze and, with prows dipping towards the east, arrived after a pleasant journey at the coast of Friesland, to be received with all ceremony by King Aldgisl and vast crowds of the heathen. With the king's permission Wilfrid preached daily to the people in the open air, telling them openly about the true God, the Father Almighty, and Jesus Christ His Only Begotten Son and the Holy Spirit who is co-eternal with Him. He preached one baptism for the remission of sin and the resurrection after death to life everlasting. In the pagans' eyes his doctrine gained strong backing by the fact that his arrival was marked by an unusually large catch of fish. Indeed the year was an abnormally fruitful one for every kind of produce. All this they attributed to the glory of the God whom the holy man was preaching. So his preaching was accepted and that year he baptized all but a few of the chiefs and many thousands of the common people, thus laying like the Apostle of the Gentiles the foundation of the faith upon which his son is still building. By his son I mean Willibrord, who was nurtured at Ripon and is now, by God's grace, a bishop. At present he is wearing himself out with toil, but shall have his reward above.[1]

1. cf. Bede, *Ecclesiastical History* v, 9–11.

## CHAPTER 27

*The king refuses the price set upon Wilfrid*

AT that time Ebroin, one of the dukes of Theodoric, king of the
Franks, sent messengers with letters for Aldgisl, greeting him with
words of peace and promising on oath a full bushel of gold solidi
– a foul offer indeed – if he would send Wilfrid to him alive, or
slay him and send his head. The king had the letter read out for
all to hear, including ourselves and the messengers, who were
feasting with his people in the palace at the time. When it had
been read out he took the scroll and tore it up for all to see and
threw the pieces on to a fire blazing in front of him. He gave the
bearers this message: 'Tell your lord what you now hear me say:
Thus may the Creator of all things rend and destroy the life and
lands of him who perjures himself before God and breaks the pact
he has made. Even thus may he be torn to pieces and burn to
ashes.'

The messengers left in confusion at the king's refusal to countenance the crime, and returned to their master.


## CHAPTER 28

*Wilfrid is welcomed by kings Dagobert and Perctarit [679]*

OUR beloved bishop (and God's) spent the winter with the Frisians
and gained many souls for Christ. At the first sign of spring he
and his companions continued on their journey to the Holy See.
They came to Dagobert, king of the Franks, and were most
graciously received. This courtesy was a return for former favours
from Wilfrid. Dagobert had been banished in his youth by enemies
who were then on the throne. He sailed away, his fortune ruined,
and came, by God's help, to Ireland. Years later his friends and

relatives learnt from travellers that he was alive, flourishing and in the prime of manhood, and sent to Wilfrid to ask him to invite Dagobert across from Scotland or Ireland and then to send him over to them as their king. This our holy bishop did; he made him welcome on his arrival from Ireland, provided him with arms and sent him back in great state with a troop of his companions to support him. The king did not forget such kindness. He now begged Wilfrid to accept the chief bishopric of the realm, Strasbourg; and when Wilfrid declined, he sent him on his way with lavish presents and with his own bishop, Deodatus, to guide him.[1] They journeyed on under God's guidance till they came to Perctarit, king of Campania, a gentle humble man, and one who held God's word in awe.[2] He received them graciously, as God bade, and gave Wilfrid this news: 'Your enemies sent messengers to me from Britain with greetings and the promise of a great reward if I would lay hands upon you as a bishop in secret flight (for so they describe you) and keep you from reaching the Apostolic See. I refused to take part in such a scandalous plot. This was the answer I gave them: "As a youth I was exiled from my own country and found refuge with a king of the Huns, a pagan. Before the idol he called his God he made a pact with me never to hand me over or betray me to my enemies. Some time afterwards messengers came from my enemies promising on oath a full bushel of gold solidi if he would hand me over to be slain. He refused, declaring that his gods would cut short his life if he broke his promise to them by this foul deed. How much more then must I, who know the true God, refuse to send my soul to perdition rather than gain even the whole world?"'

In thanksgiving for his own safekeeping Perctarit treated Wilfrid with great honour and sent him off with guides towards his long desired goal, Rome.

1. Dagobert II was king of Austrasia 676–9. He was assassinated soon after Wilfrid's visit.
2. Perctarit was king of Lombardy 661–8; he was in exile when this incident occurred.

## CHAPTER 29

*Our bishop's letters are received by the most blessed
Pope Agatho and the holy synod [679]*

GOD's beloved bishop reached Rome quite safely, only to learn
that his case had preceded him; the holy monk Cenowald had
just then arrived with letters from Archbishop Theodore. So Pope
Agatho was already familiar with the quarrel.[1] To an assembled
gathering of holy bishops and priests, more than fifty in number,
in that church of our Lord and Saviour Jesus Christ which is called
the Basilica of Constantine, the most holy and thrice blessed
Agatho, bishop of the Holy Catholic and Apostolic Roman Church,
gave the following address: 'The reason why I have summoned
you, venerable brethren, is not hidden from you. I require this
honourable assembly to understand and discuss with me the dissension which has recently arisen among the churches in the
island of Britain, where through God's grace the company of the
faithful has greatly increased. News of the quarrel has come both
from pilgrims' accounts of the situation and from a series of
written reports.'

Andrew, the most reverend Bishop of Ostia and John, Bishop
of Porto, then rose to speak.

'The ordering of the affairs of all the churches hangs on the
decision of your apostolic authority. You fulfil the office of the
blessed apostle Peter to whom the Creator and Redeemer of all,
Christ Our Lord, gave the keys for loosing and binding. In accordance with your Holiness's recent injunction, sitting in session with
our brother bishops and fellow servants we have read every letter
which the messengers from Britain brought to your Holiness, as
well as those which have come from Archbishop Theodore, who
was himself formerly sent to Britain by the Apostolic See, and the
reports from others against a certain bishop who, they allege,

1. Agatho, a Sicilian, was pope 678–81. Kindly and generous, he restored
good relations with the Eastern church.

secretly fled from his diocese and whom they believe to have come to Rome. We have gone through those presented by Wilfrid, Bishop of York and God's beloved, who has come here to appeal to the Apostolic See against ejection from his diocese by the above-mentioned holy archbishop. In these letters the accusers raise many dubious points, but never do we find Wilfrid convicted of any crime at all, on any interpretation of the sacred canons, and therefore the ejection was completely irregular. His accusers' statements cannot prove him guilty of anything leading to his degradation. Rather are we of the opinion that he refrained by his modesty from implicating himself in seditious quarrelling. After being ejected, he let his fellow bishops know the merits of the case and forthwith had recourse to the Apostolic See wherein Christ the Almighty Lord who redeemed the Church with His Blood founded the primacy of the priesthood and confirmed the authority of the Prince of the Apostles. Finally the case has been submitted to your apostolic jurisdiction for an authoritative answer.'

Then Agatho, the most holy and thrice blessed bishop of the Holy Catholic Roman Church, thus replied: 'Wilfrid, Bishop of York and God's beloved, is said to be at the doors of this assembly. Let him, in answer to his request, be admitted to address the petition he has brought.'

Our beloved bishop, on entering the sacred precincts, began: 'I beseech your Pontifical Holiness to command that this my humble petition be received and read out in your presence.'

To this the pope replied: 'Let Bishop Wilfrid's petition be received and read out before the whole gathering.'

It was then taken and read out in front of the whole apostolic council by John the notary.

### CHAPTER 30

#### The text of the petition

'I WILFRID, a humble and unworthy English bishop, with God going before to guide me, have directed my steps to this the apostolic citadel, as though to a fortress and a tower of strength, because I am confident that in that place from which the rules of the sacred canons emanate and are diffused throughout all the churches of the world to be handed down through the preaching of the bishops and received with a lively faith – there, I repeat, am I sure to be given a just judgement, unimportant though I am. I do not doubt that your Holiness has taken note both of what I stated in my letters and what I have claimed here and now in your presence; and, furthermore, I alleged when I was presented to your Holiness on arrival, that certain invaders had had the presumption to go entirely against the declared ruling of the canons and, at a synod consisting of the most holy Archbishop Theodore of Canterbury and other bishops, had, like thieves, attempted to assail the see which I, by God's mercy, had ruled for ten years and more. They succeeded in robbing me, planting themselves in my place and being consecrated as bishops. There is not just the one usurper, there are three of them. Their consecrations were, naturally, uncanonical. Because of the respect due to the archbishop I pass over the question how so venerable a man could have brought himself to consecrate, without any bishop's consent, and in face of my respectful opposition, three bishops to the see of York while I was still alive. I would rather not labour the point, for I hardly dare accuse the envoy of the Apostolic See. Should it be made clear, however, that I have been cast out of my see in contempt of the law by my enemies' spite without ever being convicted of any crime, without being guilty on any count whatsoever, let alone those for which the law reserves its severities, and should it be further proved (as I can assure you it can) that, once thrown out, I neither stirred up quarrels and sedition nor set myself to oppose my enemies but at once sought help from the Holy See, having simply protested to my fellow bishops before departure – if all this is proved and yet your Holiness and the council of bishops decide that though blameless I am still to be considered deposed, then I shall embrace your decision with humble devotion. But if I am to be restored to my diocese, I shall follow and venerate that decision with all my strength, provided you issue a decree sanctioning the ejection of the usurpers. If, on the other hand, you should think fit to appoint other bishops to my diocese, then let them be such as I can serve God with in unity, peace, and concord, so that each of us may recognize the established laws of the Church and take care to guard the flock committed to him. If it pleases the archbishop and my fellow bishops to increase the number of bishops, then let men be chosen from our own clergy, candidates whom the bishops in synod can agree upon. Do not let the Church suffer damage from strangers and outsiders; anything irregular and imprudent does nothing but give rise to quarrel after quarrel, such as can never be unravelled, appeased, nor ended. I trust that I show absolute obedience to and full compliance with the laws of the Church – to whose justice I have hastened with full confidence, having put all other matters aside in order to do so.'

## CHAPTER 31

### *Pope Agatho's answer*

THE most holy and thrice blessed Agatho, Bishop of the Holy Catholic and Apostolic Church of the city of Rome, replied thus: 'It has been a great source of satisfaction to realize, as the petition was taking its course, that Bishop Wilfrid, God's beloved, did not let his belief that he had been unjustly ejected from his see drive him into contumacious opposition, to meet, as the world would, force with force. Rather did he humbly bethink himself to seek the canonical remedies from our holy founder, St Peter, the Prince of the Apostles. Moreover he meekly awaits the decision, promising prompt obedience without cavil, vowing wholehearted assent to whatever Peter, whose office we perform, shall declare through our lips.'

## CHAPTER 32

## *The synod's reply*

THE whole synod, headed by Pope Agatho and exercising its lawful authority, promulgated, among its various decrees, the following decision:

'We decree and lay down that Bishop Wilfrid, God's beloved, is to take possession of the see which until recent times was his, according to the terms previously defined. He will summon a council to help him choose coadjutors, men with whom he will be able to live without friction, as the existing rule demands. These are to be consecrated by the archbishop. Those who, in defiance of the law, have taken over in his absence are to be expelled without hesitation. If anyone should be rash enough to attempt to resist these statutes of the synod or refuse to obey them or at any later date should try to infringe them in whole or in part, then, without regard to either their present or future rank, they shall be overthrown. This we enjoin on the authority of the Prince of the Apostles. If it be a bishop who dares to flout this holy ordinance, let him be degraded from episcopal rank and be forever anathema, and similarly with priest or deacon or minor cleric. Indeed, whether he be cleric, monk, or layman of any degree, even king, let him be made an outcast from the Body and Blood of our Saviour Jesus Christ; may he not be counted worthy to look upon Him at His awful Second Coming. But he who with sincere devotion and complete accord receives, holds, and carries out or helps to bring to perfection these our ordinances, may he see 'the goodness of the Lord in the land of the living', may his part be with those who sit at God's right hand, may he possess eternal beatitude and, with all those who have won favour in the sight of God and gained unending glory, may he be found worthy to hear, as a reward for that obedience which God prizes beyond all sacrifice, the divine voice of Our Lord Jesus Christ, the Universal

Judge, pronounce the words: "Come ye blessed of my father, inherit the kingdom prepared for you from the foundation of the world." [1]

## CHAPTER 33

### Our bishop returns [680]

WILFRID's long stay in Rome was brought to an end by the injunction of the pope and synod to return home, taking with him the orders of the Holy See which he was to show to Archbishop Theodore and King Ecgfrith. Our holy bishop carried out these commands with unwavering loyalty as he had promised, but before setting out he spent several days going round the shrines of the saints making his devotions. He managed to obtain, much to the comfort of the churches of Britain, a large supply of relics, each of which he labelled with a description of the object itself and the name of the saint. In his usual way he acquired numerous other articles to decorate the house of God, but it would be tedious to give a list of them all here. Finally he and his company set out for home in great joy with the blessing of pope and synod and with the help of God. He journeyed on, bearing the triumphal decision, up through Campania and over the mountains till he came to the land of the Franks, only to find that his faithful friend King Dagobert had been assassinated by some treacherous dukes and (Heaven defend us!) with the bishops' consent. One of these same prelates rode out to meet Wilfrid at the head of a mighty army, intending, had not God intervened, to rob the whole company, reduce them to serfdom or sell them into slavery, and to kill any who resisted. Our holy bishop was to suffer the anguish of being imprisoned and reserved for Duke Ebroin's judgement.

'What made you so bold,' they demanded, 'as to pass through the land of the Franks, seeing that you deserve to be put to death

1. *Matt.* xxv, 34.

for making Dagobert king? You it was who brought him back from exile and what did he do but lay waste our cities, spurn the advice of our elders, act like Solomon's son Rehoboam in imposing an humiliating tribute on his people, and despise the Church of God and her rulers? These are the crimes for which he was slain; this is the reason his body now lies in the grave.'

Our holy bishop answered humbly: 'In the name of Jesus Christ what I say is true; by the holy apostle Peter I swear I do not lie. It was in accordance with God's command to the people of Israel when they dwelt as strangers in a foreign land that I helped and cherished King Dagobert, then an exile and a wanderer. I raised him up not to your harm but for your good, sending him to build up your cities, to put spirit into your citizens, to counsel your senate, and, as he promised in the Lord's name, to defend the Church. Most righteous bishop, if an exile of my own country, and one of royal blood, had come to your lordship, where else would your duty have lain?'

The prelate replied: 'The Lord preserve your goings out and your comings in. Woe to me, sinner that I am! Pardon me, for, like the patriarch Judah, I see you are more righteous than I. The Lord be with you, and may the apostle Peter be your aid.'

## CHAPTER 34

### *The king flouts the decisions of the Holy See [680]*

AFTER having covered a great distance on land, and with the help of God and a ship traversed the wide ocean, he and all his train arrived at their native shore alive and unscathed, to the unbounded joy of his subjects who had been languishing and calling out with tears to the Lord for their absent bishop. He returned bearing the standard of victory, that is the decision of the Apostolic See, and peaceably presented himself before the king to show him the written judgement of the pope in which the whole synod had concurred and which each member had signed. He delivered the document all stamped with bulls and seals, then summoned the clergy and principal inhabitants of the district to the place where the synod usually met and there read out to them the decrees of the Apostolic See, sent from Rome to bring back peace to the churches. Some of them, because the document contained proposals that went against the grain or which they simply refused to accept, contumaciously rejected it. Others – and this is far more detestable – imperilled their souls by alleging that those very letters which the Holy See had sent to comfort them had been obtained through bribery. Then, at the command of king and counsellors and with the consent of the bishops who had usurped his see, Wilfrid was condemned to prison for nine months, there to be kept without any mark of honour to his rank. No sooner had the letters been opened and read out than – the very thought makes us tremble – the king flew into a rage and, urged on by his flattering minions, defied the judgement of St Peter, of him to whom God gave the power of loosing and binding; not content with this he swore by his soul's health that Wilfrid should be despoiled of all but his clothes and put in solitary confinement, that his subjects be scattered far and wide and no friend be allowed to come near him. The queen, moreover, took away his reliquary full of relics of the saints and – I can hardly bear to tell it – wore it as a necklace both at home in her chamber and when she rode forth in her chariot. But this deed brought her nothing but harm, just as befell the Philistines when, after routing the people of Israel, they carried off the ark and dragged the Holy of Holies through their cities.

## CHAPTER 35

### *Wilfrid encourages his brethren*

WILFRID, God's beloved, addressed his comrades thus: 'Keep in mind and recall to the brethren those days of old, how we read in the Old Testament that God's beloved patriarchs and his first-born, Israel, "passed from nation to nation and from one kingdom to another", awaiting the promise and not despairing. Moses too and Aaron and all the prophets of God endured men's persecution, for their trust was in the Lord. In the New Testament we read how the great Shepherd of the Sheep and Head of the Whole Church, Jesus Christ, was crucified by the Jews and his disciples scattered. Later, dispersed throughout the entire world, they and their followers after various tribulations received the crown of martyrdom. They did not forget those words of comfort which are addressed to us too as His sons, in the epistle to the Hebrews: "My son, neglect not the discipline of the Lord; neither be thou wearied whilst thou art rebuked by him. For whom the Lord loveth he chastiseth and he scourgeth every son whom he receiveth." So, brethren and helpers in Christ, in the words of that same epistle, "Let us also who have so great a cloud of witnesses over our head run with patience the race that is set before us." '

## CHAPTER 36

### Of the house lit up by God

WILFRID's words of consolation ended, the king's officers led our holy bishop away like a lamb to the slaughter to Osfrith, sheriff of the royal borough of Broninis.[1] He was confronted with the prisoner and bidden, on the king's command, to take our holy bishop into custody. Wilfrid, whose faith was so great by now that he might well have been called the light of Britain, was to be locked up in a pitch-black dungeon and securely guarded, and all this was to be kept secret from his friends. The sheriff, in loyalty to the king, carried out his urgent command. Wilfrid was hidden away, under guard, in a place which was rarely brightened by the sun during the day and where no lamp was lighted to grace the hours of the night. His guardians, hearing him continually singing psalms, looked into the cell and found the darkness of the night turned into day. Thunderstruck themselves they terrified others with the tale of his holiness.

1. Not identified.

'O Christ, Eternal light, who dost not desert those who acknowledge Thee, Thou whom we believe to be the true light illuminating "every man that cometh into this world", who in the beginning didst mark with fiery glory the hour of thy future servant's birth when he came forth from his mother's womb, now as he prayed in the darkness of his prison cell Thou didst deign to send an angel to visit him and to bring him light, just as when Thine apostle Peter was imprisoned in chains by wicked Herod. To Thee be glory and thanksgiving!'

While he was languishing in prison without the least token of respect, the king sent to offer him what was part of his own diocese and other very lavish gifts provided he acquiesced in the king's commands and ordinances and denied that the statutes sent by Rome were genuine. To this he humbly replied, showing his trust in the authority of the Holy See, that he would rather lose his head than assent to such a proposal. From this we can learn that a strong will founded on the knowledge of God cannot be confounded.

## CHAPTER 37

### He heals a woman

WHILE our holy bishop was waiting patiently in prison he was honoured with miracles, just as St John the Evangelist during his confinement on Patmos was granted visions of the mighty works of God. For at this time when, as we have said, Wilfrid was in a sorry plight, the sheriff's wife was suddenly taken ill. She went quite stiff, lost all feeling in her limbs, went cold and began to foam at the mouth, then lost consciousness and was almost breathing her last. The sheriff, realizing she was dying, rushed to Wilfrid like the centurion ran to Our Lord; he knelt before him confessing his faults and admitting the king's wrongdoing, and begged Wilfrid in God's name to help him, unworthy as he was, by coming to his dying wife. Our bishop harboured no malice. He went to the poor woman, and, standing over her, sprinkled her face with holy water. Then, calling on the Lord for help, he poured the water drop by drop into her mouth until it was well moistened. The woman opened her mouth and took deep breaths. She opened her eyes and consciousness and understanding returned. After a while warmth came back to her limbs, and she was able to raise her head and move her tongue. She thanked God aloud and then, like Peter's mother-in-law, ministered to our holy pontiff. She is still living and is now an abbess having taken the name of Aebbe in religion. She often recounts this story with tears.

## CHAPTER 38
### *His chains fall off him*

THIS same sheriff did not dare treat his prisoner decently, for fear of the king, nor, out of respect for his holiness and for fear of God's wrath, did he dare ill treat him. So he sent a message to his master.

'I implore you,' it went, 'by my life and salvation, not to force me to imperil my soul by having to punish this holy and innocent bishop any further. I would rather die than scourge him, for he is guiltless.'

This maddened the king. In reply he sent Wilfrid to his town of Dunbar under the supervision of a sheriff called Tydlin whom he knew to be more cruel. Wilfrid, despite his personal holiness and exalted rank, was to be bound hand and foot and not permitted contact with anyone. Tydlin obeyed and ordered the smiths to forge iron fetters. These smiths, with deliberate malice, put their heart into the work, but God worked against them. The irons always turned out either too small and narrow or else so big and loose that they slipped off the wrists and ankles of God's baptist and evangelist. This terrified the guards so much that they left him unbound. He sang psalms and gave thanks to the Lord unceasingly, 'Enduring,' in St Paul's words to the Hebrews, 'a great buffeting by afflictions, by reproaches made a gazing-stock, undergoing with joy the robbery of all his goods'[1]; and in Wilfrid's case the suffering had been inflicted by his own fellow-countrymen. Thus his jailers, much against their will, were forced to confine him unbound until God's appointed time.

## CHAPTER 39

### *How the queen falls ill and is healed [681]*

IN the meantime the king and queen were making their progress through the cities, fortresses, and villages with worldly pomp and daily feasts and rejoicings, in the course of which they came to the nunnery of Coldingham. The abbess, King Oswiu's sister Aebbe, was a very wise and holy woman. At this same place the queen was possessed by a devil during the night and, as in the case of Pilate's wife, the attacks were so severe that she was hardly expected to last till day. As dawn was breaking the abbess came to the queen and found her lying with the muscles of her limbs all contracted and screwed up. Obviously she was dying. Off went Abbess Aebbe to the king and with tears in her eyes gave her opinion of the cause of the calamity. Indeed she rounded on him.

'I know for a fact that you ejected Wilfrid from his see for no reason at all. He was driven into exile and went to Rome to seek redress. Now he has returned from that see that has the same power as St Peter himself in loosing and binding. And what have you done but stupidly despised its injunctions and despoiled the bishop? Then to pile injury on injury you have had him locked away in jail. Listen, my son, to your mother's advice. Loosen his bonds. Restore the relics your queen has taken from his neck and carried round from city to city like the ark of the Lord to her own doom. Send a messenger with them now. The best plan would be to reinstate him as bishop, but if you cannot bring yourself to do this, then at least let him and his friends leave the kingdom and go where they will. Do this and, as I see it, you will live and

1. *Heb.* x, 32–4.

your queen will recover. Disobey and, as God is my witness, you shall not escape punishment.'

The king obeyed the holy matron, freed our bishop, and let him depart with his relics and all his friends. And the queen recovered.

## CHAPTER 40

### *Wilfrid is welcomed by Berhtwald [681]*

So Wilfrid and his companions left their native land and set off in exile for the kingdoms of the south. God, who does not leave his saints to endure alone, sent a kind-hearted man to meet them on their way, a sheriff of noble birth called Berhtwald, nephew to Aethilred, king of Mercia.[1] As soon as he saw such honourable men and ascertained the reason for their wanderings he begged them in God's name to come and stay with him. He insisted that they accept part of his estate to settle down on. Wilfrid sincerely thanked God for having given him the consolation of somewhere to rest and without delay founded a little monastery. His monks occupy it to this day. But, alas, the ancient enemy was always on the alert and King Aethilred and his queen, Ecgfrith's sister, hearing that Wilfrid had been staying there awhile in peace, forbade Berhtwald, as he valued his safety, to harbour him another day. They did this to flatter Ecgfrith. The monks remained, but Wilfrid was spitefully driven out and made his way to Centwini, king of the West Saxons. He was not long there either for persecution followed him. Centwini's queen, Queen Iurminburgh's sister, detested him, so, because of the three kings we have mentioned, he was forced to move on yet again.

---

1. Aelthilred, son of Penda, was king of Mercia 675–704. He died in 716.

## CHAPTER 41

### *The conversion of the pagans of Selsey*
### *[681–6: cf. Bede, History iv, 13]*

BUT I am making the tale drag. His release from prison and exile
from his own province brought him no peace, for Ecgfrith stirred
up unremitting persecution against him in every country on both
sides of the Channel, as far as his power and influence extended.
There was but one place free, an area of Sussex which dense
forests and rocky coast had saved from conquest by other kingdoms. Up to this time it had remained persistently heathen, and
thither God, when all human aid failed, directed our good
bishop's steps. He sought out King Aethilwalh and told him the
whole story of his hardships and exile. Aethilwalh made a pact
with him at once, swearing such friendship as neither threat nor
sword of any of Wilfrid's enemies nor any amount of bribes
should ever frighten or tempt him into breaking. The holy man of
God, delighted with these words of consolation, gave thanks to
God and began gently to persuade the king and queen to accept
the word of God, preaching to them the greatness and blessedness
of God's Kingdom, giving them, as it were milk without guile.
Next, with divine permission and royal consent and at Wilfrid's
exhortation, the people, who never before had had the gospel
preached to them, were gathered together. Our holy bishop standing in the midst of the pagans exclaimed in the manner of our
Lord Jesus Christ and his forerunner St John the Baptist: 'Do
penance for the Kingdom of God is at hand and be baptized
every one of you in the Name of God the Father and of the Son
and of the Holy Ghost.' For many months he preached to them
at great length and with marvellous eloquence on the wondrous
doings of the Lord in the face of idolatry from the beginning of
the world. He traced these dealings for them in order right up to
the day of judgement when eternal punishment is prepared for the
wicked and life everlasting for the elect. Then our holy bishop,

God's apostle and evangelist, found favour in the king's sight and, as St Paul puts it, the great gate of the faith was laid open. Hosts of pagans, some freely and some at the king's command, left their idolatry and acknowledged the Almighty God, and many thousands were baptized in one day, as once they were by the apostle Peter. The king, whom God had filled with a spirit of gentle piety, gave up an estate of his own to Wilfrid for an episcopal seat to which he later added about ninety hides of land in Selsey. This he did out of gratitude to the evangelist who had laid open by baptism the gate of eternal life to him and all his subjects. Wilfrid gathered the brethren together and founded a community there in retreat from the world. His followers have it to the present day.

## CHAPTER 42

### Ceadwalla becomes king [686; cf. Bede, History iv, 16]

IN those days when through our bishop's efforts the Church of God was wonderfully increasing day by day and his own fame was most gloriously shining forth, an exile of noble birth came to him from the desert places of the Weald. His name was Ceadwalla. He earnestly sought our father's friendship, vowing that if Wilfrid would be his spiritual father and loyal helper he in turn would be an obedient son. This compact, which they called God to witness, was faithfully fulfilled. Our holy bishop helped and supported Ceadwalla in all kinds of ways through his many difficulties until at last he was in a strong enough position to quell his enemies and establish his sway over the whole area of the West Saxons. Wilfrid was then converting the heathens of the South Saxons and glorifying the name of God by his labours. Ceadwalla sent for him immediately, humbly summoning to his side the man he venerated as a father and loved above all others, and at once made him supreme counsellor over the whole kingdom; just as Pharaoh, in the words of the prophet, constituted Joseph on his release from prison 'master of his house so that he might impart wisdom'.

Thus God exalted our bishop through Ceadwalla's victory and Ceadwalla himself magnificently honoured his father with extensive lands and other gifts both out of natural affection and for the love of God. This new king steadfastly defended his country, preserving it from all harm by peace treaty and by the sword's edge.

## CHAPTER 43

*How peace was made with Archbishop Theodore [686–7]*

ABOUT this time Archbishop Theodore was troubled with pangs of conscience and decided to honour the injunctions of the Roman See to which he owed his own appointment. So after his long delay during Wilfrid's impoverished exile he now made hasty overtures of friendship. By this time Theodore was well advanced in years and nearly always in bad health. He invited Wilfrid and Bishop Erconwald to London. In their presence he gave a frank account of his whole life and made his confession to God.

'What troubles me most,' he said, 'is the ill I did your lordship in consenting to the kings' action when they stripped you of all your goods and sent you into bitter exile to your own harm and the detriment of your people. Before God and St Peter I confess this sin. And now, my fellow bishops, I call you to witness that to make up for my fault I will do everything in my power to restore my royal friends and their noblemen to your friendship, whether they will or no. God has revealed to me that this coming year will be my last. I therefore implore you by God and St Peter not to go against my wish which is that you should succeed me as archbishop. Here and now I appoint you my heir, for of all your race you are the wisest and most learned in the canon law of the Holy See.'

Wilfrid replied: 'God and St Peter forgive you for all the opposition you stirred up against me. Now that you have made your confession I am your friend for ever and I shall pray for you. Only first send messengers to all your friends with letters to let them know that we are reconciled in the Lord and that, since my property was formerly confiscated without just cause, they are now to restore at least part of my goods. Later, God willing, the question of a worthy candidate for the archbishopric can be discussed in council.'

After this pact of true peace Theodore sent word to Aldfrith begging him, for the fear of God and out of respect for the Holy See's commands, to be reconciled to Wilfrid by peace treaty, for thus many would be saved, including King Ecgfrith, the principal cause of his poverty and exile. The archbishop did not confine himself to this one act but strove to make friends of all Wilfrid's former enemies. He wrote to the holy virgin, Abbess Aelfflaed, urging her to have no hesitation in obeying the Holy See and making friends with Wilfrid. Aethilred, King of Mercia, was requested, as he loved Christ and his own soul, to follow his former intention and renew relations with Wilfrid. Here is the text of the letter: 'To the most glorious, most excellent King Aethilred of the Mercians, Theodore, by God's grace archbishop, sends every grace and blessing in the Lord. Dearest son, may your wondrous holiness know that I am now at peace with Bishop Wilfrid. I urge you, beloved son, and charge you by the love of Christ, to do your utmost, as long as you live, to help this devoted servant of God, as you always used to in time past; and now especially, since for a long time now, while bereft of his own goods, he has been labouring among the pagans for the service of the Lord. Therefore I, Theodore, a humble bishop, now in my declining years, put this suggestion to your beatitude. It is no more than what Rome recommended. For this man Wilfrid does indeed possess his soul in patience, as the scripture says, imitating the meekness of his Master, Our Lord and Saviour, and humbly awaiting the redress of wrongs unjustly inflicted on him. If I have found favour in your sight, come, despite the discouraging length of the journey, and let me see your joyful face and let me bless you before I die. Now, my son, do as I ask concerning this most saintly man and your charity will stand you in good stead in the world to come. Go in peace; live with Christ; dwell in the Lord; and the Lord be with you.'

What more is there to say? King Aethilred, on account of those blessed pontiffs Agatho, Benedict, and Sergius – successors each in turn to the dignity of Peter – received our bishop in fulfilment of the canonical injunctions and did so most gladly. Many monasteries were returned to him and lands which he had possessed in his own right. Aethilred treated him with the deepest respect and remained his faithful friend for ever.

## CHAPTER 44

*King Aldfrith receives our bishop [686–7]*

MANY years had rolled by; our leader was living in honourable exile and his monks, scattered throughout the whole of Britain, were mourning under the yoke of masters not their own and praying for release. Then at last news came of a woeful disaster, a battle against the Picts, in which King Ecgfrith of Northumbria and the flower of his army had been mown down. Aldfrith, his successor, proved to be a wise ruler.[1] In the second year of his reign he respectfully called Wilfrid back from exile, in obedience to Theodore. First of all he granted him the monastery at Hexham with all the possessions belonging to it and after a while, carrying out the command of Pope Agatho and the synod, he restored to him the see of York and the abbacy of Ripon together with their revenues, having driven out the usurping bishops. Like St John the Evangelist on his return to Ephesus, Wilfrid possessed them in security to the delight of his subjects, but only for five years.

## CHAPTER 45

*Enmity is stirred up between Wilfrid and Aldfrith [691–2]*

THOSE whose delight it is to stir up forgotten quarrels aroused themselves from their torpor and began disturbing the tenor of life which had up till then remained happily serene. They applied

1. Aldfrith, son of Oswiu, ruled 686–705.

themselves to their envious designs until the storm clouds
hovered and the brand of dissension was lighted afresh. For a
while all would be peace between the wise King Aldfrith and our
holy bishop, and a happier state of affairs could hardly be
imagined. Then spite would boil up again and the situation would
be reversed. And so they continued for years, in and out of friendship with each other, till finally their quarrels came to a head
and the king banished Wilfrid from Northumbria. The principal
cause of dissension was of long standing, namely the unjust
removal of land and possessions from the Church of St Peter. The
second was the making of the same monastery, which had been
given to us as our own property, into an episcopal see. This en-
tailed loss of rights that had been granted by Pope Agatho and
confirmed by five kings. The third was Aldfrith's insistence on
obedience to Theodore's edicts – not to those issued when he first
took office nor those at the end of his reign whereby he had
called all the churches to peace and concord in obedience to the
canons, but only those from the middle period when all the
trouble had started. Wilfrid refused to submit and betook himself
to his friend the king of Mercia. Aethilred welcomed him with
great honour out of reverence for the Apostolic See, so Wilfrid
dwelt on there under his and God's protection and was held in
high respect by the people of the diocese. It was the diocese the
most reverend Bishop Sexwulf had ruled until his death.[1]

## CHAPTER 46

*The council at Austerfield*[2] *[702–3: not in Bede]*

So during the reign of Aldfrith a synod was held at Austerfield
at which Archbishop Berhtwald[3] and nearly all the bishops were
present. They sent a deputation to Wilfrid asking him very civilly
to attend, on the assurance that with regard to his previous ill-

---

1. But Wilfrid ruled at Leicester, not Lichfield.
2. Near Bawtry, Yorkshire.
3. Archbishop of Canterbury 693–731.

treatment the statutes would now be honoured, so long as he did not refuse to come. Need I say more? Once he had arrived events turned out quite differently from what had been promised. Tremendous disputes and altercations broke out, fomented in the main by the avarice of some of the bishops. The peace of the Church was the last thing they wanted. They brought out all sorts of false objections, none of which was true, and in addition insisted that our holy bishop be judged according to Theodore's decrees. When Wilfrid realized the turn their arguments were taking he said that he was willing to obey in every respect, provided their decrees accorded with canon law. He went on to rebuke them at length for their contumacy, not mincing his words. For twenty-two years, he said, they had shamefully opposed the authority of the pope. How, he asked them, could they have the effrontery to set at nought the apostolic decrees sent to Britain for the good of men's souls by three successive pontiffs, Agatho, Benedict, and Sergius, and choose rather to cling to the edicts of Archbishop Theodore, decisions made in a time of great discord?

## CHAPTER 47

### *He discovers their trap*

In the meantime, while they were attempting to draw up some kind of formal reply, one of the king's officers stole out of the king's tent and came to our bishop. Wilfrid had taken him in as a helpless infant, brought him up from the cradle in fact; consequently the man was greatly devoted to him. He came in disguise, mingling with the crowd, and explained that the bishops' decision was a trap.

'They are trying to trick you completely by getting you to sign their decision at the outset, so that afterwards you will be bound by whatever they think fit to stipulate. Your hands will then be tied; you will be powerless to alter a single clause. The upshot of the transaction will be that every single parcel of land you are known to possess in Northumbria, whether belonging to the diocese or the monasteries or coming to you in any other way, will be taken from you. You will be forced to surrender to the archbishop everything you have gained in Mercia from King Aethilred. Berhtwald will then give it to whom he pleases. Finally, you will find that your own signature has condemned you to degradation from the office of bishop.'

Having given his warning, the officer returned by stealth. Our holy bishop, being a man of great strength of character, thought the matter over and was much more wary of signing anything after that. The synod demanded an immediate reply, even threatening that if an answer were not forthcoming he might well find himself sentenced and condemned. His reply was: 'First let me hear the archbishop's decision; if it agrees with the rules laid down by the holy fathers, then I will embrace it with all my heart.'

In the end the synod could no longer conceal its plan. Its motives had been publicly known for some time. They openly declared that it was their wish to strip Wilfrid of all he possessed so that he would not be able to call the smallest cottage his own in either Northumbria or Mercia. The ruthlessness of the decision, for which the king and archbishop were responsible, shocked even Wilfrid's enemies. They cried out against the wickedness of leaving completely penniless a man famous throughout the whole country and especially as no capital offence could be brought against him. So they hit upon a slightly more humane design. Wilfrid would be allowed to keep the monastery at Ripon which he himself had built and dedicated to St Peter, with all its lands and possessions, and the privileges granted to the abbot and community would devolve on him. But the grant was made only on condition that he signed a solemn promise to the effect that he would stay there quietly and never leave the monastery bounds without royal consent, nor exercise his episcopal office in any way at all, and finally that he would voluntarily lay down his rank. Thus they tried to force him to promise his own degradation on oath.

Wilfrid replied in steady fearless tones:

'Why are you trying to bring me to so sad a plight as to have

me make my own signature an instrument of self-destruction?
I have been a bishop now for nearly forty years and though
unworthy of that rank I am completely innocent of crime; yet
you would have me drag down my own name and make it a
scandal to all who hear it. After the death of those elders whom
Pope Gregory sent to us, was I not the first to root out from the
Church the foul weeds planted by the Scots? Did I not convert
the whole Northumbrian nation to celebrating Easter at the
proper time as the Holy See demanded, and to having the proper
Roman tonsure in the form of a crown instead of your old way
of shaving the back of the head from the top down? Did I not
teach you to chant according to the practice of the early Church,
with two choirs singing alternately, but simultaneously for responsories and antiphons and doing the responses and chants together antiphonally? Did I not bring the monastic life into line
with the Rule of St Benedict never before introduced into these
parts? And now, have I got to bring some hurried sentence
against myself, unconscious though I am of any crime committed? With regard to this latest novelty of yours whereby you
seek to violate my very office, I appeal in all confidence to the
Holy See. Here and now I challenge anyone who presumes to
degrade me to accompany me thither to seek judgement. You
ought to let the Roman officials, who are no fools, know what
charge you bring against me, before I submit to you alone.'

To this the king and archbishop replied: 'Now at any rate he is
guilty. Let him stand condemned for preferring their judgement
to ours.'

The king added to the archbishop's proposal: 'If you want, I
can use my army to put pressure on him and force him, this
time without the slightest delay, to say how willing he is to accept
our decision.'

But here the other synodal bishops interrupted: 'We ought to
remember that he only came here on the promise of safe conduct
from us; otherwise he would never have ventured. Let us all
return home in peace.'

## CHAPTER 48

### *Wilfrid returns to Aethilred [c. 703]*

AFTER these indecisive efforts the fruitless synod was dissolved by both sides and everyone went home. So, by God's protection, His servant was freed from the hands of his enemies and returned unharmed to the faithful King Aethilred. Wilfrid recounted the whole bitter attack made by the bishops in the face of his, Aethilred's, injunctions, and asked what sort of decrees he had made concerning the lands and privileges he had previously granted him. The king replied:

'I have no intention of adding trouble to trouble by taking away the livelihood of the monks of St Peter's Abbey. While I live, my former grant stands and on exactly the same conditions as, with God's blessing, have hitherto prevailed, until such time as I shall send either messengers or messages with you to Rome to have these urgent affairs settled. And may I find salvation in seeking to do right.'

This answer gave them both cause for rejoicing. Then they parted, each to his own home.

## CHAPTER 49

### *We are excommunicated*

WILFRID's enemies, not content with appropriating his possessions, declared that we and all who had dealings with us were no longer part of the body of the faithful. They even went so far in severing communion with us as to hold that if any of our priests or abbots should be invited to a meal by any of the 'faithful' and should bless the food on the table with the sign of the

159

cross, then that food should be thrown away as though it were meat offered to idols, and the dishes used by our men should be purified before being considered fit for use again.

## CHAPTER 50

### *His voyage to Rome [c. 703]*

WHEN we learned of the tragic calamity that had befallen both ourselves and all the congregations attached to us, we spent the time, until Bishop Wilfrid's party was ready to embark, in fasting and tears, praying and beseeching the Lord. They set sail and, with God before to guide them, reached the southern shores. Then, with the help of the holy apostles, they made their way overland and reached Rome on foot. On being presented at the papal court they went down on bended knee and begged with all urgency that the Holy See should receive the written account of the reason for their coming and show its usual kindly indulgence by disregarding the rusticity of style and lack of polish in the composition of the document.

'We wish your Holiness to understand that we have not come here to accuse anyone out of spite but simply to hear whatever objections might be brought against us by our opponents and, with the help of your clemency, to do our best to refute them if false or admit them if true. Under the protection of our Creator and with the help of the Prince of the Apostles we have sought refuge in this most glorious see, as though in our mother's lap and are completely prepared to bow to your authority.'

Pope John gave our holy prelate and his venerable priests and clergy a very warm welcome and provided free lodging for them so that they could enjoy a few days' rest while awaiting a decision from the illustrious see of Rome.[1] Archbishop Berhtwald's representatives happened to arrive at the same time as Wilfrid with written accusations and had begged a hearing for their

1. John VI, a Greek pope, reigned 701–5.

claims. The pope, therefore, called all his fellow-bishops and clergy together to form a synod. Wilfrid and his party were presented and the meeting began with a reading of his petition. It ran as follows.

## CHAPTER 51

### The text of the petition

'To the Apostolic Lord and thrice-blessed universal father, Pope John, Wilfrid, a simple and humble servant of God's servants and a bishop, pays honour. I wish to make known to your Holiness the reasons why I have come a third time to the Holy See from the far ends of the earth to seek help in your presence. They are these: First I hope to hear you confirm and corroborate all those most just and merciful decrees of your blessed predecessor Pope Agatho. Such a hope is grounded both on the belief that your action would bring about the salvation of many souls and on the fact of the undivided solidarity of judgement in the line of the popes. Secondly I would have your Holiness understand that we are only too ready to submit humbly to your commands. I have been led to make this appeal by the recent disturbances in Britain caused by that faction which, in contravention of Pope Agatho's decrees, have robbed me of my bishopric, monasteries, land, and everything I possessed. I adjured my assailants by the Most High God and by St Peter to follow the procedure laid down by Pope Sergius if they had anything to charge me with, and to accompany me hither to be judged in your presence. In view of the patent urgency of my claims I have been at pains to have a list of my humble petitions delivered to your august Eminence, in addition to which I now make bold to assail your ears with the request that your benign clemency may see fit to confirm with abounding holy benevolence all those good and just decrees made so unanimously on my poor behalf by your illustrious predecessors, the Apostolic lords St Agatho, blessed Sergius, and the glorious Pope Benedict. Moreover I myself and my companions here humbly beg you from the bottom of our hearts, should anyone appear with charges against us, to use your inflexible authority to bid him come forward and make them openly in your presence. If even the smallest accusation holds water we will gladly submit to your judgement; if, however, my opponents do not scruple to foist a pack of lies on your Holiness, backed up with false documentation, then please give us leave to clear ourselves in person. I also earnestly ask your Holiness to send orders to King Aethilred of Mercia regarding my well-being, repeating what was laid down by your three predecessors – that no one is to presume, either through foul greed or envy, to lay hands on those monasteries or their lands which Aethilred or his brother Wulfhere or anybody else may have given me for their souls' salvation. I urge you to give your orders the same force of authority as those of your forerunners. Furthermore, and this is most important, I implore you to be so kind as to advise King Aldfrith of Northumbria, in very quiet diplomatic tones, to carry out all the decrees of Pope Agatho and the synod. But if this should go against the grain with him, because of my part in the business, then use your own judgement in deciding who is best fitted to govern the see of York and all its numerous monasteries – except the houses of Hexham and Ripon which Pope Agatho included under one and the same privilege. Ask that they be restored to us with all their lands and possessions.

'To all these partitions I add this: I always show proper respect and fraternal charity towards Archbishop Berhtwald and I shall continue to do so. Only let him carry out those firmly established decrees made on behalf of my poor self by Agatho and his successors.'

## CHAPTER 52

*Pope John declares that the writings of his predecessors*
*are to be examined*

AFTER the full text of our petition had been read out and given
a hearing by the illustrious assembly, we were given leave to
retire to our lodgings and the envoys of Archbishop Berhtwald
were called in to present their documents. The accusations they
brought against Wilfrid were many and serious. The court, therefore, promised that both parties would be called at some future
date and that each count would be thoroughly examined in turn.
It then bade them withdraw and Pope John addressed his fellow-
bishops.

'Members of this holy synod, it is our duty first of all to go
through the canons of our holy predecessors, and examine the
documents treating of these injuries and wrongs sent by either
party up to now. We must bear in mind and carefully weigh
what blessed Agatho and Benedict and my holy predecessor
Sergius thought of the matter, and what orders they gave the
kings and archbishops. After that, with the help of God and the
Prince of the Apostles, we shall be in a better position to stamp
out falsehood and perceive the light of truth when we have both
sides before us in the presence of our brethren contesting against
each other. We shall follow the canons and judge according to
the rules laid down by our predecessors.'

The whole synod was pleased with this plan and proceeded
to put it into action.

## CHAPTER 53

### [The appeal is heard – 704]

So on the day appointed the most blessed John, Bishop of the Apostolic See, sitting in council with his right reverend bishops, ordered representatives of each side, both accusers and accused, to present themselves before the holy gathering. This was no sooner said than done. Our holy Bishop Wilfrid with his venerable priests and deacons came in as humble suppliants. They greeted the honourable assembly and promised to obey and carry out their decision with the greatest good-will. The archbishop's men were also present. They were given time to speak and told that they could choose any one heading from their list of accusations and speak on that and then proceed in order to the other points listed for discussion. They answered:

'This is our main charge, namely that Bishop Wilfrid here present contumaciously despised and rejected before our synod the statutes of Berhtwald, Archbishop of the Kentish Church and of all Britain and a man who was sent to us by the Apostolic See itself. We have given our view. Now let us hear the defence.'

St Wilfrid, bent under the weight of an honourable old age, rose, surrounded by his brethren, in the sight of the whole gathering.

'I speak as humble suppliant to your most excellent Holiness, asking you to condescend to hear from my own lips a true account of the actions of my unworthy self. I was indeed present at the council with my abbots, priests, and deacons, for they sent one of the bishops to ask me in the name of the king and the archbishop whether or not I was prepared to submit to the archbishop's judgement alone and zealously carry out his decisions. I answered thus: "We must be informed of the broad outlines of these decisions before we can commit ourselves one way or another." The bishop said he himself had not known and that the archbishop had declared that he would by no means let any of our party know what he had resolved upon until we had given a written promise before the synod to submit to his judgement in every single matter, and not to deviate from it one step either to left or right. "I have never in my life heard of so rigid and narrow a constraint", I replied. "I am to bind myself on oath to carry out a whole mass of decrees, no matter how impossible they may prove to be, without knowing the terms of even one of them." None the less I promised the synod my wholehearted assent to everything laid down by the archbishop, as long as it tallied with the rules and statutes of the holy fathers and with the canonical definitions and was not in conflict with the synods of St Agatho and his orthodox successors.'

After offering this defence our holy bishop was silent.

The synod fathers continued: 'Bishop Wilfrid, God's beloved, has set forth in accordance with the canons, the defence under which he seeks to shelter.'

Then they began speaking in Greek and smiled to themselves, and had a long discussion that they kept concealed from us and finally addressed our accusers.

'You are not ignorant, dear brethren, of the canonical prescription which reads: "When a number of charges are brought against clerics, if the first one cannot be proved the prosecution is not to proceed to the rest." Nevertheless, out of respect for the archbishop whom we ourselves sent to Britain and in reverence to this most blessed Bishop Wilfrid – who has been so long fraudulently despoiled – we, asking God and St Peter to reveal the truth of the matter, shall willingly put ourselves out and spend weeks and months sifting every charge, for we intend to settle the case once and for all.'

After that the synod gave our bishop and his brethren, for whom the joy of victory had already begun, permission to return to their lodgings. There they set about preparing for the skirmishes to come. Their opponents, on the other hand, returned home in confusion at the result of this first hearing. Several months later their pack of lies was blown away by the blast of wisdom, and with the help of God and St Peter the truth shone clearly forth, showing our holy pontiff completely and utterly free from anything deserving of degradation: for after seventy sessions of the council over a period of four months, in which he was refined in a veritable furnace of cross-examination, he was acquitted. The Holy See came to his aid in the following way: at Easter, on the third day of the feast, a synod consisting of one hundred and twenty-five orthodox bishops under Pope Agatho was held to root out heretical corruption. Each of the bishops witnessed to the true faith on behalf of his province and city and then confirmed the testimony with his signature. This document was read out in a loud voice before all the people, as is the custom in Rome, and in it, among other items, occurred the following passage:

'Wilfrid, Bishop of the city of York, having appealed to the Apostolic See and having been cleared by the same authority of certain definite and indefinite charges, did, together with one hundred and twenty-five of his fellow-bishops in this synod and judgement seat, confess the true and Catholic faith on behalf of all the northern part of Britain and Ireland and the islands inhabited by the Angles, Britons, Picts, and Scots, and did corroborate the same with his signature.'

When they heard this all the wise citizens of Rome were amazed. Then Boniface and Sizentius and some others who remembered him from Pope Agatho's time spoke up.

'This Bishop Wilfrid,' they said, 'is the one whom blessed Agatho sent home cleared, by apostolic authority, of every charge levelled against him; but now, alas, the malice of trouble-makers has sent him wandering from his own see. He has been a bishop now for forty years and more, yet those false accusers still do not think shame to forge documents against the venerable old man and his companions. These scoundrels, one a deacon and the rest mere laymen without the least ecclesiastical rank or dignity, have even had the temerity to arraign His Lordship before the Holy See. They deserve the harshest punishment – let them be thrown into the deepest dungeons to waste away till death.'

The citizens of Rome said they had spoken the truth. Then the pope spoke.

'We have examined the case of blessed Bishop Wilfrid, whom God loves, in numerous sessions of this council, and we can find nothing against him. Therefore, by the authority of St Peter,

Prince of the Apostles, in whom resides the power of binding or loosing from secret sins, we declare him acquitted. Moreover, unworthy though we be, we have decided, with the consent of the whole synod, to confirm whatever Agatho, Benedict, and Sergius, bishops of the holy city, decided on his behalf and delivered in writing by Wilfrid's own hand to the kings and archbishop.'

Here follows the text of the decree.

## CHAPTER 54

### *[Letter of Pope John]*

'POPE JOHN to their most noble majesties, Aethilred, king of Mercia and Aldfrith, king of Deira. We fully recognize your zeal for the faith which you received when God illumined your hearts through the preaching of the Prince of the Apostles and which you firmly hold; and we rejoice in the great increase of religion among you – may greater growth increase our joy! But the news of this tangle of dissension saddens not only ourselves but also our fellow-clergy and indeed the whole Church. The matter must now be completely disentangled, with God's help, so that you yourselves, in the presence of the Lord and Judge of all, may stand out not as despisers but as the upholders of the pontifical decrees and as our obedient sons. Some time ago, during the pontificate of Pope Agatho of blessed memory, Bishop Wilfrid came in person with an appeal to the Apostolic See. His adversaries, representatives of the holy Abbess Hilda and of Theodore of hallowed memory, archbishop of the Kentish nation by mandate of this same see, were present too. An assembly was then convened of bishops of various provinces who held a formal inquiry into the arguments of either side and decided accordingly. And this decision our holy predecessors have confirmed. Bishop Theodore is not known to have contravened this nor to have made any further accusation; on the contrary, it is quite clear from his own words that he complied. Consequently we must have recourse to God's aid to see that dissension does not continue to smoulder in one part of the Church, while in every other province clergy and people are in perfect harmony. So much for the past. Regarding the present, we have taken measures to inform your renowned majesties that a delegation recently came to us from your own island of Britain to bring accusations against Bishop Wilfrid. He himself arrived shortly afterwards and rebutted the charges by turning them back upon the accusers themselves. We had the parties debate the matter for some days before an assembly of reverend priests and prelates. Every document, old or new, adduced by either side, all their verbal statements, together with any relevant matter we could find in our archives – all this has been most carefully sifted and the findings made known to us. However, the principal protagonists in the dispute, those who started it all, were not here; but it will be necessary for them to meet and confer before the affair can be concluded once and for all. Therefore we hereby order our most reverend brother Berhtwald, whom we ourselves on the authority of the Prince of the Apostles have confirmed in office as Archbishop of the Kentish Church, to convoke a synod with Bishop Wilfrid and that, when this council has been properly constituted, he call Bishops Bosa and John to give evidence. He must hear each side and carefully weigh their claims, noting what can really be proved. If, in his opinion, the matter can be properly settled by the synod, then both ourselves and the rival factions will be satisfied. But if it turns out otherwise, he must give them formal warning in synod and admonish them privately and go over every single point at issue. They must come to Rome together and have the quarrel thrashed out in a fuller council so that a final decision may be reached on what has up to now eluded settlement. Then, by the grace of the Holy Spirit, those who have come in discord may perhaps be able to return in peace. Whoever puts off the journey or (and this we execrate) will not deign to come is to be informed that he is thereby removed from office. He must be expelled and the clergy and people of the district forbidden to receive him, for he who sets himself up against his Master is not to be counted among His ministers and disciples. Therefore, for the fear of God and out of reverence for the Christian faith and for that peace which Our Lord Jesus Christ gave to His followers, may your Royal and Christian Highnesses lend your assistance, so that these matters which with Christ's help we have so closely examined may now be happily concluded. Do so and your labours in the cause of religion will be rewarded by a peaceful reign under Christ's protection in this world and the blessed fellowship of His Eternal Kingdom in the next. Recall to mind, beloved sons, what Agatho and the bishops of the Roman Church after him have laid down on apostolic authority in this very question. For he who with rash temerity despises our commands, however high his rank may be, will not go unpunished by God and, being found guilty by Heaven, how can he escape without loss? God's grace keep your Highnesses forever safe.'

## CHAPTER 55

### Wilfrid is ordered to return home and brings back the holy relics [704]

AFTER several months of almost daily examination and close questioning Wilfrid emerged completely exonerated. His case was won. His one wish now was to remain permanently in the Holy City and there end his days, crucifying himself to the world (as St Paul said) in his old age; but he had promised humble obedience to the pope and synod and they both ordered him to leave for home. Now that his long period of affliction had been brought to an end by complete acquittal from every charge both particular and general, they bade him return to present the findings in writing to the kings and archbishops, to soothe his subjects' grief and give his friends cause for rejoicing. Our holy bishop knew how to obey. He went round the shrines of the saints with his companions making a collection of relics, each labelled with the saint's name, and he bought purple cloth and silk vestments to decorate his churches. Then, with the blessing of the saints upon him, he made his way homewards by paths rough and smooth, over mountain and plain, till after a long journey he reached the Kingdom of Gaul.

## CHAPTER 56

*Our patron falls sick and St Michael appears to him [705]*

ON the way home our holy bishop became gravely ill. At first he went along on horseback but later had to be carried in a litter. His friends mourned and wept over his condition and called upon God for aid. They brought him into Meaux scarcely alive and were convinced he was dying, for he was still breathing and warm to touch but unconscious. Nothing had passed his lips for the last four days, but on the fifth day, as dawn was breaking, an angel of the Lord in shining raiment appeared to him. 'I am Michael, messenger of the Most High God,' he announced. 'I have come to tell you that through the prayers of the ever-virgin Mary, Mother of God, and the tears of your followers, several years have been added to your life, as a sign of which your health will improve daily until you are completely well, you will reach your native land in safety, all your precious possessions will be restored to you and you will end your days in peace. I will visit you four years from now: be prepared. You have built churches in honour of St Peter and St Andrew but for the Blessed Mary, ever-virgin, who is interceding for you, you have built nothing. Rectify this omission by dedicating a church in her honour.' The angel of the Lord was taken up and disappeared from his sight. Our holy bishop arose as though he had just awoken and sat down with his friends who were weeping and chanting prayers for him.

'Where is our priest Acca?' he asked.

Acca was called in and rejoiced and thanked God with the rest of them at the sight of his master sitting up and talking. Wilfrid asked the brethren to withdraw and leave him alone with his faithful chaplain. He revealed the vision detail by detail. Acca, being a man of acute intelligence (he is now a bishop), at once recognized the parallel between this favour and that accorded Hezekiah, King of Judah, and thanked God accordingly.[1] Wilfrid's life was spared at the intercession of the Mother of God and his own followers: Hezekiah's life was lengthened by fifteen years, five because of his father David, five through the prophet Isaiah's prayers in the temple, and five of his own goodness and because he had turned his face to the wall and wept.

## CHAPTER 57

### *The return crossing [705]*

WHILE the brethren were rejoicing heartily at his recovery, our holy father washed his hands and face and took a little food and then like Jonathan 'his eyes were enlightened' and he revived.[2] They set out a few days later when he was back to his full strength, reached and crossed the breadth of the ocean and found safe harbour, by God's help, on the coast of Kent. Wilfrid's messengers sought out Archbishop Berhtwald and conferred with him. Peaceful relations were restored. The papal brief commanding obedience terrified him, so in fear and trembling he promised to mitigate the harsh decrees passed long ago by his own synod – a promise which turned out to be completely genuine. Wilfrid progressed joyfully westwards to London accompanied by a whole cortège of his abbots and laden with presents. From there he went on to visit that faithful friend whose loyalty had never wavered, Aethilred, the former king of Mercia. He was received with all the usual honours; they kissed and embraced and Aethilred was so overcome with joy that he could not restrain himself. He simply burst into tears. Wilfrid then formally greeted him in the name of the Holy See and respectfully presented the text of the papal bull properly stamped and sealed. As soon as the document had been opened and read, Aethilred prostrated himself on the ground in token of obedience.

'Never in all my life shall I think lightly of one jot or tittle of

1. Acca is praised in Bede's *Ecclesiastical History*, v, 20, as a zealous and munificent bishop of Hexham.
2. I *Kings* (A.V. I *Samuel*), xiv, 27.

this decree, nor shall I countenance those who do so. I shall do all in my power to enforce it.'

This was no idle promise. Aethilred's goodness will be rewarded above.

Not content with this, he summoned Coenred, whom he had appointed his heir, and made him swear, out of the love he bore him and in God's name, to uphold the precepts of the Holy See. This Coenred willingly promised.

## CHAPTER 58

*King Aldfrith despises him and meets his doom*

SHORTLY afterwards, on Aethilred's advice, Wilfrid sent a delegation to King Aldfrith of Northumbria. This task he entrusted to two men whom he knew well, Badwini, a priest and abbot, and Alfrith. They spoke as follows:

'Our holy bishop sends friendly greetings and begs permission to come in person to present the greetings of the Holy See together with its authoritative answer to his appeal.'

The king's immediate reply was not at all harsh. He merely arranged the date for a future meeting at which, he promised, they would receive an answer. Badwini and Alfrith duly presented themselves on the appointed day and asked what he had decided. He said what his counsellors had persuaded him to say.

'My friends, I respect you – so highly indeed that you have only to ask for whatever you want and you shall have it. But pester me no more with this business of your master Wilfrid. My kingly predecessors, the archbishop, and their counsellors arrived at a certain decision in which I myself, Archbishop Berhtwald and almost the entire body of British bishops later concurred. It still stands. As long as I live, no documents you may bring forward as emanating from the Holy See will make me change.'

But he later repented and did change his mind – completely.

## CHAPTER 59

### [Death of Aldfrith – 704/5]

THEY had no further interview, but left at once to bring Wilfrid the sad news. And now, just as the pope had promised, divine vengeance did not tarry. Aldfrith soon had to grapple with a severe illness. He at once came to his senses, realized that he had been stricken down by the power of the apostles for his defiance of Rome, and repented.

'If only Wilfrid could be persuaded to come to me now,' he lamented, 'I would quickly make amends.'

There and then he vowed to God and St Peter that if he were spared to rise from his bed he would carry out the pope's commands, let Wilfrid have his way and put everything in order.

'But if by God's will I should die, I bid my successor, whoever he may be, to come to terms with Wilfrid for the good of his soul and my own.'

This verbatim account was given us by trustworthy witnesses, among whom were Abbess Aelffled, herself a king's daughter, and Abbess Aethilberg. Many others have confirmed it. But the king's illness gained the upper hand; he lay speechless for five days, then died. Eadwulf succeeded him for a short while. Our holy bishop, who was at Ripon with Eadwulf's son, sent messengers to him as a friend – only to be answered with extreme harshness, for the deep-rooted malice of Eadwulf's counsellors had turned him against Wilfrid. This was the reply:

'I swear on my life that if you are not out of my kingdom within six days, you and any of your companions I can find shall perish.'

Shortly afterwards a conspiracy was hatched against the king and he was driven out after a mere two months' reign. The boy Osred, Aldfrith's son, took his place and became our bishop's adopted son.

## [Synod of Nidd, 706]

IN the first year of Osred's reign Berhtwald, Archbishop of Canterbury and primate of nearly the whole of Britain, came up from the south to invite the king of the northern regions together with all his bishops, abbots, and chief men of rank in the kingdom to settle Wilfrid's case in synod by the east bank of the Nidd.[1] Abbess Aelffled, the best of advisers and a constant source of strength to the whole province, was with them. Archbishop Berhtwald and Wilfrid both arrived on the same day. The whole company took their seats and Berhtwald opened the proceedings.

'Let us ask Our Lord Jesus Christ,' he began, 'to grant us peace and concord through His Holy Spirit. I have with me documents sent by the Holy See to my unworthy self and Bishop Wilfrid has others that he brought from Rome. We humbly ask your reverences' leave to read them out.'

Permission was granted and each volume was read out from beginning to end. After the reading there was complete silence. Then Berhtfrith, a nobleman, second in rank only to the king, addressed the archbishop:

'Those of us who could not manage to follow the reading would be grateful if you would explain just what the Holy See means.'

The archbishop replied:

'The papal pronouncements are couched in obscure and round-about terms but one single lesson emerges from both. Briefly it is this: The Holy See, by the power of loosing and binding first given to St Peter, and on its own authority, had decided that in my unworthy presence and before the whole synod, you prelates of the churches of this province must, as you value your salvation, put aside all long-standing enmity and be reconciled to Wilfrid once and for all. The Apostolic See leaves two ways

---

1. Exact site not known.

open to you, one of which you must choose: either to live in full and perfect harmony with Wilfrid and give him back all his former jurisdiction – the extent of which will be determined by myself and certain prudent advisers – or, if you are unwilling to take the better course, then you must all go to Rome and have your quarrels thrashed out before a higher court. Whosoever rejects both courses (God forbid that anyone should!), whether he be king or commoner, is to be excommunicated from the Body and Blood of Christ. Should any bishop or priest act like this (which would be even fouler – in fact I shudder to think of it) he is to be degraded from holy orders. That is the gist of the letters.'

But the bishops did not give way.

'Who can alter,' they claimed, 'the decrees passed by King Ecgfrith and Archbishop Theodore whom the pope sent out here to us, decisions which we, the bishops of nearly the whole of Britain, later confirmed with King Aldfrith in your Grace's own most excellent presence at Austerfield?'

Then the holy Abbess Aelffled rose and spoke these inspired words:

'Let me tell you, truly and in Christ's name, what King Aldfrith's last will and testament, the one he made on his death-bed, really was. He made a vow to God and St Peter in the following terms: "If I live I promise to fulfil all those judgements of the Apostolic See in regard to Wilfrid which formerly I had refused even to hear. If I die bid my son and heir, for the good of my soul, do the same."'

When she had finished, Berhtfrith spoke.

'The king and his earls will that the command of the Holy See and King Aldfrith's instructions be obeyed to the last detail. For when we were besieged at Bamburgh, surrounded by enemies on all sides and forced to take refuge in a narrow rocky cleft, we held a discussion on this very subject and vowed that if God granted our royal boy his father's kingdom, we would carry out the apostolic injunctions concerning Bishop Wilfrid. No sooner had we made this vow than the enemy completely changed their minds. They came rushing up to make friends with us. The gates were opened, we came out into the open air, hostilities were over and the kingdom ours.'

At this the bishops went to one side and began talking among themselves. The archbishop gave them his advice and Abbess Aelffled gave them hers. The parley ended with the decision, in which they were joined by king and counsellors, to make an unconditional peace pact with Wilfrid. And they kept it till their lives' end. He got back the two best monasteries, Ripon and Hexham, with all their revenues. Then all the bishops embraced each other and joined together in the Breaking of Bread. They thanked God for all these wonderful blessings and set off home. And Christ's peace went with them.

## CHAPTER 61

### [Peace at last]

'GOD is wondrous in His saints,' says the Psalmist, and indeed He is, for out of the love He bears the whole Church He cleansed the bishops' hearts of enmity and crowned them with peace. What a source of blessing the settlement was to both parties! Those who, after so long a tenure of Wilfrid's possessions gave them up to make amends before his death, brought down Christ's peace upon themselves; while to us their action brought new hope and restored to us all the joys of our old way of life. We had been scattered abroad as exiles in various parts of the country under strange masters. Now our misery was over and we could again enjoy community life under our beloved superior and live in peace with all who were reconciled to him.

## CHAPTER 62

### [Wilfrid's illness – c. 708]

BUT in this world no joy comes to us unmixed with sorrow and everything is by nature mortal. Our holy bishop was on his way to Hexham when the time foretold by the Archangel Michael came round. He fell suddenly ill with the same complaint that had stricken him at Meaux, only this time the attack was worse. We, the members of his household, overwhelmed with anguish, rushed to the armoury of prayer. We chanted and prayed day and night without ceasing, imploring God to prolong his life so that at least he might have time to speak to us and appoint abbots to his monasteries and divide up his possessions lest we should be left like orphans without a superior. The news of this calamity spread quickly. All his abbots and hermits came hastening in from far and wide. They even travelled on through the night in the hope of seeing him alive and refused to be turned back by rumours of his death. We were sure he would die before they arrived, but were proved wrong. Entering the house they all knelt down with one accord, beseeching the Lord to remember His promise: 'When two or three are gathered together in My Name, there am I in the midst of them', and not to take their bishop just yet. Their prayer was heard. He was given time to arrange everything that had not yet been put in order, namely to lay down the rule of life for the various houses and appoint superiors and share out his goods as he thought fit between God and man, that is to allot some for sacred, some for profane use. His reason, memory, and power of speech all came back to him; indeed the sickness left him as sleep goes on waking. We were overjoyed at this complete recovery, and having thanked God for it each went off on his own way.

## CHAPTER 63

### [Last instructions – 709]

To the great joy of his subjects our saintly master lived to enjoy another eighteen months of perfect tranquillity. He spent the time putting to rights all those affairs that had badly needed settling. Shortly before that memorable final day he summoned two of his abbots and six of his most faithful friends to Ripon. He bade the treasurer open the diocesan coffers and set out all the gold, silver, and precious stones in front of them in four separate piles. Wilfrid himself decided into which pile each object should go. The official quickly laid out the treasure and then Wilfrid addressed his trusty witnesses:

'Dearly beloved, I would have you know that it has long been my intention, God willing, to return to Rome to end my days in the See which has so often solved my difficulties for me. I had thought to take one of these four piles with me as an offering to the churches, particularly to the church dedicated to the Mother of the Lord and to offer gifts to St Paul's for the welfare of my soul. But, as happens to old people, God has disposed otherwise. Death is overtaking me here. So I am now giving orders to you, my faithful companions, to send messengers with the treasure to the churches I have just mentioned. Of the three remaining parts one is to be given to the poor of my diocese for the repose of my soul, the second is to go to the abbots of Hexham and Ripon so that they might have something in hand wherewith to secure the favour of the kings and bishops, the third is for those who laboured with me in my long exile and whom I have not already rewarded with lands or estates. Share it out between them according to their needs so that they will be able to maintain themselves after I am gone.'

He paused a while, then continued.

'Take note, brethren, that I appoint the priest Tatberht here present, as abbot of Ripon. He is my kinsman and has been my inseparable companion up to now. While I live we will rule jointly; when I die he will be in sole command. I want you to be quite clear on that point. I am making these decrees now so that, when the Archangel Michael comes to fetch me, he may find me prepared. For the signs of death are crowding thick about me.'

## CHAPTER 64

*[Future of his monasteries]*

THE meeting over, Wilfrid had a bell rung to assemble the whole community.

'Our well-beloved brother Caelin,' he began, 'has for a long time now been our leader in the observance of the Rule. He has worked extremely hard in God's service and now wants to go back to his former way of life in the wild parts of the country to serve God only by giving himself up to solitary contemplation. I will deny his wish no longer.

'Our abbots Tibba and Ebba are here from King Coelred of Mercia to ask me to go and confer with him and they have persuaded me to agree to this for the sake of the monasteries we have in that kingdom. Coelred has promised to make me his director and to follow my judgement in regulating the whole course of his life.

'I urge you to keep the rule faithfully till, if God wills it, I return. Should he will otherwise and my many infirmities overtake me, then I bid you to accept as abbot whomever my witnesses here – Abbots Tibba and Ebba, the priest Tatberht and Hathufrith and Master Alnhfrith – shall come and declare to you. The obedience you promised to God and myself and which you have hitherto rendered, you shall give to him.'

They knelt down weeping, heads bowed to the ground, and promised to fulfil all his commands; and as they prostrated themselves in prayer our holy bishop gave his blessing and commended them to God. The community never saw him again.

## CHAPTER 65

### [Death of Wilfrid, 709]

ST WILFRID set off for the south and the goodwill of the whole Northumbrian people, high and low, went with him. His abbots in Mercia were overjoyed to see him. He went round the abbeys as one who has foreseen his end and is sharing out his property among his heirs. His generosity was truly heart-warming. Every community was provided for according to its needs; some got grants of land to increase their revenues, the rest were left a legacy. To a few of the abbots he confided the full details of his will. At the end of the round his company came to the monastery at Oundle where Wilfrid had once dedicated a church to St Andrew, and here he was twice overcome by sudden illness. He knew his end was nigh and contented himself with exhorting them to follow all the good advice he had previously given. (Sometime before this, as though he knew he was soon to die, he had given his kinsman Tatberht a full account of his life one day when they were out riding.) He mentioned all the grants of land he had made to his abbots and which he now left them in his will. Hexham Abbey he gave to Acca, who afterwards succeeded him in the see. He talked a little while and blessed them, just as Jacob blessed his sons, then, quietly, without any fuss or complaint, leaned back on the pillow and rested. The brethren chanted round the bed day and night, weeping as they sang. When they came to the verse of Psalm 103 which runs 'Send forth Thy Spirit and they shall be created, and Thou shalt renew the face of the earth,' our bishop breathed his last. And the brethren heard, to their amazement, a sound in the air like a flight of birds approaching. This fact is attested to by crowds of witnesses. Wilfrid's nominee, Acca, was accepted as abbot in his place. The depth of the love he bore his father in God can be seen in the numerous practices he instituted in his honour. Acca himself celebrated a private mass daily for the repose of his soul and had every Thursday, the day of his death, kept as a feast just like Sunday. He decided to mark every anniversary of the death by giving a tenth part of all his herds and flocks to the poor – all this over and above the charity he distributed every day for the repose of his master's soul and the welfare of his own, always in Wilfrid's name.

## CHAPTER 66

### [Burial of Wilfrid]

WE looked on our holy bishop as a great man and a faithful servant of Christ, but our Lord, by the miracles worked on his behalf, made it known that he was no less than a saint living with Him in glory. It happened one day that all the abbots came to Oundle to carry away the body in a carriage. Some of them wanted to wash the corpse and have it decently vested (as indeed was only right and proper) and obtained permission to do so. Abbot Bacula spread out his robe on the ground and the brethren laid the body on it. After the washing and vesting, which the abbots themselves performed, it was taken with great reverence to the place appointed. And, lo, once again from over the monastery came the sound of birds alighting and taking off with a gentle, almost musical flapping of wings. The wiser members of the community were convinced that Michael had come with his choirs of angels to lead our bishop's soul to Paradise. The washing had been done outside the monastery buildings in a tent put up for the purpose, and the water had been emptied out in the same place. The monks erected a cross to mark the spot and many miracles were later performed there. Our monks wrapped up the holy remains in linen, placed them in the carriage, and brought it to Ripon, chanting as they came. The community came out with the holy relics to honour the cortège and hardly any of them managed to fight back his tears. They found voice, nevertheless, to sing the hymns and canticles for the reception of the corpse and led it into the basilica he himself had built and dedicated to St Peter. There he was buried with all honour in the seventy-sixth year of his age and the fortieth of his episcopate. Who can tell how many bishops, priests, and deacons he had consecrated and ordained or count the churches he had dedicated during all those years? His glory shall endure for ever. After the funeral his worthy successor Tatberht was led in surrounded by all the other bishops.

The abbot who had given his cloak for Wilfrid to be laid out on told his servant lad to take it to Wilfrid's abbess, Cynithrith. It was rather dirty from being trodden on during the washing. Cynithrith's orders were to keep it just as it was, folded up, till the abbot should visit her. At first she did as she was bidden but after a while decided to have it washed. There was a poor nun in the convent who, like the mason in the gospel, had gone about for years with a withered hand. Hearing what the abbess was doing she came and knelt before her with tears in her eyes.

'In the name of the Lord Jesus Christ,' she begged, 'and by the soul of your dear bishop, let me bathe my shrivelled limb in the washing water. I have unshakeable faith in the power of this water, mixed as it is with the saint's sweat, to cure my crooked hand and withered arm.'

The abbess, being a pious woman, dared hardly refuse the sister. To show her faith she at once picked up the lifeless hand with her good one and plunged it into the warm soapy water and rubbed it with the cloak. And, lo and behold, the fingers straightened out, the hand regained its vitality, and she got back the use of her whole arm. Like Moerisa, the woman in the gospel who was cured of an issue of blood by touching the hem of Christ's garment, her faith had made her whole, and like her prototype she gave thanks to God, praising Him for His wonderful works.

## CHAPTER 67

### [The fire at Oundle]

ON another occasion the Lord made it clear that our great and worthy bishop was a saint. There was a group of exiles, noblemen too, going round with an armed band, ravaging the countryside out of revenge. They wantonly set fire to the monastery at Oundle where Wilfrid had been called to his fathers. They did their utmost with torches and firebrands to raze it to the ground, and succeeded – except for the room where the saint had died. Here the torches, instead of setting ablaze, guttered out. Thinking that the wet thatch on the roof might have damped them out, one of the marauders pushed his way into the room to light the dry straw inside. There within stood a young man in white holding a golden cross. The man rushed out in terror yelling:

'Quick, away from here! An angel of the Lord is protecting the place.'

They quickly retreated.

There is another fact connected with the raid, which is very well vouched for. One side of the great thorn hedge round the monastery was set alight, and the flames raced along it burning all before them till they came to the place where the cross was standing, and then suddenly died out. The fire had also crept round the other side of the buildings along the parched hedge. When it reached where the corner of Wilfrid's room jutted out, the flames died away. That was the only bit of hedge saved.

God's punishment soon lighted on the evil-doers. Some of the most noble of them, going along at the head of their troops in the full light of day, were suddenly blinded. Taken unawares by their enemies they were hemmed in on all sides, thrown down and slain. Few of their companions escaped – only those who had crossed themselves.

These marvels were performed by God's saint to avenge his wrongs.

## CHAPTER 68

### The sign of the rainbow arc

Now that our holy bishop had gone to the Lord, his abbots and their subjects were afraid their old enemies might take up the attack again.

'As long as our noble leader was alive,' they said to themselves, 'we endured numerous different trials at the hands of the kings and princes of Britain, all of which ended honourably for us, thanks to Wilfrid's wisdom and sanctity and the help of his friends. We must now believe, fully and without reservation, that we have an intercessor in Heaven raised up by the power of the Holy Cross to the level of his own beloved Saints Peter and Paul, to whose patronage he and his followers dedicated all their possessions. We must trust that, there in the sight of God, he guards and defends us unceasingly.'

Their trust was soon given warrant by a sign appearing in the heavens. On the anniversary of his death all our bishops and their abbots gathered together from north, south, east, and west to mark the solemn occasion. As they were keeping the evening vigil in the church where his remains rested, certain of the less watchful brethren standing outside saw a sign appear in the sky. They kept quiet about it till the next morning. When the rest heard about it they were deeply grieved and murmured to each other that it had been kept back from them because of their sins. Their honesty was soon rewarded. When the feast that ended the solemnities was over, the whole assembly went out of doors in the twilight to sing compline. Suddenly a wonderful white arc shone out before them in the heavens, encircling the entire monastery. Apart from the lack of colour it looked exactly like a rainbow. Starting from the gables of St Peter's basilica where Wilfrid's bones were laid to rest, it stretched towards the south, then made a wide sweep to the north round the right-hand side of the monastery before bending upwards into the south-eastern quarter of the morning sky. We worshipped and praised the Lord for this sign, the Lord who is wondrous in His saints, for we clearly saw that He was with us, building a wall of protection around his chosen vineyard. Our conviction was borne out in every event that rose to affright us. Regular monastic life continued to flourish under outstanding abbots in all kingdoms on both sides of the Humber and the brethren lived to see the enemies who massed against us pierced with their own barbs. As for us, to quote the Psalmist: 'In the name of our God we shall be exalted.'[1]

1. *Psalm* xix, 6 (A.V. xx, 5).

# Bede: Lives of the Abbots of
Wearmouth and Jarrow

*Here begins the book of the lives of the holy abbots Benedict, Ceolfrith,*
*Eosterwine, Sigfrith and Hwaetberht*

### CHAPTER I

BENEDICT BISCOP, a devout follower of Christ, inspired by grace
from on high, founded a monastery in honour of the most blessed
Peter, Prince of the Apostles, on the north bank of the Wear,
towards the mouth of the river, with the help of the venerable
and holy King Egfrid who donated the land for it. For sixteen years,
despite the heavy toll exacted by his many illnesses and the burden
of all his travels, Benedict ruled over it with the same care and
conscientiousness he had given to its construction. To quote the
words of the blessed Pope Gregory when he says, in praise of an
abbot of the same name, that 'He was a man of venerable life,
rightly called Benedict since so much blessed by God. Even as a
boy he had the outlook of an old man, his behaviour belying his
age, and never gave himself to sensual pleasure.'[1] He came of
noble Angle lineage and his mind – no less noble than his birth
– was constantly fixed on the life of Heaven. He was about twenty-
five and one of King Oswiu's thanes when the king gave him
possession of the amount of land due to his rank; but he put behind
him the things that perish so that he might gain those that last
forever, despising earthly warfare with its corruptible rewards so
that he might fight for the true king and win his crown in the
heavenly city.[2] He left country, home and family for the sake of
Christ and the gospel so that he might receive a hundredfold in
return and gain eternal life.[3] He rejected the bond of earthly
marriage so that in the kingdom of Heaven he might follow the

1. Gregory, *Dialogues* ii, 1. It is highly significant that Biscop took the name
Benedict; no doubt he was inspired by the Rule and example of the great St Benedict
of Nursia.
2. cf. *Rule of St Benedict*, prologue.
3. cf. *Mark* x, 29 and *Matt.* xix, 29.

Lamb of spotless virginity.[1] He refused to bring forth children in the flesh, being predestined by Christ to raise up for Him sons nurtured in spiritual doctrine who would live forever in the world to come.

## CHAPTER 2

HE therefore left his own country and went to Rome, where, in fulfilment of his long and ardent desire, he made sure he visited the tombs of the apostles and venerated their remains.[2] Directly he returned home he devoted himself wholeheartedly and unceasingly to making known as widely as possible the forms of church life which he had seen in Rome and had come to love and cherish. Then Alchfrid, King Oswiu's son, determined to make the journey to Rome to worship at the tombs of the apostles and decided to take Benedict with him. But Alchfrid's visit was countermanded by his father who made him stay at home in his own country and kingdom. Benedict, being a young man of sound natural abilities, set out at once undeterred and completed the journey with all haste. This was during the reign of Pope Vitalian of blessed memory.[3] This time, just as on his former visit, he took a delight in amassing a good deal of useful knowledge. After a few months' stay he left for the monastery at Lérins,[4] where he entered the community, received the tonsure, took vows as a monk and followed the discipline of the Rule with all due care. After two years' training in monastic life, overcome again by love of the Prince of the Apostles, he made up his mind to tread once more the streets made sacred by the presence of St Peter's body.

1. cf. *Apoc. (Rev.)* xiv, 4.

2. This was in 653, with Wilfrid as far as Lyons. Pilgrimages to Rome and the Holy Land were already of long standing.

3. This visit should be dated about 666, a few years after the Synod of Whitby.

4. Founded by St Honoratus about 410, on the island off Cannes. In spite of its remote situation, it was an important centre of classical and Christian learning. St Vincent of Lérins was the most famous of a series of erudite bishops and monks educated there.

## CHAPTER 3

NOT long after a merchant vessel arrived and so he was able to
have his wish. At this time Egbert, king of Kent, had sent a man
named Wighard[1] from Britain as bishop-elect to be consecrated
in Rome. Wighard had been trained in Kent in every branch of
church tradition by the Roman disciples of Pope Gregory. Egbert
was eager to have him consecrated in Rome as his bishop, reckoning that, if he had a bishop of his own race and language, he
and his people would be able to enter all the more deeply into
the teachings and mysteries of their faith, since they would receive
them at the hands of someone of their own kin and blood and
hear them not through an interpreter but in their own native
tongue. Wighard arrived in Rome, but before he could be consecrated he and all his companions fell victims to the plague. The
pope, not wanting this godly embassy of the faithful to fail in its
effect because of the death of the delegates, took counsel and chose
one of his own associates to go back to Britain as archbishop.
He chose Theodore, a man endowed with both secular and ecclesiastical learning and at home in both languages, that is in Latin
and Greek.[2] As his colleague and counsellor the pope appointed
Abbot Hadrian, Theodore's equal in energy and prudence;[3] and,
perceiving Benedict's worth, wisdom, diligence and devotion, he
put the newly consecrated bishop and his companions in his
charge. He ordered him to give up the pilgrimage, on which he

1. cf. Bede, *Ecclesiastical History*, iii, 29 and iv, 1. The choice of the Archbishop
of Canterbury was particularly crucial after the Synod of Whitby. Wighard was
chosen by Oswiu, king of Northumbria and *bretwalda* as well as by the king of
Kent.

2. A native (like Paul) of Tarsus in Cilicia, Theodore had been educated at Athens
before becoming a monk. He was a member of one of the Greek monasteries in
southern Italy and a subdeacon. At the time of his consecration he was about sixty-
five years old. He died in 690 at the age of about eighty-seven after a fruitful and
eventful episcopate.

3. Hadrian was from North Africa, like Tertullian, Cyprian and Augustine of
Hippo.

had embarked for the honour of Christ, for the nobler purpose of escorting back to Egbert the teacher of truth he had so keenly desired and whom Benedict might serve in a double capacity as guide on the journey home and interpreter when teaching. Benedict did as he was bidden. They returned to Kent where they were very favourably received. Theodore was enthroned as archbishop and Benedict took charge of the monastery of St Peter,[1] of which Hadrian was later to be abbot.

## CHAPTER 4

AFTER two years in charge of the monastery he left Britain for Rome, this being the third time,[2] and completed the journey as successfully as before. He brought back a large number of books on all branches of sacred knowledge, some bought at a favourable price, others the gifts of well-wishers. At Vienne on the journey home he picked up the books he had left there in the care of his friends. When he reached Britain he thought he might pay a visit to Cenwalh, king of the West Saxons, whose friendship he had enjoyed and by whose kindness he had been helped on more than one occasion. At that very time, however, Cenwalh was carried off by a sudden and early death;[3] so Benedict went back to his own people and, turning his steps to his own birthplace, visited Egfrid, king of Northumbria. He told the king all he had done since leaving home as a young man; he revealed his ambition to build up monastic life in the area and he expounded all he had learnt of church and monastic life, both at Rome and everywhere else; and he told him how many sacred books and holy relics of the blessed apostles and martyrs he had brought back. Egfrid took to Benedict so warmly that he immediately gave him from his

1. This was the monastery of SS Peter and Paul at Canterbury, later called St Augustine's.
2. The fourth, but the third from Britain; it took place in about 671.
3. Cenwalh, the son of Cynegils who was the first Christian king of Wessex, reigned from 643 till his death in 674.

personal property an area of land comprising seventy hides[1] and ordered him to build a monastery there in honour of St Peter, the chief pastor of the church. The monastery was built, as I mentioned at the beginning, on the north bank at the mouth of the Wear, in the year of Our Lord six hundred and seventy-four, in the second indiction and in the fourth year of King Egfrid's reign.

## CHAPTER 5

ONLY a year after work had begun on the monastery, Benedict crossed the sea to France to look for masons to build him a stone church in the Roman style he had always loved so much. He found them, took them on and brought them back home with him. So strong was his devotion to St Peter, in whose honour the scheme was begun, and so fervent his zeal in carrying it out, that within a year of laying the foundations, he had the gable-ends of the church in place and you could already visualize Mass being celebrated in it. When the building was nearing completion he sent his agents across to France to bring over glaziers – craftsmen as yet unknown in Britain – to glaze the windows in the body of the church and in the chapels and clerestory. The glaziers came over as requested but they did not merely execute their commission: they helped the English to understand and to learn for themselves the art of glass-making, an art which was to prove invaluable in the making of lamps for the church and many other kinds of vessel.[2] He was also a dedicated collector of everything necessary for the service of church and altar – sacred vessels and vestments for instance – and saw to it that what could not be obtained at home was shipped over from abroad.

1. i.e. nominally enough for seventy families, a very extensive and generous endowment.

2. Recently, extensive remains of a stained glass workshop at Jarrow have been excavated by archaeologists: some reconstructed windows are exhibited in the Jarrow museum. At the nearby church are some small windows of plain glass in the chancel. All these date from the time of Bede.

## CHAPTER 6

HE was untiring in his efforts to see his monastery well provided
for: the ornaments and images he could not find in France he
sought out in Rome. Once his foundation had settled down to the
ordered life of the Rule, he went off on a fourth visit to Rome,[1]
returning with a greater variety of spiritual treasures than ever
before. In the first place he returned with a great mass of books
of every sort. Secondly, he brought back an abundant supply of
relics of the blessed apostles and christian martyrs which were
to prove such a boon for many churches in the land. Thirdly, he
introduced in his monastery the order of chanting and singing
the psalms and conducting the liturgy according to the practice
in force at Rome. To this end Pope Agatho, at Benedict's request,
offered him the services of the chief cantor of St Peter's and abbot
of the monastery of St Martin, a man called John. Benedict
brought him back to Britain to be choirmaster in the monastery.
John taught the monks at first hand how things were done in
the churches in Rome and also committed a good part of his
instruction to writing. This is still preserved in memory of him
in the monastery library. The fourth benefit Benedict brought
back, and one not to be despised, was a letter of privilege from
the venerable Pope Agatho, sought with Egfrid's permission and
indeed at his wish and exhortation, guaranteeing the monastery's
complete safety and independence by a grant of perpetual ex-
emption from external interference. Fifthly, he brought back
many holy pictures of the saints to adorn the church of St Peter
he had built: a painting of the Mother of God, the Blessed Mary
ever-Virgin, and one of each of the twelve apostles which he fixed
round the central arch on a wooden entablature reaching from
wall to wall; pictures of incidents in the gospels with which he
decorated the south wall, and scenes from St John's vision of the

1. The fourth from England, 679–80. So important were its consequences, for
England as well as Wearmouth and Jarrow, that Bede also described it in his *History*
iv, 16(18).

apocalypse for the north wall. Thus all who entered the church, even those who could not read, were able, whichever way they looked, to contemplate the dear face of Christ and His saints, even if only in a picture, to put themselves more firmly in mind of the Lord's Incarnation and, as they saw the decisive moment of the Last Judgement before their very eyes be brought to examine their conscience with all due severity.[1]

## CHAPTER 7

KING EGFRID was deeply impressed by Benedict's virtue, industry and devotion. Realizing how sound and fruitful an idea his original grant of land for building the monastery had turned out to be, he saw to it that another forty hides were added. A year later, on Egfrid's advice or, more accurately, at his command, Benedict chose seventeen monks from the community with the priest Ceolfrith as abbot to form the nucleus of a new foundation at Jarrow, dedicated to the apostle Paul and built on the understanding that the two houses should be bound together by the one spirit of peace and harmony and united by continuous friendship and goodwill. As the body cannot be separated from the head, through which it receives the breath of life, and as the head dare not ignore the body or it would die, so neither was anyone to attempt to disturb the brotherly love that would unite the two houses just as it had bound together the two chief apostles, Peter and Paul. Ceolfrith whom Benedict had appointed abbot had been the greatest help to him in every way from the beginnings of the first foundation and had gone with him at a suitable time to Rome, both for learning what was necessary and for worship. At the same time Benedict chose Eosterwine to be abbot of Wearmouth, giving him the right to rule the monastery of St Peter, so that the burden which was proving too much to be carried alone might the more easily be borne with the help of his much loved

1. Bede's concise enumeration reveals the doctrinal, musical, educational, artistic and legal importance of the varied items he brought back.

companion and fellow soldier. No one should regard it as extra-ordinary for the monastery to have two abbots at once; for it was, after all, a necessary arrangement considering both the frequency of Benedict's journeys overseas for the good of the monastery and also the uncertainty of the times of his return. History relates that at Rome the blessed apostle Peter appointed two bishops[1] to rule the church in his stead as necessity demanded; and the great St Benedict himself, Pope Gregory tells us, thought fit to appoint twelve abbots over his disciples in his stead and this, far from lessening brotherly love, did much to increase it.[2]

## CHAPTER 8

EOSTERWINE took over the monastery in the ninth year of its foundation and remained in charge until his death four years later.[3] In the world he was a nobleman by birth but, unlike some, he did not let his high rank turn to arrogance and contempt for others but used it, as befits a servant of God, as a stepping-stone to greater nobility of soul. Eosterwine was Benedict's cousin and they were both so high-minded that they thought nothing of worldly honour – so much so that when Eosterwine entered the monastery it never occurred to him to use his birth or his relation-ship to the abbot to his own advantage; nor was he shown the slightest favour by Benedict. Realizing that monastic profession put him and his brethren on an equal footing, this young man resolved that his only pride should lie in striving to keep the monastic rule in every detail. When he had turned his back once and for all on the life of the world and had ceased to be King Egfrid's thane by laying down his arms and girding himself for spiritual warfare, he kept himself so humble and identified himself so completely with his brethren that he took a positive delight

1. These were Linus and Cletus (Anacletus) according to the *Liber Pontificalis*, Bede's probable source. See also Bede's *Ecclesiastical History* ii, 4.
2. Gregory, *Dialogues* ii, 3.
3. 682–6.

in sharing their ordinary work. He took his share of the winnowing and threshing, the milking of the ewes and the cows; he laboured in bakehouse, garden and kitchen, taking part cheerfully and obediently in every monastery chore.[1] He was no different when he attained to the rank and authority of abbot, as the wise man says in Ecclesiasticus, 'If thou be made the master, lift not thyself up but be among them as one of the rest: – that is: gentle, affable and kind to all.'[2] When necessary he would correct wrongdoers according to the letter of the Rule but he much preferred to follow his normal affectionate bent and diligently admonish them by word of mouth, so that no one would think of sinning, for then their abbot's bright smile would be clouded over by anxiety on their behalf. Often as he went about on monastery business, he would come across the brethren at work and would quickly go and help them out in whatever they were doing, putting his hand to the plough along the furrow, hammering iron into shape or wielding the winnowing-fan. He was a young man of marked physical strength and gentle in speech; he was of a cheerful disposition, liberally generous and distinguished looking. He ate the same food as the rest of the monks and always ate in the same building with them, and he slept in the common dormitory as he did before he became abbot. Even when he was severely ill and had received clear signs that death was near, he still spent two more days in the monks' dormitory. The remaining five days up to the hour of his death were spent in a more secluded place. On his last day he came out for a while and sat down in the open air. He summoned all the brethren and with the compassion that was second nature to him gave them each the kiss of peace while they wept and lamented the passing of so good a father and shepherd. He died during the night of 7 March as the monks were singing matins. He entered the monastery at twenty-four and lived there twelve years, seven of them as a priest and four as abbot. And so 'leaving his earthly frame and mortal limbs'[3] he sought the kingdom of Heaven.

1. These sentences are inspired by several passages in the *Rule of St Benedict*.
2. *Eccl.* xxxii, 1.
3. cf. Virgil, *Aeneid* vi, 732.

# CHAPTER 9

AFTER this brief foretaste of the life of the venerable Eosterwine let us pick up the thread of our story. Shortly after Benedict had appointed Eosterwine abbot of St Peter's and Ceolfrith of St Paul's he set off on his fifth journey from Britain to Rome and returned, as always, with a rich store of countless valuable gifts for his churches: a large supply of sacred books and no less a stock of sacred pictures than on previous journeys. He brought back paintings of the life of Our Lord for the chapel of the Holy Mother of God which he had built within the main monastery, setting them, as its crowning glory, all the way round the walls. His treasures included a set of pictures for the monastery and church of the blessed apostle Paul, consisting of scenes, very skilfully arranged, to show how the Old Testament foreshadowed the New. In one set, for instance, the picture of Isaac carrying the wood on which he was to be burnt as a sacrifice was placed immediately below that of Christ carrying the cross on which He was about to suffer. Similarly the Son of Man lifted up on the cross was paired with the serpent raised up by Moses in the desert.[1] Amongst other things he also brought back two cloaks of incomparable workmanship, silk throughout, with which he later purchased three hides of land near the mouth of the River Wear on the south bank. It was from King Aldfrid and his councillors that this purchase was made, for Benedict learned on his return that King Egfrid had been slain.[2]

1. These paintings, comparing Old Testament scenes with appropriate ones from the New, gave visible expression to a whole range of patristic thought known as Typology. cf. J. Danielou, *Sacramentum Futuri* (1960) and G. W. Lampe, K. J. Woolcombe, *Essays on Typology* (1957).

2. Egfrid was killed on 20 May 685 by the Picts at the battle of Nechtansmere. The mention of Aldfrid's councillors (or Witan) in this connection is significant, as is the value attached to the silken cloaks.

## CHAPTER 10

THOUGH he brought joy, he found sadness awaiting him: the venerable priest, Eosterwine, whom he had appointed abbot just before he left, together with a great number of monks committed to his charge, had departed this life, stricken down by the plague that was raging everywhere. But there was this consolation – he found that a monk from the same monastery, the deacon Sigfrid, a man who was Eosterwine's equal in meekness and piety, had there and then been appointed in his place, having been chosen both by the brethren and by Benedict's co-abbot, Ceolfrith. Sigfrith was well-grounded in scriptural knowledge, possessed of the highest moral character, endowed with amazing powers of self-denial, but he was severely hampered in protecting his spiritual virtues by physical infirmity, as he struggled to preserve his innocence of heart while suffering from a painful and incurable disease of the lungs.

## CHAPTER 11

NOT very long afterwards sickness took hold of Benedict himself and began to wear him down. To prove their great zeal for the faith by means of a further virtue, that of patience in suffering, the Divine Mercy allowed them both to be cast for a short time upon the bed of sickness, so that, when their illness had been overcome by death, He might refresh them with the eternal rest of peace and light in Heaven. Sigfrith, after a long and painful internal disease, came to his last day on earth and Benedict himself, after three years of creeping paralysis, was so weakened that his lower limbs were already as good as dead and only the vital upper part of his body, on which the continuance of life depends, still functioned, being kept alive in order to give scope to his powers of patience. Both of them, in the midst of their pain, strove continually to thank their Maker and to occupy themselves in praising God and encouraging their brethren. Benedict sought to strengthen the monks who so often came to see him, in their observance of the Rule which he had given them. 'You must not think,' he said, 'that the ordinances I laid down for you were the result of my own untutored invention. No, all I found best in the life of the seventeen monasteries I visited during my long and frequent pilgrimages, I stored up in my mind and have handed on to you, to be steadfastly adhered to, for your own good.' He gave orders that the fine and extensive library of books which he had brought back from Rome and which were so necessary for improving the standard of education in this church should be carefully preserved as a single collection and not allowed to decay through neglect or be split up piecemeal. Over and over again he insisted that in electing an abbot upright life and soundness of doctrine were to be the prime considerations, not rank or family influence. 'I tell you in all sincerity,' he said, 'that as a choice of evils I would far rather have this whole place where I have built the monastery revert forever, should God so decide, to the wilderness it once was, rather than have my brother in the flesh, who has not entered upon the way of truth, succeed me as abbot. Take the greatest care, brothers, never to appoint a man as father over you because of his birth; and always appoint from among yourselves, never from outside the monastery. According to the rule of the great St Benedict, our founder, and according to the decretals of privileges of this house, you are to meet as a body and take common counsel to discover who has proved himself fittest and most worthy by the probity of his life and the wisdom of his teaching to carry out the duties of this office. You must choose as abbot him whom after kindly scrutiny you all acknowledge to be the best.[1] Then you are to summon the bishop and ask him to confirm your candidate in office with the

---

1. The clear inspiration of the *Rule of St Benedict* (chs 2 and 58) and the equally clear rejection of any 'hereditary succession', common in both Germanic and Irish monasteries, were most important for the whole future of Wearmouth and Jarrow. See Introduction, pp. 32–3.

customary blessing. For just as those who beget
generation must be governed by earthly and carn
in their choice of an heir for an earthly and car
so must they who, in a spiritual sense, bring for
God by the spiritual seed of His word, be guided sol
criteria. Let them reckon as the eldest son among
children him who is endowed with more abundant spiritual grace,
just as parents according to the flesh recognize that their firstborn
has pride of place among their offspring and must be preferred
to the rest when they share out their inheritance.'

## CHAPTER 12

I MUST not forbear to mention how the venerable abbot Benedict,
to alleviate the tedium of the long nights when his illness often
made sleep impossible, would call upon one of the monks to read
aloud the story of Job, that model of patience, or any other passage
of the Bible which might bring consolation to a sick man and lift
him out of his depression to think cheerfully of higher things. As
it was impossible for him to rise from bed to pray and difficult
for him even to find sufficient voice to recite the psalms in their
appointed order, this prudent man, spurred on by love of his faith,
had several of the brethren come to him at every hour of prayer,
both day and night. Formed into two small choirs, they sang the
usual psalms antiphonally, so that he could join in with them
as far as he was able and thus fulfil with their assistance what
he had not strength to accomplish alone.

BOTH Benedict and Sigfrith were worn out with their protracted illness; they knew that they were near to death and would never be fit to rule the monastery again. Their infirmity gave scope for the strength of Christ to be perfected within them,[1] but, physically, they were so weak that one day, when they both wished to see and talk to each other before they died, Sigfrith had to be carried on a stretcher to the room where Benedict lay on his pallet. Their attendants set them side by side with their heads resting on the same pillow – a sight to move you to tears. Though their faces were close together, they had not strength enough to turn to kiss each other, but had, even in this, to be helped by the brethren. Then, after consulting Sigfrith and all the rest of the monks, Benedict called Ceolfrith, whom he had put in charge of the monastery of St Paul, and appointed him abbot of both foundations. The virtues they shared bound Ceolfrith to Benedict more closely than any family relationship; and all the monks welcomed the appointment and judged it most admirable. Benedict thought it best from every point of view that both houses should from then on be under the guidance of one father and rector, for that way they would be kept together in harmony, unity and peace. He several times reminded them of the example of the kingdom of Israel which no foreign nation had ever been able to exterminate or damage just as long as it had been ruled by a single ruler from its own people, but when – as a result of its former misdeeds – it was divided against itself by hostile factions, it gradually perished and, once its stability was shattered, came to an end. He never ceased to warn them to keep in mind the gospel precept: 'Every kingdom divided against itself will be brought to desolation.'[2]

1. cf. 2 *Cor.* xii, 9.
2. *Matt.* xii, 25; *Luke* xi, 17.

Two months had passed after these events when the venerable abbot Sigfrith, God's well-beloved, passed through the fire and water of earthly tribulation and was led into the refreshment of eternal rest, making his supplications to God as a sacrifice of perpetual praise, in fulfilment of the vows he had assiduously made on earth with his own pure lips.[1] After another four months Benedict, conqueror of sin and valiant champion of virtue, was himself overcome by bodily weakness and came to his last hour. 'Chilly night falls as the storms of winter blow,'[2] but for that holy man it was soon to give way to the dawn of eternal happiness, light and serenity. The brethren gathered in church, awake throughout the dark night, praying and singing psalms, relieving the sorrow they felt at their father's passing by constant praise of God. Some of them stayed the whole time in the cell in which Benedict, feeble in body but strong in spirit, awaited eagerly for death to lead him into eternal life. A priest read the gospel to him, to alleviate his pain, throughout the whole of that night, as had been done on previous nights. The sacrament of the Body and Blood of the Lord was brought as viaticum for his journey when the hour of death was at hand. And so that holy soul, which had been tested and perfected by the burning pain of long but profitable suffering, left this earthly furnace of the flesh[3] and, free at last, took wing to the glory of eternal bliss. The psalm which at that instant was being sung for him witnesses to the fact that his soul made a triumphant entry into Heaven with no hindrance or delay by evil spirits. For the brethren had gathered in church at nightfall and were singing through the psalter, in order, when they came to the eighty-second psalm, which has for title 'God, who is your like?'[4] The tenor of the whole of this psalm is that the enemies

---

1. cf. *Psalms* lxv, 12–13 (A.V. lxvi, 13–14) and *Wisdom of Solomon* iv, 7.
2. Source unknown.
3. cf. *Psalms* xi, 7 (A.V. xii, 6).
4. *Psalms* lxxxii, 1 (A.V. lxxxiii 1).

of the name of Christ, whether physical or spiritual, are unceasing in their efforts to destroy and annihilate the Church of Christ and every soul in it, no matter how faithful; but by contrast they themselves will be routed and thrown into confusion and disorder and will perish for all eternity, unmanned by the Lord Himself, to whom no one can count himself equal, for He alone is the highest above all Heaven. It was rightly seen as a dispensation of Providence that the psalm should have been recited at the very moment his soul was leaving his body, so that with God's help no enemy might prevail against him. This confessor of the faith fell asleep in the Lord on the twelfth day of January, in the sixteenth year of his founding the monastery and was buried in the church of the blessed apostle Peter. In death, therefore, his body was not far from the altar and relics of him whom he had always loved during his earthly life and who had opened for him the gates of Heaven. He had ruled the monastery for sixteen years, the first eight without appointing an assistant abbot, the rest of the time with the help of the holy and venerable Eosterwine, Sigfrith and Ceolfrith, men who had the title, authority and office of abbot; the first of whom assisted him four years, the second three and the third one.

## CHAPTER 15

THE third of these, Ceolfrith, was a man of acute mind, conscientious in everything he did, energetic, of mature judgement, fervent and zealous for his faith. It was Ceolfrith, as we mentioned above, who, at Benedict's behest and with his aid, first founded St Paul's monastery, saw its completion and ruled it for seven years. Then, for twenty-eight years after this both monasteries were under his wise rule; or, to be more accurate, he was abbot of one monastery in two different places, that of the blessed apostles Peter and Paul. He promptly saw to the completion of all the notable works of piety embarked upon by his predecessor; and, in addition to the other necessities which it fell to him to provide during his long tenure of office, he built several chapels. He also enlarged the stock of church plate, altar vessels and every kind of vestment. He doubled the number of books in the libraries of both monasteries with an ardour equal to that which Benedict had shown in founding them. He added three copies of the new translation[1] of the Bible to the one copy of the old translation which he had brought back from Rome. One of these he took with him as a present when he went back to Rome in his old age, and the other two he bequeathed to his monasteries. For eight hides of land by the River Fresca he exchanged with King Aldfrid, who was very learned in the scriptures, the magnificently worked copy of the Cosmographers which Benedict had bought in Rome. The land went to the monastery of the blessed apostle Paul. Benedict, when still alive, had drawn up this arrangement with King Aldfrid, but died before the matter could be settled. Later, during the reign of King Osred, Ceolfrith traded the land together with a fair balance in money, for twenty hides at a place known locally as the township of Sambuce, because this new plot was nearer the monastery. He sent monks to Rome during the reign of Sergius of blessed memory to obtain an indult granting privileges for the protection of the monastery similar to those granted by Pope Agatho to Benedict. When it was brought back and produced before the synod, the assembled bishops and the noble King Aldfrid confirmed it with their signatures in the same way, as is well known, the former privilege was publicly confirmed in synod by the king and bishops of the time. It was also in Ceolfrith's time as abbot that Witmer, an aged and devout servant of Christ, a man well-versed in every branch of secular learning as well as in the scriptures, consecrated himself to religion in the monastery of the blessed apostle Peter, and made over to the monastery in perpetuity the ten hides of land Aldfrid had given him in the township of Dalton.[2]

1. That of Jerome.
2. Dalton-le-Dale (Durham).

## CHAPTER 16

FOR many years Ceolfrith had carried out the discipline of observance of the Rule, a discipline which its father and provider had handed down on the authority of traditional practice for the benefit both of his monks and himself. All this time he had shown a diligence equalled by none in his ceaseless daily round of prayer and chant; had proved himself remarkably zealous in restraining evildoers, yet tactful in encouraging the weak; and had practised a degree of abstinence from food and drink and a disregard for dress rarely found in those in authority. But now that he was old and full of days he realized that the defects of advanced age rendered him incapable of maintaining any longer, either by precept or by personal example, proper spiritual standards in those who were subject to him. He turned the matter over in his mind a long while and finally decided that it would be better were the brethren to choose, as the decree of their privilege and the Rule of St Benedict laid down, one from among themselves who was more suitable to be abbot. This he charged them to do. As for himself, he had it in mind to visit once more the shrines of the holy apostles in Rome, where he had gone with Benedict as a young man. This arrangement would give him respite for a while from the cares of the world and freedom to enjoy peace and solitude, and would also enable the brethren, under the more active leadership of the younger man they would elect as abbot, to follow more perfectly the way of life enjoined by their rule.


## CHAPTER 17

AT first they all opposed his plan, falling to their knees and repeatedly imploring him with sobs and tears, but in the end he had his wish. Indeed, he was so keen to start that he set off only three days after revealing his secret intention to the brethren, being afraid (and his fears turned out to be justified) that he might die before reaching Rome. At the same time he wished to avoid being delayed by his friends and the local nobility, by all of whom he was held in high esteem. Nor did he wish to be given money which he might not be able to repay at once, for it had always been his practice, whenever he was offered a gift, to give back as good as he had received, whether there and then or shortly afterwards. Accordingly, on the morning of 5 June – which was a Thursday – as soon as Mass had been sung in the church of the Blessed Mother of God, the ever-Virgin Mary, and also in the church of the blessed Peter at which those present had made their communion, he at once prepared to depart. All assembled in St Peter's church and, after he himself had kindled the incense and prayed before the altar, he gave the kiss of peace to each of them, standing on the steps with thurible in hand. Forth they went from there, the sound of their weeping interrupting the litanies, and entered the chapel of the blessed martyr Lawrence, which stood across the way from the church, in front of the monks' dormitory. He bade them his last farewell, urging them to preserve mutual love and to correct offenders, as the Gospel enjoins. He offered his forgiveness and goodwill to any who might have offended and begged any whom he might have rebuked too severely to be reconciled to him and to pray for him. They arrived at the shore; once again he gave them all the kiss of peace amidst their tears. They fell to their knees and, after he had offered a prayer, he and his companions boarded the boat. The deacons of the church embarked with them, carrying lighted candles and a golden cross. After crossing the river, he venerated the cross, mounted his horse and rode off, leaving behind him in his monasteries brethren to the number of around six hundred.

As he departed with his companions the brethren made their way back to the church and with prayers and tears commended themselves and their concerns to the Lord. A short while later, having recited the psalms for Terce, they reassembled to consider what to do. They decided to make their request at once for a new abbot to God through prayer, fasting and the singing of psalms. This decision was communicated to their brother monks of St Paul's both by a group of St Paul's monks who were present and also by a delegation from St Peter's. The monks of St Paul agreed; the two monasteries were of one mind; the hearts and voices of all were lifted up in unison to the Lord. Three days later on Pentecost Sunday all the monks of St Peter's met together in council with a good number of the senior monks of St Paul's. They were completely unanimous in their decision: and so Hwaetberht was duly elected abbot. He had been taught in that same monastery from his earliest childhood to observe the discipline of the rule and had also applied himself there to solid study of the arts of writing, chanting, reading and teaching. In the reign of Pope Sergius of blessed memory he too had hastened to Rome and had stayed there a good long while, learning, copying down and bringing back with him all that he thought necessary for his studies. At the time of his election he had been a priest for twelve years. As soon as he was elected abbot by all the brethren of the two monasteries, he set off at once with a few of the monks to find Ceolfrith who was waiting for a ship to take him across the ocean. They informed him of the result of the election. 'Thanks be to God,' he replied, and confirmed their choice. Hwaetberht gave him a letter of recommendation to Pope Gregory, some lines of which we think it well to include in this book as a record.

'To that lord who is most beloved in the Lord of lords, the thrice blessed Pope Gregory: your humble servant Hwaetberht, abbot of the Saxon monastery of Peter the most blessed Prince of the Apostles, wishes you continual health in the Lord. I, together with the holy brethren of this monastery who desire to bear Christ's most gentle yoke so that they may find rest for their souls, cease not to give thanks to the ordinance of Heaven that you, who are so glorious a vessel of election, have been appointed in our time to the government of the universal Church so that, by the light of truth and faith wherewith you are filled, God might abundantly shed, as from a brilliant star, the light of His love on those who are less exalted. Beloved lord and father in Christ, we commend to your holy grace the venerable grey hairs of our most beloved father, Abbot Ceolfrith, who has fostered and directed our spiritual peace and liberty in the calm of the cloister. We give thanks first of all to the holy and undivided Trinity that Abbot Ceolfrith should have now attained the holy joy of that rest to which he has so long looked forward, even though his departure from us caused us so much pain and grief, so many sighs and tears. In the weariness of old age he has devoutly striven to reach once more the threshold of the blessed apostles which he delighted to remember having visited, seen and venerated in his youth. He has laboured for more than forty years, continually caring for the monasteries he held charge of as abbot and now, being summoned afresh, as it were, to live the life of Heaven as a reward for his incomparable love of virtue, he has again set out as a pilgrim for the sake of Christ at the end of his days and with death looming nigh, so that the burning fire of repentance might the more easily consume in its spiritual furnace the thorns of his former worldly cares. Finally we entreat your paternal charity carefully to perform for him the last kind office of piety which we ourselves have not been found worthy to render. Though his body will rest with you, we know for certain that both you and we have in his devout spirit, whether still in the body or freed from the bonds of flesh, a mighty patron and advocate for our transgressions before the throne of grace.' And so the letter continues.

## CHAPTER 20

ON Hwaetberht's return home Bishop Acca was called and, as was customary, confirmed him in the office of abbot with his blessing. Hwaetberht, with youthful diligence, wisely saw to it that a very great number of privileges were restored to the monastery. One which especially delighted and gratified the monks was the faculty to remove the bones of Abbot Eosterwine which had been placed in the porch at the entrance to St Peter's church, and also those of Abbot Sigfrid, his former master, which were buried in a spot just south of the sanctuary.[1] He had both sets of bones placed in one casket, divided by a partition inside, and put them to rest within the church next to the body of Benedict, their blessed father in God. This he carried out on Sigfrith's birthday, 22 August, and on that very same day by God's wonderful providence, Witmer, the venerable servant of Christ of whom we have already spoken above, died and was interred in the very same place as the abbots whose disciple he was.

## CHAPTER 21

CEOLFRITH, as we said before, pushed on towards the threshold of the apostles, but was struck down with sickness and ended his days before he arrived. He had got as far as Langres[2] about the

---

1. At this time such an 'elevation' or authorized translation of holy men's bodies was equivalent to canonization. Henceforth, Eosterwine and Sigfrith were venerated as saints.
2. In Haute-Marne (Burgundy), about 40 miles north of Dijon.

third hour of the day and his soul took flight to the Lord at the tenth hour of that same day. The following day he was buried with all dignity in the church of the Three Brother Martyrs[1] amidst the tears and lamentation not only of the eighty or more English men who made up his company but also of the local inhabitants who were deeply affected at the thought of so worthy an old man being disappointed of his wish. It was hard for anyone to restrain his tears at the sight of some of Ceolfrith's party starting out to continue their journey without their father, while others revoked their intention of going to Rome, preferring to turn back for home to report the news of his burial; and the rest, in their undying love for him, remained to keep watch by his tomb in the midst of a people whose language they could not understand.

## CHAPTER 22

AT the time of his death he was seventy-four, having been in priest's orders for forty-seven years. He had been abbot for thirty-five or, to be precise, forty-three years, having been Benedict's inseparable companion from the very beginning and having worked with him and having taught the regular monastic life alongside him from the time Benedict first began to build the abbey in honour of the most blessed Prince of the Apostles.[2] He would not allow considerations of age or infirmity or the difficulties of travel to soften the rigorous standards he had accepted as part of tradition; so, from the day he set out from his monastery till

1. Speusippus, Eleusippus and Meleusippus. These, with their grandmother Leonilla, were believed to have been martyred for the Christian faith c. 155, presumably at Langres, where their supposed relics were venerated from the fifth century, and where a church and monastery were dedicated in their honour. Their legend, however, is connected with Cappadocia. cf. *Acta Sanctorum* s.d. 17 January; *Propylaeum ad Acta Sanctorum Decembris* s.d. 17 January and H. Delehaye in *Analecta Bollandiana* xxiii (1904), 427 ff.; xxiv (1905), 505 ff.; xxvi (1907), 334 ff. Later Ceolfrith's body was brought back to Jarrow where, like Benedict Biscop, he was venerated as a saint.

2. Thus he was born in 642 and ordained priest in 669. St Peter's, Wearmouth, was founded in 673, St Paul's, Jarrow, in 681.

the day he died (one hundred and fourteen days, from 4 June to 25 September) he saw to it that the psalter was recited twice, right through, every day – and this in addition to the canonical hours.[1] And even when he had grown so weak that he could no longer ride but had to be carried in a horse-litter, after Mass was sung he made daily offering to God of the Mass, apart from the one day at sea and the three days before his death.

## CHAPTER 23

HE died shortly after the ninth hour on Friday, 25 September, in the seven hundred and sixteenth year from the incarnation of Our Lord, on the sixth day of the week just after the ninth hour in the meadows just outside Langres. He was buried the next day to the south of the city, at the first milestone, within the monastery of the Three Brother Martyrs, in the presence of a vast concourse of people who came and sang the psalms – not only the English men who had come out with him, but also monks from the monastery and the inhabitants of the town. The three martyrs in whose monastery he lies buried are Speusippus, Eleusippus and Meleusippus.[2] They were triplets and not only delivered from the same womb but also born again together in the one faith of the Church, they and their grandmother, Leonilla, with them. They left behind them a memorial of their martyrdom worthy of the spot. May their kindly intercession help and protect ourselves, all unworthy as we are, and our father Ceolfrith.

1. This seems an almost incredible feat, but similar claims are made by other hagiographers. Possibly some abridged version of the psalms was used, such as that known later as the 'Psalter of St Jerome'. This (used by twelfth-century hermits like St Godric of Finchale) consisted of a few verses only from each psalm.
2. See ch. 21.

# The Anonymous History of
Abbot Ceolfrith

(Here begins the Life of Saint Ceolfrith the abbot, under whom blessed Bede received the habit of holy religion and after whose death first received the palm of eternal happiness.)[1]

1. In his letter to the Hebrews Paul the Apostle instructs us: 'Remember your leaders, those who spoke the word of God to you; consider the end of their way of life and imitate their faith.'[2] Hence it is quite clear that you do very well, dearest brothers, to order an account to be made in memory of our most reverend father and abbot Ceolfrith, who spoke the word of God to us. For truly he was such that not only his departure from a way of life devoted to God should be recorded, but also his entry into it and his progress therein; thus the constancy of his faith unfeigned should be imitated.

2. Born of noble and religious parents, he was given up to the pursuit of virtue from his early years of childhood. When he reached the age of eighteen, he chose to set aside the clothes of this world and become a monk. So he entered the monastery situated in a place called Gilling,[3] which had been ruled over by his brother Cynefrith, a devout man, well pleasing to God. Not long before, however, Cynefrith had committed the rule of this monastery to their cousin Tunbert, who was later consecrated Bishop of Hexham.[4] So Cynefrith left for Ireland to pursue the study of the

---

1. This passage occurs in the oldest (tenth-century) manuscript of this work, but is most probably not part of the author's original text: Bede died about twenty years after this Life was written.

2. *Heb.* xiii, 7.

3. Gilling (Yorkshire) was a monastery founded by King Oswy in reparation for the murder of his relative and rival Oswin, king of Deira, in 651. Queen Eanfled obtained this favour on behalf of Trumhere who built the monastery as a place of prayer 'for the salvation of both kings, slayer and slain alike'. Trumhere became a bishop in Mercia *c.* 658. See Bede, *Ecclesiastical History*, iii, 14 and 24.

4. Tunbert was consecrated bishop of Hexham in 681.

Scriptures and to serve the Lord more freely there in prayer and penance.

3. So Ceolfrith was devoutly received by his said kinsman and lived even more devoutly, being zealous in every way for study, work and monastic discipline. Not long afterwards the same Cynefrith, together with other English noblemen who had gone before him to study the Scriptures, when the plague raged far and wide, departed for eternal life through the gateway of death. Tunbert, together with Ceolfrith and not a few monks of his monastery, then left at the invitation of Bishop Wilfrid to the monastery of Ripon. There Ceolfrith, subject to the customary way of life of the rule, was chosen in due course by this bishop for the priesthood at the age of about twenty-seven. Soon afterwards he left for Kent to study more fully the rules both of a monk's life and that of a priest, which he had undertaken.

4. He also came to East Anglia to see the monastic observance of Abbot Botulf, known everywhere as a man of outstanding life and teaching, and one filled by the grace of the Holy Spirit.[1] Ceolfrith returned home as well informed as possible after a short stay, so that no one could be found more learned than he in monastic and clerical rule. Yet neither through consideration of his order, nor of his learning, nor of his noble status could he, like some people, be drawn away from his attitude of humility; rather he took care to be subject in everything to the discipline of the rule. Indeed for a considerable time he held the office of miller-and-baker, in which he applied himself to learn and practise the priesthood's ceremonies while he ground the flour, cleaned and lit the oven and baked the loaves. At this time also he was told to instruct the brothers in the observance of the rule, which task included both teaching the ignorant and correcting the contumacious, thanks to his acquired learning and his burning zeal for God.

5. As the time drew near when the heavenly Judge had decided

1. Botulf (d. 680), an East Anglian monk, built a monastery at Iken (Suffolk) from 654. He had previously been chaplain to a nunnery, one of whose inmates, Liobsynde, became first abbess of Wenlock (Shropshire), initially dependent on Botulf. Her monastery was large and its estates were of comparable size to those of Wearmouth and Jarrow. Liobsynde was of royal birth and her monastery estates formed an important block of land in a border area. See *Oxford Dictionary of Saints*, s.v. Botulf and references.

for him to become a ruler over faithful souls, our pastor and abbot Benedict of holy memory, knowing of his learning, religion and diligence, when he had decided to found this monastery where God's goodness has gathered us, obtained that Ceolfrith be given to him by his bishop (Wilfrid) as his helper and fellow-worker in its foundation.[1] This he obtained although such an experienced man as he did not need his teaching for his own instruction as, having travelled overseas many times in Gaul, Italy and the Islands, he had already acquired detailed knowledge of the statutes of long-established monasteries.

6. Moreover he often used to say that he had learnt the rule which he taught from seventeen ancient monasteries, and whatever he had found most valuable anywhere he had (as it were) hidden in his inmost heart and brought back to Britain and delivered to us to be followed. But just as the apostle Barnabas, a good man full of the Holy Spirit and of faith, when about to teach in Antioch first came to Tarsus (where he knew Saul was), who he remembered had already given great signs of virtue soon after receiving the faith, so that using this helper he might fulfil the ministry of the word as he had planned; or just as Moses, elected and trained by God himself to lead the people of Israel, lest he shrink from bearing the full weight of so great a charge, asked the help of his brother Aaron and thus fulfilled his office with the help of a priest and prophet;[2] so also the famous abbot Benedict, even though very learned in all monastic discipline, sought Ceolfrith's help in building his monastery. He would both strengthen monastic observance by equal zeal for doctrine and discharge the office of the altar through his priest's orders.

7. They began to build the monastery close to the mouth of the river Wear in the year of our Lord 674, the second indiction, the fourth year of King Egfrith's rule, having received from him initially fifty hides of land. Afterwards this was increased considerably by gifts from him and others. In the second year of this foundation Benedict crossed the sea and asked for master-builders from Abbot

1. Wilfrid, bishop of York from 669, was exiled from Northumbria *c.* 680, reinstated 686–91, and exiled again until 705, when his jurisdiction was reduced to the diocese of Hexham: he died in 709. See pp. 22–8.

2. Cf. *Acts* xi, 25–xiii, 3 and *Exodus* xxviii, 1–xxix, 46.

Torthelm, a friend of long standing, by whose direction and work he could build a church of stone: when he obtained them, he brought them from Gaul to Britain.

8. Meanwhile Ceolfrith found his office of prior irksome: the freedom of monastic peace appealed to him more than the care of ruling others. He suffered acutely from the bitter attacks of certain noblemen who could not endure regular discipline, so he returned to his monastery and hastened to resume his former way of life. But Benedict followed him there and asked for his return. At last, overcome by this request of charity, Ceolfrith went back and with Benedict sedulously continued all they had begun in the foundation and organization of this monastery.

9. When the church of excellent workmanship had been built very quickly and then dedicated in honour of St Peter the Apostle, the most reverend abbot Benedict decided to go to Rome to bring back home a plentiful supply of sacred books, the sweet memorial of the blessed martyrs' relics, pictures of biblical events worthy of reverence, and other gifts from overseas, as was his custom. Above all however he planned to bring back teachers: these would establish in the church he had just founded the order of chant and ceremonies according to the usage of the Roman rite.[1]

10. Ceolfrith accompanied him on this journey, hoping to learn more in Rome than he could in Britain about the practice of the priesthood. Eosterwine, a priest and a relative of Benedict, was left in charge of the monastery until their return. With God's help their plan was accomplished: they learnt in Rome many of the Church's laws and they brought back with them to England John, the arch-cantor of the Roman Church and abbot of St Martin's monastery, who generously taught us the order of chanting both by word of mouth and by his writings.[2]

11. Eight years after they started the foundation of this monastery mentioned above, King Egfrith was pleased to donate for the redemption of his soul another estate of forty hides, on which a church and monastery of St Paul could arise: this was not to be separated from the community of the former monastery but united

---

1. See Bede, *Lives of the Abbots*, ch. 6 (above, pp. 190–91) and *Ecclesiastical History*, iv, 18, which reveals the national rather than local importance of Abbot John of Tours.

2. It is conjectured that John also taught the monks how to write uncial script.

to it in everything in single-minded brotherhood.[1] Ceolfrith
energetically accomplished the task entrusted to him. He took with
him twenty-two monks, of whom ten were tonsured and the other
twelve awaiting this grace, and came to the place where he first
built everything necessary for monastic life. He began the same
observance of the monastic rule and the same canonical method of
chanting and reading as in the first monastery, although by no
means all those who came with him knew then how to sing the
psalms, still less read in church or sing the antiphons and
responsories. But the love of religious life helped them, as did the
example of their learned ruler: until he planted a deep root of
monastic observance he would often frequent the church with the
brothers at all the canonical hours, and would eat and take his rest
with them, so that if any corrections had to be made or the novices
taught, he would be present to perform these tasks himself.

12. In the third year from the foundation of the monastery he
began to build the church to be dedicated to the name of St Paul the
apostle, for which Egfrith himself had marked out the site of the
high altar. The work proceeded so fast that, although the workmen
were few, the dedication day was reached in the second year after
its beginning. At the same time that the most reverend Benedict
had sent Ceolfrith there, he also appointed Eosterwine (mentioned
above) as ruler of the first monastery. This was not because one
and the same monastery should have two abbots, but because
Benedict often used to be called to the king for his innate wisdom
and mature counsel. He did not always have the time necessary for
ordering and guiding all monastic matters, so he sought a
colleague by whose help he could carry the necessary burden of
office more lightly and peacefully. Moreover he was hastening to go
to Rome to bring back to the monasteries he had founded those
goods which were necessary.

13. While he delayed overseas, a sudden outbreak of plague
struck Britain and devastated it far and wide. This carried away to
God many monks from each of his monasteries and also the
venerable and beloved-by-God Abbot Eosterwine in the fourth year
from his appointment. In his place the monks with Abbot

---

1. This unusual arrangement is emphasized also by Bede.

Ceolfrith's advice chose as their abbot Sigfrith, a deacon of the same monastery, a man of wonderful holiness who was very learned in the Scriptures and specially devoted to their study.[1]

14. But in the monastery which Ceolfrith ruled, all those who could read or preach or were able to sing the antiphons and responsories were carried off by the plague except the abbot himself and one small boy, who has been brought up and taught by him and who until the present day holds the rank of a priest in the same monastery and commends the abbot's laudable actions in words and writings to all who wish to know them. Because of the plague the abbot was very sorrowful and ordered the previous custom to be interrupted and that the whole psalter except at Lauds and Vespers should be recited without antiphons. But when this was done for the space of only one week with many tears and laments, he felt unable to bear it any longer so he decided that the psalms with antiphons should be resumed as before. With everyone trying their best, he completed this by himself but with the help of the boy mentioned above, with no small labour, until he trained sufficient companions in the work of God or else obtained them from elsewhere.[2]

15. But when Benedict returned home, laden as always with goods from abroad, he was deeply grieved by the disaster which had taken place. He rejoiced however that Sigfrith, beloved by God, had been chosen as abbot in place of Eosterwine: he told him to take vigorous care of the monastery he had received, while he himself would help by teaching and by praying. But not long afterwards both of them fell ill, and as their infirmities increased with time, both were confined to bed and were even unable to sit up.

16. After taking counsel with the monks, Benedict then called Ceolfrith and appointed him abbot of each monastery, enjoining that it should really be one single monastery although situated in two places, and that it should always be ruled by one abbot and made safe by the same protection of privileges. In conformity with the written privilege which he had received from Pope Agatho as well as the rule of the holy father Benedict, he stipulated that the

---

1. See Bede, *Lives of the Abbots*, chs. 11–14 (above, pp. 197–202). Note the importance of biblical studies for any future abbot.

2. The boy described has often and probably rightly been identified as Bede himself.

abbot of this same monastery should never be chosen by hereditary succession, but 'for his way of life and the soundness of his teaching', and so he had appointed Ceolfrith to his present post.[1] He indeed was linked to Benedict by spiritual rather than carnal affinity, while Benedict also had a physical brother who was very close by blood but far distant from him in mind because of the emptiness of his heart.

17. Ceolfrith then was appointed abbot there in the third year of King Aldfrith, the first indiction on 12 May in the eighth year since his foundation of the monastery of St Paul. And in the same year the venerable abbot and deacon Sigfrith, tested by long illness, departed for the kingdom of heaven on 22 August of the third year since he became abbot. Moreover, at the beginning of the next year, on 12 January, abbot Benedict, beloved by God, after the furnace of long infirmity in which his custom was always to give thanks, also attained to the rest and light of heaven after ruling his monastery for sixteen years.[2]

18. He had in fact ruled the monastery of St Peter the apostle for eight years, and he had devoted another eight to the monastery of St Paul through Ceolfrith. During the first four years he had ruled the monastery of St Peter (as said above) with Eosterwine as his helper, for the next three he had Sigfrith and for the last year Ceolfrith as his coadjutor. Benedict was buried to the east of the altar, where afterwards the bones of the very reverend abbots Eosterwine and Sigfrith were translated.

19. When Benedict had been taken from death to life, Ceolfrith took charge of both monasteries (or rather of the one monastery on two sites) and cared for it with watchful skill for twenty-seven years. He was a man of keen mind, energetic action, burning with zeal for justice, glowing with both the love and fear of God, severe in correcting wrongdoers yet mild when encouraging the repentant, and assiduous in keeping and teaching the rules of monastic life. He was also kindly in relieving the poor and in almsgiving, generous with money whether by giving what was asked from him or making rewards for gifts offered to him; he

1. *Rule of St Benedict*, chs. 2, 64.

2. Benedict Biscop died in 689; Bede's sermon on him is printed in D. Hurst (ed.), *Bedae Opera Homiletica* (*Corpus Christianorum Scriptorum Latinorum*), vol 122, pp. 88–94.

was also committed with holy regularity to both psalmody and prayer.

20. Thus he enriched the monasteries he ruled, externally with substantial wealth and internally with spiritual resources no less important. In order to make them more secure from attacks by the wicked, he sent envoys to Rome who asked for and obtained a letter of privilege from Pope Sergius (of happy memory) similar to that which his predecessor Benedict had obtained from Pope Agatho.[1] He also substantially enriched the monasteries with vessels for the service of church and altar, and copiously increased the library which he and Benedict had brought from Rome. Among other projects he had three Pandects copied: two of them he placed in his monasteries' churches so that all who wished to read a chapter of either Testament could quickly find what they wanted, while the third one he decided to offer when he was going to Rome as a gift to St Peter, Prince of the Apostles.

21. When he realized that he was worn out by old age and could no longer set his earlier vigorous example to his disciples, he thought out an appropriate plan: he would leave the rule of the monasteries to younger men and himself go on pilgrimage to the thresholds of the apostles. Once there and free from earthly cares, he could await the day of his death amidst unhindered application to prayer. Thus he would follow the example of his brother Cynefrith, who (as we said above) left the care of his monastery to pursue the contemplative life, and by voluntary exile for God's sake exchanged one fatherland for another.

22. Ceolfrith therefore prepared a ship and drew up a list of monks he would send to Rome: he decided which gifts to offer to St Peter and obtained enough of everything for the journey. For a time he hid from the monks that he too would be going, lest if what he planned became openly known, his friends would either forbid or delay his departure, or else many people might give him money which he had neither the time nor the ability to repay. For he

---

1. These documents of Agatho (678–81) and Sergius I (687–701) are the earliest extant papal privileges for English monasteries and were probably based on earlier ones in favour of Bobbio, founded by Columbanus. They were followed by others in favour of Chertsey, Bermondsey, Evesham and Malmesbury some twenty years or more afterwards.

always retained the outlook of a really generous soul, so that if any gift were made to him by anyone of either high or low status, he would not send him away unrewarded, but more often than not would give his benefactor something more valuable in return.

23. When everything was ready and the day of his departure was near, he called to the church all the monks of St Peter's monastery and told them what he intended. They all wept at the news: some fell on their faces and grasped his feet. They besought him with tears not to go away so suddenly, but rather to remain with them for at least one more day. He agreed to their request and stayed with them for a day and a night (it was the Tuesday before Whit Sunday), and in the morning, accompanied by many, he went to the monks living in St Paul's monastery and spoke to them also, explaining the reasons for his going. They also were very grieved and much disturbed by his sudden departure. He spoke gently and reasonably to all, asking them to keep the rule he had taught them, to remain in the fear of God and not to impede the journey he intended by their entreaties and tears. If he had ever acted intemperately or unjustly, he asked their forgiveness, while he with all his heart forgave all who had offended him in any way: he also desired that God would be merciful to them all, both then and for ever.

24. After they had resisted him for no little time and he had obtained (with many tears) that they would allow him to depart with their favour and approval (as was right), they insistently asked him that if he reached the apostles' holy places he would commend them to God in frequent prayer; but if he should die first, he would always remember to intercede for their salvation.

25. He left St Paul's on the same day, eagerly longing to go but driven to dismay at the grieving monks. He told them to choose as abbot for themselves with his blessing, according to the Rule of St Benedict and their statute of privileges, whoever they thought most worthy from their own community. Returning to St Peter's monastery as soon as morning dawned, they sung Mass at St Peter's and at St Mary's and those present received communion.[1]

---

1. This passage probably indicates the presence of two small churches on the same axis, as in contemporary Canterbury, Malmesbury and elsewhere.

Then he called all the monks to St Peter's church, asked them to pray for him and said the collect himself. Then he lit the charcoal and, taking a thurible in his hand, stood on the steps where he had been accustomed to read, and gave the kiss of peace to most of them. He was prevented by their grief and his from giving it to them all. He went out with the thurible to the oratory of St Laurence the martyr, which is in the monks' dormitory. The monks followed him, singing the antiphon from the prophet: 'The way of the just is right and the journey of the holy is prepared' and 'going from strength to strength', adding psalm 66: 'May God have mercy on us and bless us, lighten his face and have mercy on us.'[1] Then, having burnt the incense, he went out and again told them all to keep peace with each other, to beware of quarrels, detractions and scandals; to reprove sinners as the Gospel commands (first alone, then with two or three together) and make every effort to bring them back to the way of truth. If reward follows their efforts, let them rejoice; but if not, then let them bring forward the faults in public. They should preserve concord and unity with the brothers at St Paul's and remember that they both formed one monastery, to be ruled by one abbot. So if the bond of brotherhood were broken from within, the door should not be opened to harmful interference from outside, as in the case of the Jewish people who, when divided against themselves through the folly of Solomon's son, never had respite from external disaster.[2]

26. When his sermon was finished, they repeated the antiphon with the psalm already mentioned and went out towards the river, leading their father with sad songs as if he was already departing this life. As before, he gave to each one the kiss of peace, while their song was often interrupted by tears. After praying on the shore, he went on board ship and sat down in the prow. Deacons sat beside him: one held a cross of gold he had made himself, the other lighted candles.

27. As the ship sailed across the river, he looked towards the brothers mourning his departure and heard the sublime sound of

---

1. Cf. *Isaiah* xxvi, 7; *Psalm* lxxxiii, 8 and lxvi, 1.
2. Cf. *Matthew* xviii, 15–20 and 1 *Kings* (3 *Kings*) xi–xii; see also J. R. Porter, *The Illustrated Guide to the Bible* (1995), pp. 92–5.

their song mixed with grief; he could not prevent his sobbing
and tears. He repeated frequently this prayer: 'O Christ, have
pity on this band. Lord Almighty, protect this community. For
I know very well that I have found none better than them or
more inclined to obedience. O Christ, O God, defend them.' Then,
leaving the ship, he bowed to the cross, mounted his horse
and departed, his material cares set aside; he hastened away from
the English people, his kindred, to be a stranger in foreign lands
so that he might with greater freedom and purity of heart
devote himself to contemplation with the legions of angels in
heaven.

28. The brothers returned to the church and when the office was
ended took counsel what to do. It seemed right that with prayer
and fasting they should seek from the Lord whom they should
appoint as abbot over them. But since the venerable father (when
leaving) had said that none of them were to fast on the day of his
departure but rather all hold a greater feast, and had even told
some of those accompanying him on no account to wait with them
until the end of the midday meal (it was the Thursday before Whit
Sunday), it seemed proper to fast the following day and night and
refresh themselves on the Saturday at the ninth hour, for they
could not prolong the fast further because of the vigils of the
Sunday solemnity. They would also add several psalms to each of
the appropriate hours of canonical prayer and all would implore
the Almighty that on the day when He sanctified the beginning of
His Church through the coming of the Holy Spirit, He should also
indicate to them, who were truly a part of that Church, a worthy
abbot through the grace of the same Spirit.

29. When these matters were thus concluded, there came from
the monastery of St Paul several brothers on the day of Pentecost,
and by unanimous consent they chose Hwaetberht as their new
abbot. He had passed his life in the same monastery from an early
age and had been well trained in ecclesiastical as well as monastic
learning: at this time he already exercised priestly orders. As soon
as he was elected abbot, he wrote a letter to the apostolic pope
commending his father and predecessor. At the same time he
prepared presents to send and, following in Ceolfrith's footsteps
with some of the brothers, he read the letter to him and showed the

gifts he was to deliver, having found him in Ælfberht's monastery, situated in a place called *Cornu Vallis*.[1]

30. Ceolfrith gladly accepted the community's choice and confirmed it with his blessing. He also gave him full instruction how to govern the monastery in many matters. The letter begins as follows:

'To the lord most beloved by the Lord of lords and thrice blessed Pope Gregory, Hwaetberht, your humble servant, abbot of the monastery of the most blessed Peter, Prince of the Apostles, situated in the land of the Saxons, sends perpetual greetings in the name of the Lord.

'I do not cease to give thanks (together with the holy brothers who in these places desire with me to bear the most sweet yoke of Christ to earn rest for their souls)[2] for the decision of the heavenly Judge to appoint you, a glorious vessel of election, to govern the whole Church in our times, so that through this light of truth and faith with which you are filled from heaven all those of lower degree may be illumined with the radiance of its goodness. We commend to your holy kindness, most beloved father and lord in Christ, the venerable grey hairs of our most beloved father Ceolfrith, abbot and provider and guardian of our spiritual freedom and of our peace in monastic quiet. First indeed we give thanks to the holy and indivisible Trinity, that although he departed from us accompanied by our intense sorrow, groans, grief and tears, he has nevertheless reached the joy of his longed-for rest. Now, even though worn out with age, he has devoutly sought again those thresholds of the apostles which (as he often told us) he had approached, seen and venerated in his youth. After the long labour and continuing care of over forty years, during which he presided with abbatial authority, ruling our monasteries with unique love of virtue, he once more begins as if newly summoned to the society of heaven, although worn out with old age and already near the point of death, to live as an exile for Christ: thus the glowing fire of penance may more freely burn away the old thorns of earthly cares in the furnace of the Spirit. Finally we venture to ask your Fatherhood to diligently fulfil for him (which we have been unworthy to do) the last acts of kindness, as we know for certain that although you have his body, yet we too have his spirit devoted to God, whether remaining in the body or freed from bodily ties, as a strong intercessor with God for our transgressions, and as a heavenly protector.'

31. Ceolfrith set out from his monastery on Thursday 4 June, intending to embark by sea at the mouth of the river Humber. On

---

1. That is, 'Horn of the Valley'. Possibly Hornsea (East Yorks) is meant, or else the monastery of Wilgils, situated on a headland between the river Humber and the sea, mentioned in Alcuin's *Life of St Willibrord*.
2. Cf. *Matt.* xi. 28–30.

Saturday 4 July he boarded a ship, which before it reached the coast of Gaul landed in three provinces, in each of which he was received with honour by all because he had decided to crown the grace of his earlier perfection with an example of outstanding excellence.

32. This journey ended when he reached Gaul on Wednesday 12 August. Here too he was warmly welcomed by all, especially King Hilperic himself,[1] who besides offering gifts gave him letters for all parts of his kingdom so that in all places he could be received in peace and nobody could delay his journey. Moreover he recommended him and all his followers to the kind treatment of Liutprand, king of the Lombards.[2] He arrived at Langres, a city of Burgundy, on Friday 25 September, where, worn down by great age and by sickness and declining in a good old age, as the Scriptures say, 'he was gathered to his fathers'.[3] For he was seventy-four years of age and had served the Lord in priest's orders for forty-seven years and held the office of abbot for thirty-five years.

33. He left in his monasteries a company of soldiers of Christ, more than six hundred strong, with land of nearly one hundred and fifty hides, according to the usual English computation.[4] From the time he left his monastery until he ended his last day, he chanted the psalter of David right through three times a day besides the canonical psalmody; thus he increased his former practice by which for several years he had habitually recited the whole psalter twice a day. On no day did he omit to offer to the Lord the sacrifice of the Eucharistic offering both for himself and for his friends, not even when he was unable to ride through considerable weakness and had to be carried in a horse-drawn litter. The only exceptions were when he was tossed all day at sea for one day, when storms were beating on the ship, and the four days before his death.

1. Hilperic is Chilperic II, king of Neustria 715–20, and of all Gaul under Charles Martel 720–21.

2. Liutprand was king of the Lombards 712–44; in 726 he visited Rome as a pilgrim and Gregory II as his friend.

3. Cf. *Gen* xxxv, 8.

4. Our author agrees with Bede in describing both monasteries as the home of 600 monks with 150 hides of land to support them.

34. In his company were about eighty men, assembled from different places, who all followed him and cherished him like a father. For he had told his attendants that if they found anyone accompanying him was without provisions of his own, they were to give him either food or money.[1] For indeed Ceolfrith was very kind-hearted and a great benefactor of the poor. This was why, when he was on the point of departure and actually leaving, the general lamentations by the poor and the homeless indicated that they were being deprived (as it were) of their father and supporter. He took care to practise assiduously this kind of virtue, not only as commended by the fear and the love of God but also as something acquired from his father by hereditary right. When he held a noble office in the king's household, his father always took great pleasure in works of mercy on behalf of the poor. On one occasion when he had prepared a splendid banquet for the king but the necessities of war had prevented his coming, then he gave thanks to Providence and at once caused all the poor, the strangers and the sick to be summoned from all sides to the feast; so with the goods he had intended for entertaining an earthly king and his thanes he welcomed instead the King of kings in the person of his humble followers and for the sake of eternal reward. He indeed discharged all the service of his male guests while entrusting to his wife the lowliest service to the women.[2]

35. Ceolfrith reached Langres about the third hour of the day on 25 September (as we have said) at the beginning of the fifteenth indiction; when he arrived at the countryside around this city, he was gladly received by Gangulf, the lord of this region. He indeed had previously met Ceolfrith on the way and invited him to come and stay with him and assured him of a warm welcome even if he himself were not present. He urgently pressed him not to depart until he was well, or, if God so willed it, to await his entry into the life of heaven by the tombs of the holy martyrs.

36. It happened on the very day that he arrived, he departed to the Lord at about the tenth hour. On the next day, with a great

1. These eighty men formed a large, secure group of travellers, less vulnerable through number to the attacks of marauding robbers.

2. This precious account reveals not only the practice of Ceolfrith's parents, but also a glimpse of noble Anglo-Saxons' generosity to the poor.

company of his own followers and of the local inhabitants, his body was brought for about three miles to Gangulf's monastery about a mile and a half from the city, on the south side. It was buried in the church of the holy martyred brothers whose names are Speusippus, Eleusippus and Meleusippus, who were born triplets of their mother and were crowned with martyrdom there in times gone by. They were buried in the same place where their grandmother called Leonella was buried, who had also left this life by the confession of a martyr.[1]

37. So when the father had been buried, some of the brothers who had escorted him returned home to tell in his own monastery where and when he had died; some however completed the proposed journey to Rome to deliver the presents which he had sent. Among these was the Bible (as we have said) translated from the Hebrew and Greek originals according to the interpretation of the blessed priest Jerome, which had written at its beginning verses as follows:

To the body of sublime Peter, justly venerated, whom ancient faith declares to be head of the Church, I, Ceolfrith, abbot from the furthest ends of England send pledges of my devoted affection, desiring that I and mine may ever have a place amidst the joys of so great a father, a memorial in heaven.[2]

38. Moreover some preferred to dwell in that same city of Langres through love of their father buried there, but afterwards these fulfilled their resolve and desire to visit Rome. The companions of the most reverend abbot found such great favour with Gangulf that he entertained them all to a splendid feast after the funeral and also provided guides to those who departed in different directions as well as supplies for their journeys. He also arranged for an allowance for those who stayed on, for as long as they wished to remain.

39. The letter which the apostolic pope sent in reply tells how highly he thought of Ceolfrith and his gifts. It begins as follows:

---

1. See p. 209, note 1.

2. This is the subsequently altered dedicatory text of the *Codex Amiatinus*, now in Florence; see above, pp. 37–8.

'Bishop Gregory, servant of the servants of God, to the religious abbot Hwaetberht.

'We have read the content of your writings of admirable piety, which show that you rejoice in the truth by whose grace "those things which are not" are called as "those that are"[1] with regard to our promotion, and that you profess yourself willingly subject to the authority of the apostolic law, whose duties we, although unworthy, discharge. For this reason, sharing in prayer with him whose supremacy you welcome, you should pray more earnestly that he may benefit himself and you and many others. Furthermore, he whose venerable grey hairs, dedicated to God, you were anxious to commend to us, was by God's summons removed from temporal matters to eternal ones before we could receive him, after he had sent as an everlasting memorial a gift to our lord and patron in common the blessed Peter, Prince of the Apostles. Approving of his faith in offering us this gift, we have judged him worthy of constant commemoration. We pray that this most approved teacher of the holy precepts of the rule may show the way in God's sight to worthy disciples. May divine grace, which has taken him away, perfect his merits like those of Aaron and Moses, the holy leaders of the chosen people who were called away before they reached the promised land, or like Elias, suddenly removed to heaven. May it also adorn Ceolfrith's disciple, who survives and succeeds him, along with the followers he is to govern, with the spiritual gifts and dignities of Joshua, the admirable leader, and of Phineas and Elisha. Farewell.'[2]

The companions of our father, beloved of God, who returned to us, used to tell us how in the night after his venerable body had been committed to the tomb, while three custodians of this church were keeping their night watch (as was usual), the fragrance of a wonderful smell filled the whole church. This was followed by a light, which remained for no short time, and at last arose to the roof of the church. They quickly went out and saw the same light rise quickly to the sky, so that all the places around seemed to be lit up by its glow as if it were day-time. Thus they clearly understood that ministers of eternal light and perpetual sweetness had been present and had consecrated by their visit the resting-place of this holy body. Thus a custom arose among the inhabitants that through the various hours of day and night

---

1. Cf. *Rom.* iv, 17.

2. The sense of this passage is that Gregory prays that Hwaetberht, as Ceolfrith's successor, may be in relation to him what Joshua was to Moses, Phineas to Aaron and Elisha to Elijah. Plummer in *Baedae Opera Historica* (1896) suspected that the text is corrupt here.

prayer, when the canonical office of psalms was ended, all the men should go to kneel at his tomb. Reports also were spread abroad that other signs and cures took place there by the grace of Him who is accustomed to help His saints as they strive in this present life, and to crown them as victors in the life to come. Amen.

# The Voyage of St Brendan

1 SAINT BRENDAN, the son of Findlug, great-grandson of Atla of the line of Eogen, was born in the marshy region of Munster. He led a very ascetical life, was renowned for his powers as a miracle worker, and was spiritual father to almost three thousand monks.

One evening, while he was engaged in spiritual warfare in the place known as Brendan's Meadow of Miracles,[1] a monk called Barinthus,[2] one of Brendan's own kinsmen, came to visit him. Brendan questioned him at length and, when the interrogation was over, Barinthus began to weep. He threw himself full-length on the ground, and remained there a long time in prayer until Brendan lifted him to his feet, kissed him, and said, 'Father, your visit ought to be filling us with joy, not sadness. Surely you came with the intention of cheering us up, so preach the word of God to us and then regale our spirits with an account of the wonders you have seen on your voyage over the sea.'

In answer to this request Barinthus started to tell them about an island he had visited:

'My son Mernoc, the steward of Christ's poor,' he began, 'fled from my sight in order to live the life of a hermit. He discovered an island called the Island of Delights, situated near a rocky mountain. A long while later I received news that there were many other monks with him on the island, and that God had worked numerous miracles through him. So I went to visit him myself.

'After a three days' journey I reached the island and found Mernoc and his brethren hurrying down to the shore to meet me – the Lord had revealed to him that I was coming. As we went round the island monks poured from their cells like a swarm of bees to look at us. The cells were scattered far and wide over the island, but the monks lived in close

1. 'Meadow of miracles' (*saltus virtutum*) = 'Cluain Ferta', Clonfert in Galway.
2. Abbot of Drumcullen and spiritual confidant of Brendan.

spiritual union with each other, bound together in faith, hope, and charity: they all ate at the same table and always sang the Divine Office in common. Their diet was made up of apples, nuts, roots, green vegetables, and nothing else. At night, when compline was over, each monk had to go to his cell and remain there till cockcrow or until the rising bell was rung. My son Mernoc and I stayed awake to wander round the island during the night. He led me to the western shore where there was a small boat moored. "Father," he said, "let us embark and row away westwards to the isle which is called the Land of Promise of the Saints, that land which God will give to us and our successors on the last day." We boarded ship and sailed away.

'Clouds came down and covered us on all sides, so completely that we could scarcely make out the prow or stern of the vessel, but after we had sailed an hour or two a brilliant light shone round us and a country appeared before us, spacious, green, and exceedingly fruitful. The ship put in to land and we disembarked to make a tour of the island. We walked for fifteen days and still did not reach the farther shore. All the plants we saw were flowering plants and every tree was a fruit tree; the very stones beneath our feet were precious. On the fifteenth day we came to a river flowing from east to west. We stood and thought of all the marvels we had seen and wondered what direction we should take: we were eager to cross the river but were waiting for God to show us His will in the matter. Our ponderings were interrupted by the sudden appearance of a man surrounded by an aura of shining light. He greeted us by name and said: "Be of good cheer, brethren. The Lord has shown you this land which is intended for His saints. The river you see before you divides the island in two. You may not cross it; go back, therefore, the way you came." I asked him where he came from and what was his name. "Why do you ask me where I come from or what is my name?" he answered. "Why do you not rather question me about the island itself? From the very beginning of the world it has remained exactly as you see it now. Do you need any food, drink, or clothing? You have been here a whole year already without tasting food or drink. You have never felt the need for sleep, for it has been daylight all the time. Here there is no obscuring darkness but only perpetual day, the Lord Jesus Christ being Himself our light."

'We set out at once and the man accompanied us as far as our boat. He disappeared from sight when we boarded the vessel, and we sailed back through the same dense cloud as before and arrived at the Island of Delights. When the brethren caught sight of us they rejoiced greatly and expressed their sorrow over our prolonged absence. "Why, fathers," they complained, "did you leave your sheep to wander about in a wood without their shepherd to tend them? We are becoming accustomed to our abbot's leaving us quite frequently to go we know not where and to stay there for perhaps a week, a fortnight, or even a month." I tried to comfort them. "Brethren," I said, "please do not think ill of us. You are living before the gate of Paradise. Not far from here is that island which is called the Land of Promise of the Saints, where night never falls and day knows no ending. It is to this place that Mernoc, your abbot, so often goes. Have no fear, for an angel guards him on his journey. Can you not tell by the smell of our garments that we have been in Paradise?"

' "Father," they answered, "we know that you have been to God's Paradise over the sea, but exactly where it is we do not know. We have often been able to smell the fragrance issuing from our abbot's garments for forty days after his return."

'I had stayed with my son for two full weeks on the Island of Promise without eating a bite or drinking a mouthful, yet we felt so replete that anyone might well have thought we were full of new wine. After forty days on the Island of Delights I received the blessing of the abbot and his monks and left with my companions to return to my own cell – I shall arrive there tomorrow.'

St Brendan and his whole community prostrated themselves, glorifying God and saying 'The Lord is righteous in all His ways: and holy in all His works.' When they had finished praying, Brendan said: 'Let us take some refreshment and carry out the Lord's "new commandment".'[1] The following morning St Barinthus received the brethren's blessing and set off for his own cell.

2 St Brendan chose out fourteen monks from the community, shut himself up with them in an oratory, and addressed them thus: 'My most beloved co-warriors in spiritual conflict, I beg you to help me with your advice, for I am consumed with a desire so ardent that it casts every other thought and desire out of my heart. I have resolved, if it be God's will, to seek out that Land of Promise of the Saints which our father Barinthus described. What do you think of my plan? Have you any advice to offer?'

As soon as their father in God had made known his intentions, they all replied, as with one voice: 'Father, your will is ours too. Have we not left our parents and set aside our earthly inheritance in order to put ourselves completely in your hands? We are prepared to come with you, no matter what the consequences may be. We seek to do one thing alone – the will of God.'

---

1. *John* xiii, 34: 'A new commandment I give unto you: that you love one another as I have loved you.' This verse is sung at the Washing of Feet in the Maundy Thursday liturgy.

3  St Brendan and his companions observed a series of three-day fasts, to cover the period of forty days before they were due to set out. At the end of forty days, Brendan bade farewell to the body of his community, commended them to the prior's care (this prior later succeeded Brendan as abbot), and set out westwards with his group of fourteen monks to the island of a holy monk called Enda.[1] There they remained for three days and nights.

4  At the end of their stay Brendan received the blessing of Enda and of all his monks and set out to the most distant part of the region, where his parents lived. He did not wish to visit them, but, rather, pitched his tent on the top of a mountain that extended far out to sea, in the place that is called Brendan's seat.[2] Below, at the water's edge, there was room for only one boat to put in. Brendan and his companions made a coracle, using iron tools. The ribs and frame were of wood, as is the custom in those parts, and the covering was tanned ox-hide stretched over oak bark. They greased all the seams on the outer surface of the skin with fat and stored away spare skins inside the coracle, together with forty days' supplies, fat for waterproofing the skins, tools and utensils. A mast, a sail, and various pieces of equipment for steering were fitted into the vessel; then Brendan commanded his brethren in the name of the Father, Son, and Holy Spirit to go aboard.

5  As Brendan was standing alone on the shore blessing the harbour, three of his own monks, who left the monastery in search of him, approached. They fell down in front of their abbot's feet. 'Father,' they begged, 'let us go with you. If you refuse we will remain here and die of hunger and thirst, for we are determined to go with you as pilgrims all the days of our life.' Seeing their plight he ordered them aboard: 'Your will be done, my sons, though I know what you have come for. One of you has done well and God will reward him with the place he deserves. The other two have a terrible judgement awaiting them.'

Then he stepped aboard, the sails were hoisted and they set

---

1. Abbot of Ardmere and a friend of Brendan.
2. St Brendan's Mountain in the Dingle Peninsula.

off towards the summer solstice; the wind was fair and they needed to do no more than steady the sails. After fifteen days' sailing the wind fell and they rowed and rowed until their strength failed. 'Have no fear,' said Brendan, losing no time in encouraging the brethren, 'for God is our helper. He is our captain and guide and will steer us out of danger. Just leave the sails and let Him do as He will with His servants and their boat.' They ate every day about the time for vespers, and from time to time the wind would fill their sails, though they knew neither whence it came nor whither it was taking them.

6 Forty days passed and they found themselves without food. Then one day an island came in sight towards the south. It looked very high and rocky, and as they drew in to the shore they saw a bank, built high like a wall, and several streams gushing down from the crest of the island into the sea. They could find no harbour at which to put in. Being sorely tormented with hunger and thirst, some of the monks picked up their flasks to fill them from the streams. The saint reproved them for this: 'Stop, brethren! What a foolish thing to do! Since God does not intend to show us a way in just yet, why must you start assaulting the place? In three days' time Our Lord Jesus Christ will show us a harbour and a place in which to stay and refresh our weary bodies.' They circled round the island for three days and on the third, about the ninth hour, found a harbour just big enough for one ship. Brendan at once stood up and blessed it. On each side loomed a rock, cut away sheer like a wall and tremendously high. When they had all disembarked and were standing on dry land, St Brendan forbade them to bring any gear out of the boat. While they were wandering along the shore, a dog ran towards them down a path and sat at Brendan's feet as though he were its master. 'You must admit,' said Brendan, 'that God has sent us a trustworthy messenger. Let us follow him.' He and his monks followed the dog till it led them to a group of buildings.

They entered and saw before them a vast hall, well furnished with seats and couches. Jugs of water had been put out for them to wash their feet. When they had sat down, St Brendan charged them: 'Be on your guard, brethren, lest Satan lead you into temptation. I can see him persuading one of those three brethren who followed us to commit an awful theft. Pray for his soul, for his body is given over to the power of the devil.' The walls of the room were hung with vases of various kinds of metal and bridles and drinking horns chased with silver.

Brendan told the monk who normally served their food to prepare supper. This monk found a table already laid, with cloths, rolls of extraordinarily white bread, and fishes. When everything was set out, Brendan blessed the food, praying thus: 'Let us praise the God of Heaven who gives every creature its food.' There was also plenty to drink. When the meal was over and they had finished the canonical hours for the day, the saint told them to sleep. 'Take your rest,' he said, 'for there is a good, well-covered bed here for each of you. You need rest; you are worn out with over-exertion.'

After they had fallen asleep, St Brendan witnessed the machinations of the evil one. He saw a little Ethiopian boy holding out a silver necklace and juggling with it in front of the monk. At once the saint arose and persevered in prayer till dawn. At daybreak they went briskly about their business of singing the divine office, so that they might be able to get down to their boat in good time. When they had finished singing, a table appeared before them, already laid for a meal, just as had happened on the previous day. For three days and nights God provided for His servants in this way.

7 Then they set out on their voyage with this warning from Brendan: 'Take care, brethren, not to take anything with you from this island.'

'Far be it from us,' they rejoined, 'to mar our journey with theft.'

'What I forecast yesterday has now come to pass. That brother of ours is hiding a silver necklace in his bosom; a devil handed it to him last night.'

At this the monk flung the necklace from him, fell at Brendan's feet, and cried: 'Father, I have sinned. Pardon me and pray for me lest I perish.'

The rest of the monks cast themselves to the ground and begged the Lord to save their brother's soul. Brendan lifted the culprit to his feet and the rest of the monks stood up – to see a little Ethiopian boy pop out of the culprit's breast and cry out: 'Man of God, why are you expelling me from the home I have lived in these past seven years? You are casting me off from my inheritance.'

'In the name of Our Lord Jesus Christ,' Brendan replied, 'I forbid you to harm any man from now till the Day of Judgement.' Then, turning to the monk, 'You must receive the Body and Blood of the Lord, for your body and soul are soon to part company. You will be buried here, but that brother of yours who accompanied you out of the monastery will rest only in hell.'

The monk received Communion, his soul left his body and was borne heavenwards by angels of light, as the brethren stood looking on. Brendan buried him where he had died.

8 St Brendan and his monks reached the shore of the island where the boat was moored and, just as they were embarking, a young man arrived carrying a basket full of bread and a large jug of water. He greeted them, saying: 'Accept a blessing from the hand of your servant. You have a long journey ahead of you before you will find the fulfilment of your desires, but at least you will not lack food and water between now and Easter.' They received his blessing and sailed out into the open sea, where they refreshed themselves with food and drink every two days, while their barque was borne hither and thither over the face of the deep.

9 One day they sighted an island close at hand. A fair wind sprang up after they had set course for it and saved them from being overtaxed by the effort of rowing. On arrival, the man of God ordered them all out, but was himself the last to disembark. A tour of the island led to the discovery of springs gushing forth to form vast streams teeming with fish. 'Let us sing the divine office here,' said Brendan, 'and offer to God the spotless victim of the Cross, for today is Maundy Thursday.' They stayed there till Holy Saturday.

In their walks round the island they came across several flocks of sheep, all the same colour, white, and so enormous that their great bulky forms quite blotted out the ground from view. St Brendan called his brethren together and told them: 'Take as many sheep as we shall need for the coming feast.' They hurried away to carry out his order. One animal was singled out and its horns were tied. One of the monks took the cord attached to its horns and the sheep trotted along behind him, like a domestic pet. On their return Brendan repeated his command to one of the monks, saying: 'Take an unspotted lamb from among the flock.' The monk hastily did as he was bidden.

When all preparations had been made for the following day, a man suddenly appeared before them, carrying a basket full of bread baked in hot ashes, and other victuals. He put these down in front of Brendan and fell down three times full length on the ground at the saint's feet, crying out: 'What have I done, you pearl of God, to deserve the honour of providing meat and drink for you by the sweat of my brow during this holy season?' Brendan raised him up and kissed him. 'My son,' he said, 'Our Lord Jesus Christ Himself has indicated the place in which we are to celebrate His holy Resurrection.'

'Father,' the man replied, 'you will celebrate Holy Saturday here, but God has decided that you will celebrate the Easter Vigil and tomorrow's masses on the island you can now catch a glimpse of.' Then the man began to wait on the servants of God and started collecting together whatever they would need the next day. He packed these supplies and carried them down to the coracle, then said to Brendan: 'The boat can hold no more, but in eight days' time I shall bring across to you everything you will need in the way of food and drink, sufficient to last you till Pentecost.'

'And how,' asked Brendan, 'do you know where we will be in eight days from now?'

'By tonight,' the man rejoined, 'you will be on that island you see close by and you will remain there till the sixth hour[1] tomorrow. Then you will sail westwards to another island, called the Paradise of Birds. There you will remain till the octave of Pentecost.'

St Brendan asked him how the sheep could possibly grow to so great a size – they were as big as bulls.

'There is nobody on the island to milk them, and since there is no winter to make them go thin they stay out at pasture and feed the whole year round. That is why they are bigger than sheep in your country.'

They blessed each other, then St Brendan and his monks set out for their boat and were soon rowing away.

1. About noon.

10 Before reaching the neighbouring island, their vessel came to a standstill and the monks, on their master's advice, jumped into the shallows and fixed ropes to either side of the boat to enable them to drag it in to the shore. The island was rocky and bare, there was hardly a grain of sand on the beach and only an occasional tree here and there. The monks landed and passed the whole night in prayer in the open, but Brendan stayed on board. He knew perfectly well what kind of an island it was but refrained from telling the others, lest they should take fright.

When morning came, he told the monks who were priests each to say his own mass, and this they did. After Brendan had sung mass in the boat, the monks took out of the coracle joints of raw meat and fish which they had brought over with them from the other island, and sprinkled them with salt. Then they lighted a fire and put a cooking-pot on it. When they had built the fire up with sticks and the pot began to boil, the island started to heave like a wave. The monks ran towards the boat, imploring their abbot to protect them. He dragged them in one by one and they set off, leaving behind all the things they had taken ashore. The island moved away across the sea, and when it had gone two miles and more the monks could still see their fire burning brightly. Brendan explained the situation: 'Brethren, does the island's behaviour surprise you?'

'Indeed it does! We are almost petrified with fright.'

'Have no fear, my sons. Last night God revealed to me the meaning of this wonder in a vision. It was no island that we landed on, but that animal which is the greatest of all creatures that swim in the sea. It is called Jasconius.[1]'

11 They rowed towards the island on which they had previously made a three days' stay. They climbed its summit, which faces westwards across the sea, and from there they espied another island close at hand. It was grassy, covered with flowers, full of glades, and separated from the island they were on by only a narrow strait. They sailed round it, looking for a harbour, and put in at the mouth of a stream on the southern shore. This stream was about as wide as the coracle. The monks disembarked, and

---

1. A proper name, derived from the Irish 'iasc' = 'fish'.

Brendan instructed them to fix ropes to the sides of the coracle and pull it, with himself on board, as hard as they could, against the current. He was conveyed about a mile upstream to the source. 'Our Lord Jesus Christ,' he said, 'has led us to a place in which to stay and celebrate his Resurrection.' Then he added: 'I think that, even if we had brought no supplies at all, this spring would provide us with all the nourishment we need.'

Beyond the spring, on higher ground, there was an exceptionally tall tree growing, with a trunk of colossal girth. This tree was full of pure white birds; so thickly had they settled on it that there was hardly a branch, or even a leaf, to be seen. Brendan wondered why so vast a number of birds should have flocked together. So keenly did he long to unravel the mystery that he threw himself on his knees in tears and prayed silently: 'O God, to whom nothing is unknown and who can bring to light every hidden fact, you see how anxious I am. I beseech your infinite majesty to deign to make known to me, a sinner, this secret design of yours which I see before me. I presume to ask, not because of any merit or dignity of my own, but solely on account of your boundless clemency.'

He sat down in the boat and one of the birds flew down from the tree towards him. The flapping of its wings sounded like a bell. It settled on the prow, spread out its wings as a sign of joy, and looked placidly at Brendan. He realized at once that God had paid heed to his prayer. 'If you are God's messenger,' he said to the bird, 'tell me where these birds come from and why they are gathered together.'

'We are fallen angels,' the bird replied, 'part of the host which was banished from Heaven through the sin of man's ancient foe. Our sin lay in approving the sin of Lucifer; when he and his band fell, we fell with them. Our God is faithful and just and, by His great justice, we were placed here. Thanks to His mercy, we suffer no torment: our only punishment is to have no part in the vision of His glory which those who stand before His throne in Heaven enjoy. Like the other messengers of God, we wander through the air, over the bowl of Heaven, and upon the earth, but on Sundays and holy days we take on this physical form and tarry here to sing the praises of our Creator. You and your companions have completed one year of your journey; six more years remain. Every year you will celebrate Easter in the same place as you are going to spend it today, and at the end of your travels you will achieve your heart's desire – you will find the Land of Promise of the Saints.' With that the bird flew away from the prow of the boat and rejoined the flock.

When it was almost time for vespers, the birds all began to sing in unison: *'Thou, O God, art praised in Sion: and unto thee shall the vow be performed in Jerusalem . . .'*, beating their wings against their sides, and they continued singing the verse antiphonally for a whole hour. To the man of God and his companions the rhythm of the melody combined with the sound of their beating wings seemed as sweet and moving as a plaintive song of lament.

'Let us eat something,' said Brendan to his monks, 'to keep up our bodily strength; our souls have already been fully nourished today with heavenly food.' After supper they sang the divine office and, when it was over, went to sleep till the third hour of the night. St Brendan stayed awake and called the brethren for lauds of Easter Sunday, himself intoning the 'O Lord, open thou my lips'. When he had finished praying, the entire flock of birds started to flap their wings and sing 'Praise him, all ye angels of his: praise him, all his host . . .' They sang for an hour, just as they had done previously at vespers.

As dawn came up in splendour, the birds sang *'And may the splendour of the Lord come upon us . . .'* in the same measure and psalm tone as they had used at lauds. At terce they sang *'O sing praises unto our God; O sing praises, sing praises unto our king, sing ye praises with understanding . . .'*; at sext *'Let thy face, O Lord, shine forth upon us, and be thou merciful unto us . . .'*; at none *'Behold how good and joyful a thing it is, brethren, to dwell together in unity . . .'* – day and night they praised the Lord.

Brendan made sure that Paschaltide was a source of spiritual refreshment for the brethren, by having them celebrate the full eight days of the Easter octave. When the feast days came to an end, he said: 'Up to now we have used this spring, near which we are standing, only for washing our hands and feet; it is time for us to use it to replenish our supply of drinking water.' Hardly had he finished speaking when the man who had been with them for three days before Easter, and who had stocked them up with provisions for the feast, arrived with a boat full of food and drink. He unloaded the supplies and said: 'Men and brothers, you have here enough to last you till Pentecost. On no account drink water from that spring. It is too strong to drink. Let me tell you what its properties are: it flows from a spring and looks and tastes like ordinary water but, if anyone drinks it, he immediately falls fast asleep and remains in that condition for the next twenty-four hours.' Then he received Brendan's blessing and returned home.

The monks stayed where they were till the octave of Pentecost and were constantly regaled by the singing of the birds. On Whit Sunday, after Brendan had sung the community mass, their steward arrived with all they could require for celebrating the feast. 'You have still a long way to travel,' he told them, when they had all sat down at table. 'Fill your flasks with water from this other spring[1] and take with you loaves of dry bread which will keep till next year.' At the end of the meal he received a blessing and set off home.

After the octave day of the feast Brendan loaded the coracle with everything their steward had brought them, and had all the flasks filled with water running out from the spring. When all the gear had been carried down to the shore, the bird that had previously spoken to Brendan flew quickly towards them and perched on the prow. The man of God realized it had a message for them. It addressed them in a human voice: 'Next year you will celebrate Easter Sunday and the rest of the time up to the octave of Pentecost here with us, and you will celebrate Maundy Thursday in exactly the same place as you did this year. Easter Eve, too, you will spend in the same spot as this year, on the back of Jasconius. In eight months' time you will come across an island called the Island of the Community of St Ailbe. You will spend Christmas there.' The bird left as soon as it had finished speaking. The monks hoisted the sails and put out to sea, with the birds singing *'Hear us, O Lord, thou that art the hope of all*

---

1. The text is not clear whether there are two springs or whether the steward has changed his mind about the soporific spring.

*the ends of the earth, and of them that remain in the broad sea ...'*

12 The saintly abbot and his monks spent three months sailing hither
and thither across the wide expanse of the ocean, and all the
while they had nothing to look at but the sea and the sky. They
took food every two or three days. One day they sighted an island
close at hand, but, when they were approaching the shore, a
breeze blew them back out to sea away from the harbour. Round
and round the island they sailed for four days without being able
to find anywhere to land. The monks, with tears in their eyes,
implored the Lord to come to their aid, for they had come to the
end of their strength and were completely exhausted. After three
days of fasting and unceasing prayer, they came upon a small
inlet, so narrow that only one boat could enter. Near by there
were two springs, one clear and one muddy. The brethren were
hurrying off to fill their flasks when Brendan called after them:
'My sons, do not take anything that does not belong to you without permission from the elders who live on this island. They will
be willing to let us have water, if only we ask. There is no need
to take it by stealth.'

As they were all standing on the beach, looking round and
trying to decide which direction to take, an extremely grave and
dignified old man with white hair and a shining face came up
to them and prostrated himself three times on the ground. The
brethren helped him to his feet. He kissed each of them, was kissed
by all in return, and then, taking Brendan's hand, led them to
a monastery about a furlong away. At the monastery gates
Brendan stopped and asked him who the abbot was and where
the monks came from. Brendan repeated his question in several
different ways but could elicit no response at all from the old man,
except the gentlest movement of the hand indicating that the rule
of silence ought to be kept.

As soon as Brendan realized that monastic silence was in force
there, he instructed his monks to observe it. 'Keep guard over
your tongues,' he said, 'or you will destroy the spirit of recollec-
tion of the monks here with your buffoonery.' The attention of
the brethren was distracted from this admonition by the arrival
of twelve monks who came in procession, bearing crosses and
reliquaries, to give them formal welcome. They were singing as

they came and greeted Brendan and his company with the following verse: 'Rise up you holy ones of God, from your abode, and
set out on the way of truth. Hallow this place with your presence,
bless the people, and vouchsafe to keep us, your servants, in
peace.' When the verse had been sung, St Ailbe[1] the abbot came
forward and kissed Brendan and the brethren in turn, then each
of the monks in procession did the same. Everyone gave everyone
else the kiss of peace, the guests were led inside, and prayers were
recited as they went, as is customary in monasteries in the East.
Then the abbot and community washed their guests' feet, singing
the antiphon: *'A new commandment I give unto you . . .'* After this
the abbot preceded them into the refectory in profound silence,
a bell was rung, and they all washed their hands and were told
to be seated. A second bell was rung, and one of the community
rose from his place and laid out on the table roots and loaves
of wonderfully white bread. The roots were incredibly tasty. The
seating was so arranged that, all the way down the table, guests
alternated with monks of the community. Loaves were shared
one between two. Then a third bell went and the drink was served.
With great amusement the abbot exhorted his guests to drink,
saying: 'Now you can have your fill, with joy and fear of the
Lord, of the water which, a short while ago, you wanted to take
by stealth from the clear spring. That other spring, the muddy
one, we use every day for washing our feet, because the water
is always warm. Where the bread comes from or who brings it
to our cellar are facts unknown to us. All we know is that God,
in His kindness, sends it to us by one of His creatures. Every day
we have twelve pieces of bread, cut from two large loaves; on
Sundays and feast days God adds a roll for each of us, so that
the pieces left over from dinner may be eaten for supper; and
now, on your arrival, we have been given double rations. Christ
has been used to feeding us in this way from the time of St
Patrick and St Ailbe, our holy founder, to the present day. It is
eighty years since this began and we never feel any older or more
feeble. On this island we feel no need for cooked food, nor do

1. Patron Saint of Munster.

we ever suffer from extremes of heat or cold. When it is time for mass or the night hours, the church lamps which, by divine ordinance, we brought with us from our country, are always already lighted for us; they burn till daybreak and the flames never diminish.'

They drank three times, then the abbot rang the bell, and the monks rose from the table in a body and, with great solemnity and in complete silence, filed out into church, with St Brendan and the abbot at the end of the line. As they entered the church, St Brendan was surprised to see a group of twelve monks hastily genuflect and leave the building. 'Father abbot,' he said, 'why did they not eat with us?'

'Because you are here. The refectory table is not long enough to accommodate us all at once. They are going to have their meal now; they will not go hungry. Let us sing vespers now, so that the rest of the monks will be able to come in and sing their vespers as soon as they have eaten.'

When the evening office was over, St Brendan looked round the church to see how it was built. It was square and had seven lamps inside – three hanging before the high altar in the middle of the church and two each in front of two other altars. The altars were square blocks of crystal and the sacred vessels – patens, chalices, cruets – and other articles used in divine worship were made of the same substance. The twenty-four seats placed round the church were of crystal too. The abbot's seat was flanked on either side by a choir of monks. He would begin a line of chant, the choir on one side would take it up, and then he would conclude it; then the next line would be picked up by the choir on the other side. No monk in either choir would presume to start a line of singing: that was the abbot's privilege. Silence reigned throughout the monastery – none of the community would take it upon himself to speak or make any noise. If anyone needed anything, he would go up to the abbot, kneel down, and make a simple and sincere request for whatever he required. The abbot at once would take his stylus and write down on a tablet whatever God had revealed. This he handed to the monk who had made the petition. Brendan pondered over all this for a while, then said:

247

'Father abbot, it is time to betake ourselves to refectory, so that we may eat while it is still light.'[1] They did so and the usual meal-time order was followed.

The day's routine over, they all hastened to compline with great alacrity. After the abbot had intoned the *'O Lord, make haste to help us'* and had sung the *'Glory be to the Father ...'* in praise of the Holy Trinity, the monks inserted the following: *'We have acted unrighteously and done evil. Pardon us, O Lord, our merciful father. I will lay me down in peace and take my rest; for it is thou, Lord, only, that makest me dwell in safety.'* Then they continued with the rest of compline.

After finishing the day's office, each monk retired to his cell, taking with him one of the guests. Brendan and the abbot stayed behind in church to await the coming of the light. Brendan inquired about the way of life in the monastery and about the rule of silence, wondering whether it were not too severe for human nature to bear. With great respect and humility the abbot replied: 'Father, I testify before Christ that it is eighty years since we first came here and yet the only time we ever hear a human voice is in choir. There is never a sound heard from the twenty-four of us; sometimes the older brethren might express themselves with a glance or gesture, but only the older ones. And we have never known illness, either physical or mental, since we arrived.'

'May we have permission to stay here?' Brendan asked.

'No,' came the reply. 'That cannot be. It is not God's will. Why do you ask, father? Before you set out, did not God tell you what you had to do? You and your brethren must one day return to your own monastery. It is the will of God that you should be buried there. Of those two other monks, one will journey to the Isle of Anchorites, the other is doomed to everlasting death in hell.'

As they were speaking, a flaming arrow shot through the window and lighted all the sanctuary lamps. As soon as they were lit, the arrow shot back out the window, but the precious

---

1. The *Rule of St Benedict* (ch. 41) enjoins that meals should be taken during daylight hours.

fire remained burning in the lamps. Brendan wanted to know who extinguished them in the morning. 'Come and examine the mystery for yourself,' replied the abbot. 'You see these candles burning in the lampstands – they never burn lower nor do their wicks leave any ash, because their light is spiritual.'

'But how,' Brendan protested, 'can material substance be on fire with spiritual light?'

'Have you not read of the bush on Mount Sinai, how it burned and was not consumed?'

They kept watch the whole night long, and when it was day, Brendan asked permission to set off on his journey.

'No father, not yet. You must first spend Christmas here with us and then stay on until the octave of the Epiphany.'

Brendan complied with the old man's request and stayed the required length of time in the monastery of twenty-four monks on the Island of the Community of St Ailbe.

13 At the end of the Epiphany festivities St Brendan and his followers were given a good supply of victuals and received the blessing of the whole community. They set off in their little boat with all possible speed and voyaged hither and thither, sometimes sailing and sometimes rowing, till the beginning of Lent.

Their supplies ran out, and three days later they caught sight of an island not far off. They immediately began to row hard towards it, for, by that time, the pangs of hunger and thirst had become severe. St Brendan blessed the place where they landed and they all disembarked. There before them was a sparkling spring set in the midst of a profusion of greenery. A rivulet led from the spring and it was full of every kind of fish pushing their way down to the sea. 'Brethren,' exclaimed the saint, 'what refreshment God has prepared for us after all our toil! Catch enough fish for supper, roast it, and pick salad and roots to go with it.' They did as he bade them. Then, as they were pouring out the water, he warned them: 'Be careful, brethren, not to drink too much of this water, in case it does you harm.' His words, unfortunately, were not interpreted with uniform strictness by every monk – some had one glass, some two, and some three. They all fell asleep – some for one day and night, some for two, and the rest for three. St Brendan prayed unceasingly, begging God to pardon what they had brought on themselves by their own ignorance.

When at last they were all awake again, their holy father addressed them: 'Come, my sons, let us flee, before worse befall us. This place is death to us. God provided us with food and drink, but you abused the gift and have done yourselves harm. Get in enough water, fish, and roots to last us till Maundy Thursday – calculate at one fish, one root, and one cupful of water per head each day. Then let us be off.' The sails were hoisted and the boat set off southwards laden with all the supplies St Brendan had ordered.

14 Three days later the wind dropped and the calm was so great that the sea looked as though it had curdled. 'Ship your oars!' Brendan shouted. 'Unfurl the sails and let God steer us where He will.' And so they were carried back and forth for twenty days till God raised up a fair west wind for them. They hoisted the sails, at the same time manning the oars for greater speed. They ate every three days.

15 One day an island appeared in the far distance, like a cloud on the horizon. 'Do you recognize that island, my sons?' cried Brendan.

'No, not at all!'

'Well, I do. It is the island where we celebrated Maundy Thursday last year; that is where our good steward lives.'

Overcome with joy they started to row with all the strength they could muster. 'Do not be so foolish!' Brendan shouted. 'You will tire yourselves out. Is not the Lord our captain and helmsman? Then leave it to Him to direct us where He wills.'

Their steward ran down to meet them coming in and guided them to the place where they had disembarked the previous year. Praising God, he kissed their feet, beginning with St Brendan and going down in order to the lowliest monk, saying as he did so: 'God is wonderful in His saints; the God of Israel is he who will give power and strength to his people. Blessed be God.' Having unloaded the boat he erected a tent and got ready a bath for them – because it was Maundy Thursday – and dressed them all out in new clothes and waited on them during the sacred Easter triduum. Up till the Easter vigil the monks were occupied in celebrating the Passion.

Once the Holy Saturday ceremonies were over, mass had been offered, and they had received Holy Communion, the steward made the following suggestion: 'Board your vessel and depart to the place where you celebrated the holy night of Christ's Resurrection last year. You shall do so again this year and shall remain there until the sixth hour tomorrow. Afterwards you shall sail to the island called the Paradise of Birds, where you spent from Easter to the octave of Pentecost last year. Take with you all necessary food and drink. I shall pay you a visit next Sunday.' This they did. The steward stocked up the boat with as much bread and water, meat, and other delicacies as it could hold. St Brendan gave him a blessing and climbed aboard, and they sailed away.

They disembarked at the same place as before and there, in front of them on the ground, was a cooking-pot they had left behind a year ago. St Brendan stepped ashore, sang the *Hymn of the Three Children*[1] and warned his monks: 'My dear sons, watch and pray, lest you fall into temptation. Remember how God, without the slightest trouble, tamed, for our benefit, the fury of a monstrous beast.' The monks scattered themselves round the island and kept vigil until time for lauds. Later each priest offered mass. This brought them to the third hour of the day. Then St Brendan celebrated the sacred mysteries, offering to God the unspotted Lamb, His Son: 'A year ago,' he said, 'I kept the feast of the Lord's Resurrection here. I want to do the same now.' Then they journeyed on to the Island of Birds.

At their approach all the birds burst out in chorus: 'Salvation to Our God who sits upon the throne, and to the Lamb. The Lord is God and He hath shone upon us. Appoint a solemn day, with shady boughs, even to the corner of the altar.' Their cries resounded with loud flappings of wings for almost half an hour, until Brendan and his party, having disembarked and removed all their belongings from the boat, were finally settled into their tent.

1. The *Benedicite*, from *Daniel*, iii.

When the Paschal feast was over, the steward arrived, as he had promised, on the first Sunday after Easter, bringing with him all the necessaries of life.

As soon as they had sat down to a meal, the bird who had spoken to them last year flew down and perched on the prow of the coracle, stretched out its wings, and made a noise like some great church organ. St Brendan surmised that it had a message to impart. It began: 'God has mapped out four places for you, one for each of the four seasons of the year, where you shall stay every successive year till your pilgrimage is at an end. Maundy Thursday you spend with your steward; the Easter vigil is passed on the back of the whale; you are here with us from Easter till the octave of Pentecost; and Christmas you spend with the Community of St Ailbe. After seven years, not without great and diverse trials, you will find the Land of Promise of the Saints which you have sought so long. There you will stay for forty days and then God will take you back to the country of your birth.' The holy abbot and his monks flung themselves to the ground thanking and praising their Creator. When the venerable old man rose to his feet, the bird flew back to its place in the flock.

At the end of the meal the steward said: 'With God's help I shall return with provisions on the day of the Descent of the Holy Ghost on the Apostles.' St Brendan and all the monks gave him a blessing and he went off home. They remained till Pentecost, and when the festival was over Brendan ordered them to get the boat ready and fill their flasks with spring water. The coracle had already been drawn down to the sea when the steward arrived with a boat full of food. All this he transferred to Brendan's vessel, kissed all the brethren, and went back whence he had come.

16 Our venerable father and his companions put out to sea and sailed for forty days. Looking round one day they espied a creature of gigantic proportions writhing along in their wake. It was still far off but was charging towards them at top speed, ploughing up the surface of the water and shooting out spray from its nostrils. It looked as though it would devour them. 'Good Lord, deliver us!' they yelled. 'Do not let the beast consume us!' Brendan tried to console them: 'Do not be afraid, O you of little faith!' he cried.

'God has always looked after us and He is sure to save us from this monster and from all perils to come.' Great waves buffeted the boat, heralding the sea-monster's approach, and the monks' fear increased. St Brendan raised up his hands to Heaven and prayed: 'Lord, deliver your servants now, as of old you delivered David out of the hand of the giant, Goliath. Deliver us, O Lord, as you rescued Jonah from the belly of a great whale.' Just as Brendan had finished, another huge sea-monster lunged from the west towards their attacker and, spewing out fire, began to give battle. 'My sons,' cried out Brendan, 'look at the wonders of Almighty God. See how the creatures obey their Creator. The fight will soon be over and, far from its being harmful, you will be able to set down this event as one of the glories of God.' The wretched animal that had assailed the servants of God was chopped into three parts before their very eyes; the victorious monster swam back the way it had come.

The following day they sighted an island, wide and well set with trees, and, when they drew in, the rear quarters of the dead monster were lying on the beach. 'Ha!' cried Brendan. 'That creature was going to eat you; now you are going to eat it. We shall remain here a good while, so drag the coracle high up the beach and look round in that wood yonder for a safe place for our tent.' He himself chose the spot to pitch the tent.

When they had put all the gear into the tent, Brendan told them to cut enough meat from the carcass to last them three months – 'For animals will come in the night and pick it clean.' They did as they were bidden and stored away as much meat as they would need. When this task, which kept them busy till vesper time, was completed, they asked, 'How, father, will we be able to survive here without water?'

'Do you imagine God finds it harder to provide water than food? Walk towards the southern shore. There you will find a sparkling spring and plentiful vegetation. Bring me some, but not too much.'

They found everything as he had said. Their stay on the island was lengthened to three months, because foul weather at sea – heavy rain and hail storms – kept them from putting out. The monks went to see if what Brendan had said would happen to the fish had in fact taken place. When they reached the spot where the carcass had been, they found nothing but bones. Back they came at once. 'Father,' they said, 'you were right about the beast.'

'I knew you would not be satisfied until you had seen for yourself. Here is another piece of information for you; a great lump of fish will be washed up tonight and will provide a meal for you tomorrow.' The next day the fish was lying on the beach, just as he had foretold. The monks took as much as they could carry. 'Preserve it carefully in salt,' said Brendan. 'You will need it later. God will give us fine weather today, tomorrow, and the day after tomorrow, and the sea will be calm. Then we shall leave.'

Three days later he ordered them to load the coracle, fill their leather water-bottles and any other vessels, and to gather shoots and green plants for his own use – for, since his ordination, Brendan had never eaten meat. Everything was loaded on board, the sails were spread and they set off southwards.

17 One day they saw an island in the distance. 'Do you see that island?' Brendan asked.

'Yes, we see it,' they replied.

'There are three groups of people living there: boys, young men, and elders. One of our party will leave us to go and live with them.'

The monks were eager to know who it was and persisted in asking till, seeing how crestfallen they were, Brendan gave in. 'That monk there,' he said, pointing to one of the three who had left the monastery to follow him at the beginning of the voyage.

The boat came close in to the shore. The island itself was remarkably flat and low, and seemed to be literally at sea level; it was completely bare of trees or of anything which could act as a windshield. It was very wide and was covered with purple and white *caltae*.[1] Three bands of men could be discerned, just as Brendan had said, and they were standing apart from each other, the distance between them being roughly as far as a stone could be cast by a sling. They moved about continually except when one band stopped and sang 'The saints shall go from strength to strength, the God of gods shall be seen in Sion.'

---

1. The meaning of '*calta*' is uncertain. It is either a fruit or a flower.

When the group came to the end of the verse, another band would take it up again, and so the singing went on unceasingly. The first band, the boys, was dressed in pure white garments, the second group in jacinth apparel, and the third in purple dalmatics.[1]

Brendan's party landed about the fourth hour. At sext the groups sang in unison *'God be merciful unto us ...'* – which was sung right through to the end, *'Haste thee, O God, to deliver me ...'* and, as a third psalm, *'I believed, and therefore will I speak ...'* and then a prayer. At none they sang another three psalms: *'Out of the depths have I cried to thee, O Lord ...'*, *'Behold how good and joyful ...'*, and *'Praise the Lord, O Jerusalem ...'*. The psalms for vespers were: *'Thou, O God, art praised in Sion ...'*, *'Praise the Lord, O my soul ...'*, *'O Lord, my God ...'*, *'Praise the Lord, ye servants ...'* and then, one after another, the fifteen 'Songs of Degrees'.[2] These latter were sung sitting down.

An astoundingly white cloud came down over the island at the end of the singing and made everything invisible, such was the density of vapour; but the singing continued audibly till it was time for lauds. The psalms for lauds were: *'O praise the Lord of Heaven ...'*, *'O sing unto the Lord a new song ...'*, and *'O praise God in his holiness ...'*. Then twelve psalms were sung, one after the other, as they occur in the psalter. The cloud lifted at daybreak and the three groups at once sang three psalms: *'Have mercy upon me, O God ...'*, *'O God, thou art my God; early will I seek thee ...'*, and *'Lord, thou has been our refuge ...'*. At terce they sang another three: *'O clap your hands together, all ye people ...'*, *'Save me, O God, for thy name's sake ...'*, and *'I am well pleased ...'* with the *Alleluia*. Then the divine victim was offered up and all received Communion, saying: 'Receive this sacred Body and Blood of your Lord and Saviour unto life everlasting.'[3]

Two boys came out at the end of mass, carrying a basket of purple *caltae*, which they put into the boat, saying: 'Take with

---

1. The colours symbolize respectively innocence, vigour, and maturity.
2. *Psalms* cxix–cxxxiii (A.V. cxx–cxxxiv).
3. This verse, ascribed to St Sechnall, is said to be the oldest Latin Eucharistic hymn extant.

you some of the produce of this island of steadfast men. Let your brother come with us, then set out in peace.' St Brendan called the monk who was about to leave them. 'Kiss your brethren,' he said, 'and go with those who are calling you, for you have been found worthy of a place in this wonderful fellowship. Blessed was the hour in which your mother bore you!' The monk kissed his abbot and fellow monks and Brendan bade him farewell: 'My son, remember all the many benefits God has given you in this world. Go in peace, and pray for us.' The monk followed the two youths to their group.

Our venerable father and his companions began to row away. At the ninth hour Brendan told them to restore their strength with *caltae* from the island of steadfast men. He picked out one himself and was astonished to find it so huge and full of juice. 'Never in my life,' he exclaimed, 'have I heard, or even read, of *caltae* of this size.' They were all the same size, large and globular in shape. He asked for a cup, and from one fruit alone squeezed out a quart of juice. This was shared among the twelve monks and for the next twelve days the party lived on one fruit each day. The *caltae* left a constant taste of honey in their mouths.

18 When the fruit had all been eaten, Brendan ordered a three-day fast. At the end of the third day an enormous bird flew straight towards the boat, carrying in its beak a branch of some unfamiliar tree. On the end of this branch hung a large bunch of bright red grapes. The bird dropped the branch into Brendan's lap. Calling together the monks he exhorted them to eat: 'Look at the meal God has sent us! Take and eat.' Each of the grapes was as big as an apple. Brendan shared the bunch out, grape by grape, and it lasted twelve days. After this they fasted again.

The island they came upon three days later was thickly set in every part with trees bearing the same kind of fruit as the bird had brought them. These trees were all the same colour and so full of fruit – it was incredible – that the branches were bowed down to the ground. No other species of tree was to be found and not one of the fruit trees was sterile. They put in to the shore. Brendan disembarked to beat the bounds of the place, and the monks stayed on board till he came back. The island exhaled a fragrant odour, like the smell of pomegranates pervading the rooms of a house. They were so much refreshed by the sweet smell wafting over them that the edge was quite taken off their fast. Meanwhile Brendan had discovered six springs set in the middle of a patch of lush ground which was thick with green plants and shoots. He came back with his arms full of the first fruits of the island's produce. 'Come ashore!' he shouted. 'Fix the tent and take your fill of these prime fruits of the land to which God has led us.' For forty days they fed well on grapes, salads, and shoots. Then they left, taking with them as much as the boat could hold.

19 They hoisted sail and drove before the wind. As they were sailing along, a bird appeared in the distance, flying towards them. It was a gryphon. The brethren cried out to Brendan in consternation, 'Help! That thing is coming to eat us.'

'Fear not,' Brendan replied. 'God has been our helper up to now and will not fail us this time.'

The gryphon was stretching out its claws to catch the monks when, suddenly, the bird that had brought the grapes swooped rapidly down upon it. The gryphon tried to devour it but the other defended itself and finally gained the upper hand. It tore out the gryphon's eyes and the gryphon then flew higher and higher, till it was almost lost from sight. The other bird gave chase and killed it; the carcass fell into the sea near the coracle. The victorious bird flew back to where it had come from.

20 St Brendan and his mariners caught sight of the Island of the Community of St Ailbe a few days later. Christmas was spent there, and after the festivities were over Brendan's party received the blessing of the abbot and community and sailed across the ocean for a long while. The only rest they had from navigating was at Christmas and Easter, which they spent at the usual places.

21 St Peter's Day was celebrated by St Brendan at sea, and the water was so clear that the monks could see every movement of life beneath the boat; so clear, indeed, that the animals on the ocean bed seemed near enough to touch. If the monks looked down into the deep, they could see many different kinds of creatures lying on the sandy bottom like flocks at pasture, so numerous that, lying head to tail, and moving gently with the swell, they looked like a city on the march.

The monks urged their master to say mass silently lest the fish, hearing his voice, might rise up and attack them. Brendan chaffed them: 'I am surprised at your foolishness. What – are you afraid of these creatures? Have you not several times landed on the monarch of the deep, the beast who eats all other sea creatures? Why, you have sat down on his back and sung psalms, have even gathered sticks, lighted a fire and cooked food – and all this without showing fear. Then how can you be afraid of these? Is not Our Lord Jesus Christ the Lord of Creation? Can he not make all creatures docile?' Brendan sang at the top of his voice, causing the brethren to cast an anxious eye in the direction of the fish, but at the sound of singing the fish rose up from the sea bed and swam round and round the coracle. There was nothing to be seen but crowds of swimming forms. They did not come close but, keeping their distance, swam back and forth till mass was over. Then they scurried away on their own tracks over the paths of the ocean, out of sight of the servants of God. St Brendan journeyed on, and after going at full sail for a week, with fair winds every day, still had not crossed the open sea.

22 One day, when the masses were over, they noticed a column rising out of the sea. It seemed quite near at hand but turned out to be a good three days' journey away. When they reached it, Brendan gazed upwards but could hardly see the top because of its great height: it was higher than the sky. This column was covered with a most unusual canopy – so strange indeed that the coracle could pass through the openings in it but no one could tell what substance it was made of. It was the colour of silver and seemed harder than marble. The column itself was of pure crystal.[1]

'Ship the oars!' Brendan commanded. 'Take down the sails and hold back the ribs of the canopy.' The canopy was so big that it extended a mile on either side of the column and went down into the sea. 'Now draw the boat through the opening,' Brendan continued, 'and let us inspect the wonders of God, our Maker.'

---

1. The sudden appearance of the column and canopy is bewildering and there is no explanation given in the text. The incident suggests a meeting with an iceberg. Details of shape and size seem to have been taken from *Ezekiel* xl and xli, or ch. xxi of the *Apocalypse*.

They entered and gazed all round: the sea was as transparent as glass and everything in it was clearly visible; they could look at the foundations of the column below the surface and see the top of the canopy reflected in the water. The sun shone inside the canopy as brightly as on the open sea. Brendan measured four different apertures in the canopy and found them each four cubits long.

They spent a whole day in rowing along one side of the canopy and could still feel the heat of the sun until the ninth hour, despite the shade cast by the canopy. The length of each side was one thousand four hundred cubits. Brendan measured a side of the towering canopy a day, and as there were four sides the task took four days to complete. A chalice, made of the same substance as the canopy, came to light in the southern reaches on the fourth day; with it, lying on a niche in the canopy, was a paten the same colour as the column. St Brendan immediately picked up the vessels. 'This miracle,' he said, 'is the work of Our Lord Jesus Christ. These two gifts have been given to me so that the story of our travels may be widely believed.' He ordered them to sing the Divine Office and then to take some food, because the sight of the column had cast out of their mind all thought of food and drink.

The following day they set off southwards. Some of the brethren held back the ribs of the canopy to let the others get the mast and sails ready for hoisting as soon as the boat would be clear of the opening. Once the mast and sails were hoisted they were caught by a good strong wind, which carried them north for eight days, so that all they had to do was keep an eye on the steerage and rigging.

23 The eighth day found them near a stony island quite without grass or trees. The countryside was wild and dotted with slag heaps and numerous forges. 'Brethren,' said Brendan, 'that island makes me feel uneasy. I have no desire to land nor even to go near, yet the wind is taking us straight towards it!' They had only gone forward about a stone's throw when the blowing of bellows and the clang of hammer on anvil dinned in their ears like thunder. Crossing himself with the sign of Christ's victory, he prayed: 'Lord Jesus Christ deliver us from this island.' Hardly

had he finished the prayer when one of the inhabitants, a very swarthy, evil-looking man, with a bright red face, came out of a forge to perform some task or other. He caught sight of the coracle approaching and turned back. St Brendan crossed himself again. 'My sons,' he shouted, 'let us flee from this place. Up with the sails and row as fast as you can.' He had just finished the sentence when the savage rushed down to the beach carrying a huge piece of blazing slag in a pair of tongs. This he hurled at the boat, but it shot over their heads and fell about a furlong beyond them. It struck the water and seethed like a live ember from a volcano. Smoke rose up from the sea as from a fiery furnace.

When the boat had sailed about a mile from where the slag fell, all the inhabitants of the island rushed down to the beach, each carrying a glowing mass of slag. Some aimed at the servants of God, but the rest pelted the embers at each other. Then they ran back to the forges and set them alight. Soon the whole island was like a blazing furnace and the sea hissed like a cauldron of stew boiling over a good fire. All day a long drawn-out wail could be heard. An intolerable, fetid stench emanated from the island and was still perceptible after they had lost sight of it. Brendan tried to comfort his flock: 'Soldiers of Christ, put on spiritual arms and stand firm in faith unfeigned. Watch and play the man, for we are at hell's gates.'

24 The next day a high mountain came up towards the north. At a distance it seemed wreathed in light cloud, but the cloud turned out to be smoke belching from its peak. The wind carried them swiftly towards it. The cliffs at the water's edge were so high that the summit was obscured; they were as black as coal and wonderfully sheer, like a wall.

One of the three monks who had followed Brendan out of the monastery suddenly leapt overboard and started wading to the bottom of the cliffs, calling out: 'Woe is me, father, I am being torn away from you and am powerless to turn back.' The monks hastily pushed the boat off, crying out to the Lord: 'Have mercy upon us O Lord, have mercy!' Then they witnessed the wretch being led off to torment by a group of devils. He and they would burn together. 'Woe to you, my son!' exclaimed Brendan. 'What a dreadful doom you have brought upon yourself.' A fair wind carried them away southwards, and, when they looked back from afar, they saw the mountain, clear of clouds, vomiting forth flames sky-high and then sucking them back upon itself, so that the whole mass of rock, right down to sea-level, glowed like a pyre.

25  Seven days after this fearful sight, St Brendan espied a shape in the sea that looked like a man perched on a rock. A length of cloth, the size of a cloak, hung down in front of it from two spits. The whole thing was being battered by the waves like a skiff in a whirlpool. Some of the monks said it was a bird, others a ship. 'Put an end to the discussion,' said Brendan, 'and turn the boat towards it.'

As Brendan approached, the waves retreated as though turned to jelly, revealing a swarthy and disfigured man crouching on the rock. When the waves surged in, they crashed right over his head, and when they retreated the rock stood out stark and bare. The sheet of cloth would alternately billow out, leaving him exposed to the gale and then, caught by the wind, would lash in and smack him hard about the face and eyes.

The saintly abbot asked him who he was and what crime he could have committed to have deserved such a fate.

'I am of all men the most wretched,' came the answer, 'for I am Judas Iscariot who foully bargained away the life of his Master. Jesus Christ's unspeakable mercy, not my own desert, has put me here. To me this is no place of punishment. It is the spot where my loving Saviour grants me respite in honour of His Resurrection. Sitting here is like being in the Garden of Delights, compared to the torments to which I can look forward this evening. My punishment is to burn like a lump of molten lead in a crucible, day and night, in the middle of yonder mountain, the home of Leviathan[1] and his allies. I was there when that brother of yours was swallowed up. The mountain shot out great flames then, as though leaping for joy – that is the usual welcome for a damned soul. I come here to rest from first to second vespers of every Sunday, from Christmas to Epiphany, from Easter to Whitsun, and on the feasts of the Purification and the Assumption of the Mother

---

1. Biblical monster ( *Job* xli, *Isaiah* xxvii).

of God. The rest of the year I am torn in hell with Herod and Pilate, Annas and Caiaphas. I implore you, therefore, to beg Our Lord Jesus Christ, the Redeemer of the World, to let me stay here till sunrise tomorrow, so that the devils may not take your arrival as a sign to come to torture me and drag me off to the destiny I purchased at so horrible a price.'

'God's will be done,' the saint replied, 'the devils will not gnaw you till morning. But tell me, what is that cloth for?'

'It is a sheet I gave a leper when I was the Lord's treasurer, but since it was not mine to give – it belonged to Him and His brethren – it is more hindrance than help to me now. These iron spits to which the cloth is tied are those I gave the temple priests as a stand for cooking pots. This rock I sit on used to lie in the open street, where I flung it into the gutter to trip up passers-by, before I became His disciple.'

No sooner had twilight begun to close in over the deep than a vast cloud of demons wheeled about, yelling at the top of their voice: 'Keep out of our way, man of God! We cannot reach our colleague if you stay close to him, and, without him, we dare not face our prince. So give us our tasty morsel, do not shield him from us tonight.'

'It is not I who shield him, but the Lord Jesus Christ. He has granted him respite here until tomorrow morning.'

'How can you invoke the Lord's name over His own betrayer?'

'I command you,' Brendan retorted, 'in the name of that same Jesus Christ, not to lay hands on him till tomorrow.'

Once night was past and the man of God had set sail, an endless press of demons covered the face of the deep, yelling hideously and calling out: 'O man of God, cursed be your goings out and your comings in! All night long we have been flogged with the utmost severity for not bringing our prince that damned slave.'

'Your maledictions shall light on yourselves, not on us; for whomsoever you curse is blessed, and cursed is he whom you bless.'

'Because you shielded him from us last night, he shall receive twice as much punishment these next six days.'

'Neither you nor your leader have power to do so; that decision lies with God. Therefore I command both you and him, in the name of Our Lord Jesus Christ, to torment Judas no more severely than before.'

'Why should we take notice of what you say? Do you think you are Lord of all?'

'No. I have no power except what God has given me, but I am His servant and whatever I command in His name shall be done.'

The demons followed Brendan till Judas was out of sight, then they turned back and violently snatched away the miserable wretch with a loud plangent cry.

26 St Brendan and his co-warriors in Christ sailed away in a southerly direction, glorifying God in all things. The appearance of a small island in the distance towards the south made them row more spiritedly. 'Do not row too fast,' Brendan advised them, as they were approaching it. 'You will soon tire yourselves out. You have toiled quite enough – this coming Easter will mark the seventh anniversary of our leaving our homeland. In a short time you will meet Paul the Hermit, a very holy man. He has lived on that island for the past sixty years without a mouthful of food. For thirty years before that an animal used to bring him food.'

The cliffs were so sheer that it was impossible to find a landing place. The island itself was small and round, about a furlong in circumference and as high as it was wide. On top of the cliffs there was no soil, only bare, jagged flint. They sailed round and round and came upon a narrow harbour, barely wide enough to let the prow of the boat pass through. They had difficulty in clambering out of the boat. 'Wait here,' Brendan instructed them, 'till I return. You may not have access to the island without first obtaining permission from the servant of God who dwells here.'

He climbed up to the summit and saw two caves with their mouths facing each other, on the eastern side of the isle, and a tiny spring gushing out from a rock in front of the mouth of the cave where the soldier of Christ was sitting. The spring water, as it fell, was at once absorbed by the rock. While Brendan was peering into the mouth of one cave, the old hermit emerged from the cave opposite, saying: 'Behold how good and joyful it is for brethren to dwell together in unity.' Paul told Brendan to call the monks up from the coracle, kissed them when they arrived, and addressed them each by name. This prophetic gift of knowing their names added to their astonishment at his attire: he wore no clothes at all, yet only his face and eyes were visible, the rest of his body being covered from head to foot with his hair, beard and body hair – all of which was snow white on account of his age. Brendan felt sad within himself at the sight: 'How ashamed I feel, I who wear the habit of a monk and have jurisdiction over many monks in our order, when I see this mortal man living like an angel and wholly free from the sins of the flesh.'

'Venerable father,' the hermit replied, 'God has worked many astounding miracles on your behalf, such as have never been vouchsafed to any of the holy fathers. You say you are not worthy to wear the habit of a monk, yet you are higher than any monk. A monk has to support himself by the sweat of his brow, but, for the past seven years, God has secretly fed and clothed you and your family of monks.'

In answer to Brendan's questions where he had come from, how he had come and how long he had borne so hard a life, Paul replied: 'For forty years I was brought up in St Patrick's monastery, where I was caretaker of the cemetery. One day the prior told me to dig a grave in a certain spot for one of the monks. As I was digging, an old man, whom I did not recognize, came up to me and said: "Do not dig the grave there, brother. That plot of ground is for someone else."

'"Who are you, father?" I asked.

'"What! Do you not know me? Do you not recognize your abbot?"

'"St Patrick is my abbot," I answered.

'"I am he," the apparition replied. "Yesterday I departed this life and here I am to be buried." He pointed to another spot. "Dig a grave here for the brother who has died recently, and do not repeat what I have told you. Go down to the shore tomorrow and you will find a small boat waiting. Step into it and it will take you to the place where you are to await the day of your death."

'The following morning I went down to the shore and found a boat, just as St Patrick had said. I boarded it and sailed for three days and nights. From the fourth day onward I let myself sail with the wind and on the seventh day I sighted this island and the vessel came straight towards it. Once landed I pushed the boat off with my foot and back it went to my native land, furrowing swiftly through the waves. And here I have remained. Every third day, at the ninth hour, a sea-otter would emerge from the water on its hind legs, with a fish for my dinner in its mouth and a small bundle of twigs between its front paws for kindling a fire. It put down the fish and the bundle of twigs and returned to the sea. I lit a fire with flint and iron and cooked the fish. For thirty years the otter fed me. I ate a third part of the fish each day and, thank God, never experienced thirst, for on Sundays a trickle of water flowed from a rock. This provided me with drink there and then and I used to fill a flask to last me for the rest of the week. I did not discover these two caves nor the spring until I had been here thirty years. From then on I lived – indeed am still living – on spring water and nothing else. I have lived ninety years on the island – for thirty of which I lived on fish, and the remaining sixty on water from this spring – and I was fifty when I left my own country; so I am now one hundred and forty years old. And here, in this mortal flesh, I shall soon see my judgement day dawn. Away you go now, and fill your bottles at the spring. You will need water: you have a forty-day journey ahead of you between now and Holy Saturday. You will celebrate Holy Saturday and Easter Sunday and its octave in the same places as you have done these past six years. But this time, when you have received your steward's blessing, you will journey to the Land of Promise of the Saints, and after forty days spent there the God of your fathers will bring you back safe and sound to the land of your birth.'

27 St Brendan and his monks received the old man's blessing and set off southwards. During the whole of Lent their little barque was carried hither and thither over the ocean and their only source of nourishment was the water they had brought with them from Paul the Hermit's isle. Yet they were quite content: one drink every three days perfectly satisfied their appetite for food and drink.

On Holy Saturday they arrived at the island where their steward was waiting for them. He was so overjoyed to see them that he lifted them bodily out of the coracle, one by one. When the office of the day was over, he set before them a meal, and on the evening of that same day they put to sea again, taking the steward with them.

They found Jasconius in the usual place, climbed out on to his back, and sang to the Lord the whole night, and said their masses the next morning. After the last mass, the whale swam away and all the brethren called out: 'Hear us, O God of our salvation, thou that art the hope of all the ends of the earth, and of them that remain in the broad sea.'

'Have no fear,' said Brendan, trying to comfort them. 'The beast will not harm you; it is helping us on our way.'

The whale swam in a straight line towards the Island of Birds, and there they stayed till the octave of Pentecost.

When the solemn season had ended, the steward said to Brendan: 'Fill your water-bottles from this spring here and go back on board. This time I shall be your guide and companion, for without me you will never find the Land of Promise of the Saints.' As they left, all the birds called out: 'May the God of our salvation grant you a safe journey!'

28 The steward took them back to his island and stocked up the coracle with all they would need on the forty days' journey east which they were about to undertake. He led the way, sailing on in front of them. On the evening of the fortieth day they were enveloped in darkness, so thick that they could hardly see each other. 'Do you know what this darkness is?' the steward asked.

'No,' said Brendan.

'It swirls round that island which you have been seeking these seven long years.' An hour later a brilliant light shone round them – their boat had reached the shore. Before them lay open country covered with apple trees laden with fruit. The monks ate as much as they wanted and drank deeply from the springs. The island was so wide that forty days' wandering still did not bring them to the farther shore. One day they came upon a vast river flowing through the middle of the country. 'What are we to do?' asked Brendan. 'We have no idea of the size of the country and we cannot cross this river.' While he was standing pondering, a young man approached, kissed the monks joyfully, called them each by name, and said: 'Blessed are they that dwell in thy house, O Lord. They shall praise thee for ever and ever.'

He turned to Brendan. 'Now, at last, you have found the land you have been seeking all these years. The Lord Jesus Christ did not allow you to find it immediately, because first He wished to show you the richness of His wonders in the deep. Fill your ship brim-full with precious stones and return to the land of your birth. The day of your final journey is at hand; you shall soon be laid to rest with your fathers. After many more years have rolled by, this island will be revealed to your successors at the time when Christians will be undergoing persecution. This river divides the island in two. You must be thinking that it is autumn and the fruit has just ripened – it is like this the whole year round; dusk and darkness are unknown, for Christ Himself is our light.'

They gathered fruit and all kinds of gems, bade the young man farewell, dismissed their steward with a blessing, and sailed away into the belt of darkness. Once they had passed beyond it, they soon came to the Island of Delights. After a three days' stay they set off, with the abbot's blessing, on a direct route for their own monastery.

29 Brendan's community was rapturous with joy at his return, and glorified God for His kindness in letting them once more enjoy the sight of their father from whom they had been separated so long. St Brendan returned their affection and recounted everything he remembered of the voyage and all the wonders God had deigned to show him. Finally he informed them of the prophecy made by the young man on the Island of Promise, assuring them that he had not long to live. Events proved him right; he put all his affairs in order, and very shortly afterwards, fortified with the sacraments of the Church, lay back in the arms of his disciples and gave up his illustrious spirit to the Lord, to whom be honour and glory, world without end. Amen.

The end

# Further Reading

**On Brendan:**
C. Selmer, ed., *Navigatio S. Brendani Abbatis* (Notre Dame, Indiana, 1989)
T. Severin, *The Brendan Voyage* (London, 1978)
R. Sharpe, *Medieval Irish Saints' Lives* (1991)

**On Cuthbert:**
B. Colgrave, ed., *Two Lives of St Cuthbert* (Cambridge, 1940)
C. F. Battiscombe, ed., *The Relics of St Cuthbert* (Oxford, 1956)
M. Baker, 'Medieval Illustrations of Bede's Life of St Cuthbert', *Journal of the Warburg and Courtauld Institutes*, xli (1978). pp. 16–49
G. Bonner, ed., *St Cuthbert: his cult and his community* (1989)
M. P. Brown, *The Lindisfarne Gospels: society, spirituality and the scribe* (London, 2003)

**On Wilfrid:**
B. Colgrave, *Eddius' Life of St Wilfrid* (Cambridge, 1927)
E. S. Duckett, *Anglo-Saxon Saints and Scholars* (Cambridge, 1947)
W. T. Foley, *Images of Sanctity in Eddius Stephanus' "Life of Bishop Wilfrid"* (Canada, 1992)
D. P. Kirby, ed., *St Wilfrid at Hexham* (Newcastle, 1973)
D. P. Kirby, 'Bede, Eddius Stephanus and the Life of Wilfrid', *English Historical Review*, xcviii (1983), pp. 101–14
H. Mayr-Harting in *Studies in Sussex Church History* (ed. M. J. Kitch, 1981), pp. 1–17

**On the Wearmouth-Jarrow Abbots:**
P. Hunter Blair, *The World of Bede* (London, 1970)
G. Bonner, ed., *Famulus Christi* (London, 1976)
R. L. S. Bruce-Mitford, *The Art of the Codex Amiatinus* (Jarrow, 1976)
P. Meyvaert, 'Bede and the Church Paintings at Wearmouth–Jarrow', *Anglo-Saxon England*, viii (1979), pp. 63–77

**General Background:**
J. Campbell, *The Anglo-Saxons* (1982)
F. M. Stenton, *Anglo-Saxon England* (Oxford, 1946)
K. Hughes, *The Church in Early Irish Society* (London, 1966)
H. Mayr-Harting, *The Coming of Christianity to Anglo-Saxon England*, 3rd edn (London, 1996)
A. Gransden, *Historical Writing in England, c. 550–c. 1307* (London, 1974)
D. H. Farmer, ed., *Benedict's Disciples*, 2nd edn (Leominster, 1995; reprinted 2002)
D. H. Farmer, *The Oxford Dictionary of Saints* 5th edn (Oxford, 2003)

The British Isles at the time of Bede

Western Europe at
the time of Bede

# Index

(Note: Anglo-Saxon proper names often survive in more than one form. This is partly because they were translated into Latin, when the letter 'thorn' was read as a 'd', partly because greater simplification was sometimes desirable, particularly for names difficult to pronounce. Sometimes the less correct form, such as 'Wilfrid', 'Ceolfrid', 'Sigfrid' has become more popular, similarly 'Oswy' is more widely used than 'Oswiu'. Absolute consistency has not been possible in this volume; it is hoped that the index will make it clear when the same person is referred to under a slightly different form of name.)

# THE STORY OF PENGUIN CLASSICS

**Before 1946** ... 'Classics' are mainly the domain of academics and students, without readable editions for everyone else. This all changes when a little-known classicist, E. V. Rieu, presents Penguin founder Allen Lane with the translation of Homer's *Odyssey* that he has been working on and reading to his wife Nelly in his spare time.

**1946** *The Odyssey* becomes the first Penguin Classic published, and promptly sells three million copies. Suddenly, classic books are no longer for the privileged few.

**1950s** Rieu, now series editor, turns to professional writers for the best modern, readable translations, including Dorothy L. Sayers's *Inferno* and Robert Graves's *The Twelve Caesars*, which revives the salacious original.

**1960s** The Classics are given the distinctive black jackets that have remained a constant throughout the series's various looks. Rieu retires in 1964, hailing the Penguin Classics list as 'the greatest educative force of the 20th century'.

**1970s** A new generation of translators arrives to swell the Penguin Classics ranks, and the list grows to encompass more philosophy, religion, science, history and politics.

**1980s** The Penguin American Library joins the Classics stable, with titles such as *The Last of the Mohicans* safeguarded. Penguin Classics now offers the most comprehensive library of world literature available.

**1990s** The launch of Penguin Audiobooks brings the classics to a listening audience for the first time, and in 1999 the launch of the Penguin Classics website takes them online to a larger global readership than ever before.

**The 21st Century** Penguin Classics are rejacketed for the first time in nearly twenty years. This world famous series now consists of more than 1300 titles, making the widest range of the best books ever written available to millions – and constantly redefining the meaning of what makes a 'classic'.

The Odyssey continues ...

*The best books ever written*

PENGUIN CLASSICS

SINCE 1946